SCIENCE, SYSTEMS, AND PSYCHOANALYSIS

Robert Langs

SCIENCE, SYSTEMS, AND PSYCHOANALYSIS

Robert Langs

Foreword by

W. W. Meissner

Introduction by

Karl H. Pribram

Karnac Books
London 1992 New York

First published in 1992 by
H. Karnac (Books) Ltd.
58 Gloucester Road
London SW7 4QY

Distributed in the United States of America by
Brunner/Mazel, Inc.
19 Union Square West
New York, NY 10003

British Library Cataloguing in Publication Data.

Langs, Robert
Science, Systems, and Psychoanalysis
I. Title
150.19

ISBN 1 85575 036 8

Printed in Great Britain by BPCC Wheatons Ltd, Exeter

To Anthony Badalamenti, Ph.D.,
whose creative devotion to the research
on which this book is founded
has inspired and shaped the struggles and thinking
that have given this work its ultimate form.

ROBERT LANGS, M.D. is a classically trained psychoanalyst, engaged once again in clinical practice, and in teaching and psychotherapy research. He is the author of 30 books and 70 papers on the nature of unconscious communication and the psychotherapeutic process—and related topics. He is the Executive Director of the Psychoanalytic Center for Communicative Education in New York City, and Visiting Clinical Investigator at The Nathan S. Kline Institute for Psychiatric Research in Orangeburg, New York. He is also Visiting Clinical Professor of Psychiatry at the Mount Sinai School of Medicine in New York City.

CONTENTS

PREFACE

This book has been written for a broad audience. It is addressed to anyone who is at all concerned with a scientific grounding for the art of psychotherapy and psychoanalysis, and for the understanding of the human mind and its outputs via emotionally charged communication. These compelling issues deserve the serious attention of mental health professionals of all persuasions, as well as a wide range of nonprofessionals—anyone who gives thought to the intricacies of the human condition.

Our grasp of the nature of emotional life and of the workings of the many forms of psychotherapy designed to ameliorate emotional dysfunctions has blossomed yet languished during the hundred years since Sigmund Freud established the mental domain as a subject for scientific investigation. With this as its heritage, psychoanalysis, broadly defined, has been the form of therapy that has served as the main arena for the struggle to achieve a science for the full spectrum of treatment modalities and their theories. It is for this reason that this book unfolds around issues related to psychoanalysis, even though its subject matter and findings are of importance to all treatment forms (see Smith, 1991)—and to emotional life in general.

As discussed in the book, it seems advisable to think in terms of a rather basic definition of psychoanalysis as a branch of the *science of emotional cognition* (Langs & Badalamenti, 1992)—the exploration of the emotional realm. The history of the science of psychoanalysis indicates that until recently it has been carried forward almost entirely through qualitative and unmeasured general observations. This unstructured early phase is as inevitable as the requisite, now, for a more systematic and formal research methodology. This advance to a quantitative and mathematically grounded science is sorely needed, lest therapists and their patients suffer unduly from the inescapable misconceptions and errors characteristic of all grossly observational sciences. Given that the understanding of human emotions is a vital aspect of the search to know ourselves, and that psychotherapy is an intervention made into the lives of millions of people each year, it seems self-evident that we can no longer afford the luxury and dangers of anything less exact and less substantial than a grounding in formal science.

For the many reasons detailed in this book, the communicative approach to psychoanalysis and psychotherapy has proven to be uniquely positioned to establish a pathway from the prevailing impressionistic and statistical modes of science to a formal, mathematical science for the field (Smith, 1991). Indeed, one major goal of this book is to show how this theory, an elaboration of the seminal writings of Freud (1900a), evolved to a point where such a science became a growing necessity and, eventually, a sought-for goal (Langs & Badalamenti, in press). The key factors in this process were (1) the creation of a unique and valid means of listening to and formulating the direct and encoded meanings contained in the communications from both patients and therapists, and (2) the development of a systems theory for psychoanalysis and psychotherapy that supplemented and complemented the usual focus clinically on psychodynamics, self, and interpersonal issues (Langs, 1989c). As described on these pages, the communicative approach not only provided fresh insights into the psychotherapeutic process, but it also took on an evolutionary trajectory that was punctuated by the emergence of several critical anomalies that would not allow the theory to rest easy. The resolution of these unsolved puzzles (Kuhn, 1962) proved to be elusive with the use of the usual clinical methods; a more systematic and definitive strategy was needed. Drawing upon a number of unusual resources, planned and unplanned, the outcome was the realization of the goal of a scientific foundation for psychoanalysis—and for all forms of psychotherapy.

* * *

The book begins by establishing the need for a formal science of psychoanalysis and then presents the distinctive features of the communicative approach that moved it towards the creation of that science. Next, it shows how this development was facilitated by a return to the psychoanalytic art of model-making (of the human *mind*), an activity that was rewarded with many new perspectives on emotional functioning and the therapeutic interaction. From there, the book turns to a presentation of an elaborate, clinically grounded systems theory for psychoanalysis and psychotherapy; systemic thinking proved to be a vital element in the transition from qualitative to quantitative science. This is followed by a critique of present-day psychoanalytic science, one that stresses its constricting Aristotelian qualities and points the way to a Galilean and post-Galilean form (see also Langs, 1987c, 1988d). Finally, a formal science of psychoanalysis is introduced, along with some initial results. The evolution from critique to definitive findings, and from descriptive to mathematically based science, is thereby accomplished.

In moving towards a formal science for psychoanalysis, it will prove helpful to understand that the term "science" is used in this book in three distinctive ways (for details, see Langs & Badalamenti, 1992, in press). The first alludes to the descriptive or Aristotelian mode of science—psychoanalysis as a science in the sense that Freud first defined it. We now call this *domain science* because it is established by fiat through the claim to an aspect of nature not previously investigated with scientific spirit. Domain science is a qualitative and impressionistic form of science that is typically both highly imaginative and virtually certain to embody grave and unrecognized errors; it must in time be supplemented with the development of two other modes of science.

The advance to the first of these additional forms of science was initiated for psychoanalysis some 50 years ago with the development of *statistical science*, which introduced quantification, controlled study, and a host of other, more rigorous methods and standards as compared to domain science (Langs & Badalamenti, 1991b, 1992, in press; Shulman, 1990). However, this science is one that summarizes huge amounts of data with single numbers in a fashion that limits the insights it can generate and renders it, in general, of only minor consequence to psychoanalytic theory and its adherents.

The transition to the third mode of psychoanalytic science, *formal science*, is made through *stochastic models* that attempt to summarize the trajectories of quantified time-series data with *post hoc* mathematical equations that take into account both random and deterministic factors. Although this transitional mode of science cannot define deep laws, it does advance the level of the mathematical techniques that are invoked and the kinds of insights that can be developed through these scientific efforts.

Finally, there is *formal science*, which requires the use of commonplace, yet vital, dimensions that can be both quantified and studied from moment to moment. Here the search is for the laws of nature and for individual variations in how these laws are obeyed. Beyond these basic achievements, as shown in preliminary fashion in the final chapter of this book, this mode of science offers the promise of a definitive and quantified approach to many complex and uncertain issues in psychotherapy and psychoanalysis. This potential is illustrated by bringing formal science results to bear on the basic issues of defining sound therapy techniques and identifying the presence of countertransference in a psychotherapist. This effort is offered as the first of what hopefully will be many important, practical applications of these new methods.

* * *

For the record, chapters three and five were adumbrated by a paper on a systems theory for psychoanalysis that appeared in *Contemporary Psychoanalysis* (Langs, 1989c), and chapter six is a modified version of a paper that was first published in the same journal (Langs, 1987c). I am grateful to the editor-in-chief of the journal, Arthur Feiner, and to his editorial board for permission to publish reworked versions of this material in this book. Chapter seven was developed and written in collaboration with Anthony Badalamenti, Ph.D., to whom this book is dedicated. The good fortune of working with him, and the inspiration and ideas he brought to our partnership (our emergent research system), gave vitality and fulfillment to my own expanding efforts.

* * *

This book wends its way through the various modes of science until a formal science is established. The intention is to show how the communicative form of psychoanalytic theory leads to the beginnings of a formal science that can be broadly applied to all forms of psychotherapy and to emotionally charged interactions in everyday life. Along the way, the clinical and scientific utility of each step taken down this unusual path is delineated and defended. Many unprecedented clinical ideas come forth as we proceed. The hope is to present a convincing sequence that enables the reader to extend his or her purview and understanding on many interrelated levels—clinical, psychodynamic, systems dynamic, and scientific. Indeed, it is this uniquely varied yet comprehensive approach that seems to distinguish this volume most. And it is this investigation of multiple levels of interaction, communication, mental processing, and the like, carried out with a variety of conceptual and scientific tools and ideas, that gives freshness to this work—a vitality that has hopefully been passed on to the reader. There is, in all, a diversity here that becomes integrated into a unified theory that provides, it is hoped, fresh vantage points and new perspectives into the remarkable complexities of psychotherapy, psychoanalysis, and human emotional life.

Robert Langs, M. D.
New York

FOREWORD

W. W. Meissner

Robert Langs has established himself through his contributions over the last score of years as a major contributor to the disciplines of psychoanalysis and psychotherapy. He has been one of the prominent advocates of the bipersonal emphasis—his view of the field of interaction arising between therapist and patient as a "bipersonal field" is well known. Those who have followed the development of his ideas over the years will not be surprised by the line of thinking in this new work, since it is essentially an attempt to systematize and articulate his basic clinical insights in a more scientifically consistent and acceptable way.

This effort comes at an opportune time. The body of theory Langs addresses is psychoanalysis, and that collection of theoretical perspectives and principles is under dire attack from many sides. In a climate of opinion created by the onslaughts of a group of psychoanalytic thinkers—including many followers of the late David Rapaport: George Klein, Robert Holt, Roy Schafer, Philip Holzman, Merton Gill, and others—the basic psychoanalytic metapsychology has been put under exhaustive and challenging scrutiny. In that climate of doubt and uncertainty, Adolf Grunbaum (1984) launched his detailed and magisterial criticism of psychoanalytic epistemology and methodology. Grunbaum's onslaught elicited staunch defence on the part of psychoanalytic defenders—Wallerstein, Wallace, Meissner, Van Spruiell—some of whom Langs cites. The outcome of the debate was somewhat uncertain, but clearly Grunbaum's astute argumentation had struck a sensitive chord, if not an Achilles' heel of psychoanalysis. The issues that the argument brought into focus and that have challenged and continue to challenge the best efforts of current psychoanalytic theoreticians are twofold: (1) can psychoanalytic concepts be formulated in a manner consistent with other scientific disciplines; and (2) is it possible to articulate an understanding of the epistemological basis of psychoanalysis that would respect the derivation of psychoanalytic formulations within the clinical context, independently of any further extraclinical verification.

The first issue involves the question regarding the nature of psychoanalysis as a scientific discipline: can it qualify as a natural science or not? Grunbaum argued that it was, but that it was confined to serving only an heuristic role, and that because of built-in sources of contamination of the data it could not play any role in validation or verification of its heuristic propositions. Langs seems to accept this verdict and responds to it by a dual strategy. The first involves the translation of psychoanalytic terms into the language of information systems theory. Previous efforts to make this translation have been only partially successful, but Langs adds an important note that may have a saving grace. He insists that systems theory must be complemented by a psychodynamic perspective. The suggestion is intriguing since the dynamic aspect is often what seems to be omitted or glossed over in systems theory formulations—as though psychoanalysis could become a kind of sophisticated cognitive control theory. Langs avoids this pitfall, but it remains somewhat unclear what the final form of his theory would be and to what degree it succeeds in covering the real data base of psychoanalysis.

The second part of Langs' strategy involves the use of data derived from actual clinical experience in the form of recorded analytic and therapeutic sessions. The strategy is one that has been under development by research analysts such as Merton

Gill and Hartvig Dahl. The approach has definite advantages, especially in the light of the revolutionary growth of capacity to store, retrieve, and process data provided by advances in computer technology. Langs is not slow to make use of these resources. But he does not address the problems inherent in the use of such clinical recordings, nor does he consider the built-in limitations such an approach imposes (Meissner, 1989). What is happening in the respective minds and hearts of both analyst and patient is not available in any kind of recording, audio or video. Even with such recording, there are no facts without interpretations. That message was brought home clearly in the recent Rodney King videotape. Moreover, reliance on such data runs the risk of reducing the analytic experience to the objectivized data available in these recordings. We would have no resource for meeting Spence's (1982) demand for an unpacking of the analytic process. But this touches the heart of the matter—what are the analytic data, and can they be utilized in a manner consistent with scientific needs? My own view is that the situation is much more complex than Langs' account conveys (Meissner, 1991).

Langs' approach to the second issue—can the clinical data of analysis serve as a scientific data base that does not require extraclinical verification to substantiate its claims to scientific legitimacy—is not so clear. Here his attempts to dichotomize and to disparage the accomplishments of traditional psychoanalysis will not please many of his readers. The distinctions he draws between the two types of "psychoscope," the F-scope and the C-scope, may be more caricatures than real, more strawmen serving pedagogical ends than reflecting the true character of psychoanalytic data processing in given historical contexts. The F-scope is the approach to analytic data characteristic of classical psychoanalysis that aims at defining the infrastructure and unconscious meanings in the therapeutic dialogue, whether on the part of the patient or the therapist, by way of the translation of hidden meanings and motives into manifest symptoms or mental contents. Langs' trenchant criticisms of this approach to analytic data leave little doubt that he finds it not only useless but misleading. Whatever deficiencies are found in the Freudian F-scope, these are remedied by the Langian C-scope, which is communicative and interactional, and dynamic as opposed to the static quality of the F-scope. The C-scope seems to add the interactional component that Langs finds lacking in the F-scope—that, for example, the dream content is not merely the result of unconscious latent drive-dependent dream thoughts coming to expression via defensive channels, but it is in part the result of interactional input that triggers a preliminary response on both conscious and subliminal levels, thus eliciting the dream images. The caricature of pre-Langian F-scope psychoanalysis will strike many as overly simplistic, excessively reflecting concentration on a long-outdated Freudian model, and not congruent with much of current psychoanalytic thinking.

But Langs is clearly trying to establish his idea of the data base of psychoanalysis—an effort that many will applaud and support. Again there is risk of over-simplication—the F-scope may still have its place and function, even as the C-scope finds its proper application. Here again the issue of the heterogeneity of the psychoanalytic method and the diversity of its data and interpretive methods raises its problematical head.

The contribution here should be saluted and respected as it enters the field of dispute and challenge. The effort to clarify the data base and to rationalize its implementation in scientifically and methodologically acceptable terms is both courageous and praiseworthy. Many will find its terms and methods troublesome, many more will find the approach debatable, but the effort demands respect. It is one thoughtful and creative psychoanalyst's attempt to join the issues that are so fundamental and worrisome in the current climate of anti-analytic and anti-scientific criticism. Langs has outlined a systematic approach to the study of psychoanalytic and psychotherapeutic processes. I find the models he provides of conscious and unconscious mental processing worthy of careful scrutiny and assessment in relation to the full range of clinical experience. If they seem more encompassing of research findings, will they provide a solid basis for clinical application? Can the models hold their own as representations of the total range of psychic functioning rather than as more sophisticated cognitive processors—even though they seem to encompass the complexities of integrated conscious and unconscious mental processing. Comparison to the models of the *Project* or the famous seventh chapter of *The Interpretation of Dreams* would prove not only interesting but illuminating. The question for the reader and for the field of clinical study that is the focus of such scientific interest is whether the epistemology and methodology here presented satisfy the scientific need of the field and sufficiently reflect the nature and quality of clinical experience. That verdict must await the test of time. But the field of psychoanalysis and its related forms of psychotherapy cannot fail to be enriched by this thoughtful and thought-provoking study, one that will challenge analytic thinkers to rethink their attitudes towards psychoanalysis as a scientific discipline even as it points the way towards a possible solution to this difficult and perplexing problem.

INTRODUCTION

Karl H. Pribram

At a dinner meeting of the San Francisco psychoanalytic society, I found myself sitting happily between Ken Colby and Alan Newell. Ken was enthusiastically telling us of a computer program he had devised, which was based on psychoanalytic premises into which were entered the interactions between Colby and one of his patients. Every weekend Colby would attempt to predict the following week's sessions. When prediction failed, he would error-correct the program to include the new data.

Newell was equally enthusiastic about how well his General Problem Solving program was faring in winning chess games against more and more formidable antagonists. He too error-corrected his program, updating it whenever a chess master defeated the computer. This was accomplished by asking the master what strategies he was implementing and adding these to the General Problem Solver.

I chimed in with the observation that both Colby and Newell were obviously using practically identical techniques. Further, I felt that Colby was enacting in his program the procedure developed by Freud, which has been the essence of psychotherapy and the resultant psychoanalytic theories (which are, when they become formal, fairly similar to computer programs). We joked that we have a choice: either computer science is not *really* a science (an accusation that has so often been tendered against psychoanalysis), or else psychoanalysis is, and always has been, a science.

Bob Langs, in this new book, aims to take the psychoanalytic enterprise a step further in its development into a mature science by adding measurement and a more formal (i.e. quantitative and perhaps logical) systems approach. How well he succeeds, I leave readers to judge for themselves. For my part, I am sufficiently impressed to accept his invitation to write this introduction. In doing so, I wondered what I might say that would illuminate his aim. The answer to this question came to me in the context of a concern that has been a focus of discussion among my colleagues in the computer sciences: just what kind of science is computer science?

Here I want to make this question a more general one: what kind of science characterizes the classical natural sciences? Is the science of biology similar or different? And what about the behavioural sciences? What is the role of formalism and mathematics in these various sciences?

To begin to answer these questions, I hark back to the epilogue of *Plans and the Structure of Behavior* (1960) where George Miller, Eugene Galanter, and I declared ourselves to be subjective behaviourists. *Plans* has often been cited as heralding the coming cognitive revolution in experimental psychology. What has rarely been realized, however, is that in *Plans* we proposed a new method for the behavioural sciences: the method of re-enactment, of simulation of observed behavioural relationships:

> Life is more than a thing, an object, a substance that exists. It is also a process that is enacted. We have a choice in our approach to it. We can choose to describe it, or we can choose to re-enact it. Description in its various ramifications is the traditional approach of the scientist. Re-enactment has been the traditional approach of the artist. And just as description depends upon an Image, re-enactment depends upon a Plan.

> Re-enactment has lived on the technological borders of pure science for a long time—the planetarium is an astronomer's re-enactment of the solar system, the model is an engineer's pre-enactment of his structure, the wind tunnel is an aeronautical re-enactment of the atmosphere—but it has usually played a supporting role. If a description is correct and accurate, re-enactments based upon it should closely resemble the natural phenomenon that was described. Now, however, re-enactment is emerging as a scientistic alternate in its own right. The development of modern computing machines, more than anything else, has given scientists the tools required to re-enact, or simulate, on a large scale, the processes they want to study. The program for a computer that re-enacts a process is becoming just as acceptable a theory of that process as would be the equations describing it. There is still much that needs to be clarified in this new application of the artist's ancient attitude, but clarification will not lag far behind application. [pp. 213–214]

Lang's use of systems theory fits this paradigm and places his theory squarely within the frame of cognitive science.

Is re-enactment limited to the cognitive sciences? I don't believe so. In biology, the biochemist uses *in vitro* test-tube simulations of *in vivo* physiological chemical processes in a most fruitful fashion. Interestingly, both these and the simulation pursued in the cognitive sciences are based on apparatus formed of silicon.

Interestingly, both in chemistry and in computer science, two avenues have been opened and become established: intelligent computational systems and organic chemical ones depart from their behavioural and biological roots to create technological miracles. By contrast, biochemistry and the neural network aspect of artificial intelligence attempt to further knowledge regarding brain, behaviour, and experienced relationships.

Finally, even in physics, re-enactment may have gone unrecognized. Perhaps the formalisms of mathematics are really to be seen as re-enactments—or, better, pre-enactments—of physical processes. The idea that these formalisms are descriptive has led to considerable worry that Gödel's theorem is operative and that, when applied to the computer sciences, formalism becomes a dead end—that is, that the computer science itself may come to a dead end.

But in physics formalism has been a liberating influence when the formalism is accompanied by conceptualization. This must mean that the formal structure of physics is indeed a simulation, a pre- and re-enactment, which can be played with to further understanding. Viewed in this light, perhaps what science itself is all about has up to now been misinterpreted in some quarters.

Re-enactment is, however, not the only differentiating characteristic of current cognitive science. Equally important is its cross-scale approach. Systems theory is cross-scale and is practised in two forms: (1) General Systems Theory, which demonstrates that there are formal identities among scales, and these identities are expressed as self-similarities among *models* of various levels of inquiry (self-similarities such as those demonstrated by fractals are an example); (2) transformations, the transfer functions that relate models at different levels of inquiry to one another (see, Pribram, 1991, p. 2). It is this second use of systems theory that informs Langs' conceptualizations of the relation between unconscious and conscious processes.

In *Freud's 'Project' Re-assessed* (1976), Merton Gill and I pointed out that

> Whereas behaviouristic psychology had an apparently clear theoretical field in which to develop its clinical applications, cognitive scientists will find in classical psychoanalysis and all of its offshoots a venerable [cognitive] psychology formulated on its own terms. [p. 9]

At the end of the epilogue of our re-assessment, Gill and I concluded:

> Reductive explanation of psychoanalytic knowledge is not what either of us espouses. Pribram, however, feels there is a place in the scientific scheme for investigators and practitioners working at the interface between disciplines. Further, he feels that often, though not always, the most significant advances in understanding and in practice arise at such interfaces. Pribram proposes two examples: the meaning of a phrase of music is certainly largely independ-

> ent of the characteristics of the medium in which that music is realized; a high-level programmer can function reasonably well without knowing whether his program is going to be realized with an IBM or a CDC computer. But *somebody* has to know—a conductor, a taping expert, an assembler of machine language, etc.—else the music and program remain unrealized. Gill feels, on the other hand, that a knowledge of the medium in which the music or program is realized tells us nothing about the music *as music* or the program *as program*.
>
> Pribram feels that it is important that this volume addresses and finds audience in these 'somebodies' working at the brain–behaviour–experience interfaces. Specifically, he urges psychologists in the physiological and in the cognitive areas to review the *Project* for currently relevant, comprehensive and detailed theories of thinking and consciousness. Gill also feels that they ought to read it, and that psychoanalysts will profit by sympathetic study of Freud's *Project* because it is, in important respects, considerably more explicit than Chapter 7 of *The Interpretation of Dreams*—their current source for metapsychological understanding. Where we differ is that Gill feels that psychoanalysis must go its own way and that means purging it of its natural science metapsychology, while Pribram welcomes psychoanalysis back into the natural sciences. Pribram doubts that the differing views of the two authors are really, in the long run, incompatible, while Gill finds them irreconcilable. [pp. 168–169]

I am therefore personally delighted that some 15 years later Langs has taken up the challenge on my side of this friendly exchange.

Description and re-enactment are now brought together in Langs' fresh approach to the psychoanalytic enterprise. There is still a great deal to be done, of course. But the following pages provide a most promising beginning.

PART ONE

OBSERVATION, THEORY, AND PRACTICE IN PSYCHOANALYSIS AND PSYCHOTHERAPY

CHAPTER ONE

The call for a science of psychoanalysis

> So, I for one, think it is gratuitous for anyone to enquire into the causes of the motion towards the centre when once the fact that the earth occupies the middle place in the universe, and that all weights move towards it, is made so patent by the observed phenomena themselves.
>
> Ptolemy, *Almagest*

As we approach the twenty-first century and celebrate the one-hundredth anniversary of Freud's great innovation, classical psychoanalysis, we do well to pause to reflect on the state of the field. There is much that has been accomplished: we have a theory that has moved through a number of transformations, from a basically topographic and instinctual drive configuration to one that now embraces object relations (both internal and external), self, mental structures (ego, id, and superego), a theory of personality and development, and much more. There is, as well, a body of clinical precepts that offer a flexible guide to therapeutic practice, enabling both formal psychoanalysis and dynamic forms of psychotherapy as they are applied to a broad range of psychopathological dysfunctions. And, of late, there is also a growing body of clinical research—including a measure of science—that has in some broad and general sense tended to support prevailing psychoanalytic ideas (for example, the importance of a therapeutic alliance between patient and therapist [e.g., Alexander & Luborsky, 1986; Marmar, Horowitz, Weiss, & Marziali, 1986]).

Indeed, for most clinicians—and at the moment, virtually everyone in the field, including most of those engaged in formal research, is basically committed to clinical practice—the existing conceptions of dynamics and genetics are sufficiently rich to fulfil substantially their needs for an adequate and workable clinical theory. Then, too, their actual clinical work is by and large equally satisfying: most practising therapists find contentment with their clinical accomplishments, and they are in some self-reassuring way able to account for the occasional failures of their therapeutic efforts. Calm seas prevail.

On a loftier level, the absence of a definable science of psychoanalysis is also no great cause for concern; by and large, it is a void that is seen as a result of the special attributes and uniquely undefinable characteristics of the psychotherapeutic encounter (Bornstein, 1989; Edelson, 1984, 1989; Wallace, 1989). Some writers believe that the situation will remain as such for years to come, while others hold to the belief that in time a more scientific stance will be developed. Existing efforts to broaden the base of psychoanalytic thinking—for example, by introducing information theory into its domain (Peterfreund, 1971; Rosenblatt & Thickstun, 1977, 1984) or by providing the field with a systems point of view (Newton, 1971, 1973, 1989; Peterfreund, 1971)—have been met with relative indifference or refutation (see, for example, Wallerstein, 1986). There is evidently little felt need for much that extends beyond the fundamental base of dynamic and genetic classical thinking—and its elaboration by way of self psychology and object relations theory (see also Smith, 1991).

I do not mean to imply that psychoanalysis is without its critics, since this is far from the case. However, most of the doubts that have been raised come from psychotherapy researchers and others who are far from the main stream of the field. Indeed, some of the themes I attempt to develop here have been touched on by prior writers (see, for example, Holt, 1985), though none of these critiques has enabled us to forge a pathway to science—the ultimate goal of this book. Still, there is little that can be said that has not been foreshadowed by others; one can only hope to garner fresh evidence and additional lines of thought in attempting to assess fairly and identify soft points in the current psychoanalytic position.

To cite a few examples, Holt (1985) has written of the disorder in the field and the untestability of commonly accepted psychoanalytic propositions—an observation supported by many other writers, including a number who have attempted to design relevant research studies (e.g. Ford & Urban, 1963; Kiesler, 1966; Orlinsky & Howard, 1978).

Inconsistencies in the practice of therapists working on the basis of shared propositions has been widely observed (e.g. Glover, 1940; Kiesler, 1966). Along different lines, Strupp and Bergin (1969) have tellingly pointed out that psychotherapy research has yet to produce a significant unanticipated finding and is yet to affect profoundly the field at large. Then, too, Rieff (1979) has discussed the distinct ambivalence shown by psychoanalysts towards existing research efforts and their results.

Of course, a close look at any field will bring into bold relief the inconsistencies and uncertainties that are generally overlooked by most practitioners. For the moment, it is well to realize that these are isolated voices barely heard as a whisper over the crowd of undaunted clinicians, and at this point essentially without a solution to the generally noted chaos. We need a more definitive critique, and certainly one that leads us towards new avenues of methodology and understanding.

* * *

To continue the development of my own critique, it seems fair to state that psychoanalysis (a term I will use to refer to all forms of dynamic psychotherapy informed by any notion of unconscious experience or communication) at the moment stands apart from other sciences in somewhat splendid isolation, content to operate within its own domain, with little clamour for substantial change. On the clinical level, there are minor discontents and some debate among those advocating one or another version of standard theory (if such a theory can be defined to any degree of general agreement), but small advances are made from year to year, and they are sufficient to maintain the general status quo.

Given this general sense of satisfaction, I find it difficult to disturb this universe and argue that there may well be a considerable measure of self-deception in this complacency. Viewed from within, the psychoanalytic system is completely self-contained and self-perpetuating. While critics emerge here and there, there is no organized voice—from within or without—of scepticism and no sense of basic flaw. When seemingly minor clinical uncertainties crop up, slight revisions are made in the basic theory to account for the anomalies. If certain patients prove to be unanalysable, it is because of a certain type of masked psychosis or due to a failure to analyse unrecognized narcissistic transferences properly. Either psychoanalysis has reached its golden age of near-total wisdom, or it has unwittingly created another science in which epicycles—the kind of modifications within modifications that sustained for over one thousand years the Ptolemaic theory that the earth was the centre of the universe—constituted as adjustments in the central dogma are serving in some significant way to cover over basic flaws in thinking.

In introducing the problem of psychoanalysis as science—a topic that concerns us throughout this book—it behoves us to acknowledge Freud's (1917a, 1933a, 1940a) insistent position that psychoanalysis is a science, albeit a psychological science, and that the field must accept not only the canons and requisites of the physical sciences, but also has no choice but to accept the *Weltanschauung* (the world view; cf. Freud, 1933a) of science as its own as well. Freud wrote knowingly of the initial crudeness of this science, at the time less than fifty years old; his discussions stress scientific methodology, the elusive search for ever-changing truths, hypothesis testing, and the like. However, a careful reading of his ideas reveals that Freud sees the analytical clinical setting as a laboratory in which this work could be carried out, largely though hypotheses related to unconscious processes whose existence could be verified through clinical judgement. In the end, then, Freud's science is, at best, a kind of pseudo-science (Conti, 1989) that lacks the necessary rigours of quantification, controlled study, and other essential safeguards of the scientific method. Freud's statement nonetheless represents the hopes of the field for scientific status—a quest we will explore as we go on.

* * *

Turning now to our search for indications that psychoanalysis is actually a field in difficulty, we may take as our first sign that there is a the striking absence of clear signs of trouble. This lack of major and disquieting unsolved puzzles (to use Kuhn's, 1962, term) in our vast clinical literature—problems that would goad both clinicians and theorists or researchers into coming face-to-face with the insufficiencies in current analytic theory and practice—creates a situation that is also all too reminiscent of the classical mechanics of Newton, which seemed to explain exactly how the entire universe—past, present, and future—operated on the most fundamental levels. (Of course, Newtonian physics was based on quantification and formal science rather than qualification and impression—the sources of psychoanalytic theory.) It required persistent unsolvable puzzles, such as the spectra given off by black body radiation and the perihelion of the planet Mercury, to create an unceasing pressure for new solutions before quantum theory and relativity—two distinctly new paradigms—emerged from the fountainhead of the Newtonian physics, which they both so radically revised.

In a sense, this absence of anomalies touches on a recurrent problem that has been something of an irritant for psychoanalysis: the falsifiability issue (Grunbaum, 1984; Popper, 1959). A debate has stirred the field regarding the question as to whether psychoanalysis can produce hypotheses that are experimentally or even clinically falsifiable. There are many who feel that this cannot be done because of the individuality of each therapeutic experience for the patient. It seems clear that present psychoanalytic clinical theory and its accompanying research has not produced these falsifiable hypotheses, nor has it called into question or invalidated a major psychoanalytic postulate. From another vantage point this is tantamount to saying that there are no clearly defined unsolved puzzles for the field; for this to be the case, an errant hypothesis or a major unexplained clinical phenomenon—a thorny issue of some kind—would have to exist.

The history of science speaks strongly for the likelihood that psychoanalysis will go through a typical developmental pathway that begins—indeed, has already begun—with a generally qualitative and impressionistic phase during which there is a prevailing sense of great—almost unbounded—explanatory power and little sense of limitation. This phase is characteristically sustained by individuals with impressive gifts of persuasion and deep, generally shared, needs for the status quo. Change is difficult to foster, because those involved are mainly clinicians whose clinical work is based on the very tenets that would need to be challenged if evolution and science were to advance.

Such a state of affairs is likely to be maintained as long as there is no solid means of quantifying psychoanalytic data. As Kuhn (1962) has cogently noted, in a field where qualitative impressions prevail, disputes as to the validity of one or another theoretical position are all but impossible to resolve. At such junctures, unconscious needs play an especially significant role in one's choice of ideology and belief—and even what one professes to observe. Paradoxically, it is the presence of unsolved puzzles, so difficult to establish through general and qualitative impressions, that is the prime mover of a field towards measurement; anomalies stimulate the use of quantification, because it is a most powerful means of finding satisfactory solutions to newly discovered and disturbing dilemmas. As a rule, it also requires a significant and basic departure from accepted theory to create any notable pressure for change during this phase of contentment, and as such, the new theory—experienced as an enigma and threat to complacency by those allied to existing theory—will inevitably have great difficulty finding general acceptance. It is indeed a wonder that science progresses at all, yet it always does so—whatever the inertial lag.

Where, then, are the unsolved puzzles of psychoanalysis? Surely they must exist. And how do we find the lens—the new paradigm—through which they may be defined and eventually understood, thereby substantially modifying existing thought?

To answer these important questions, we must find a way to create a foundation for a science of psychoanalysis—and then a science itself. For once the anomalies are identified, there can be no other sound way to resolve them except through the use of a definitive scientific method for the field. Anything less measured permits an ambience in which the seeming new solution is very likely to be nothing more than another qualitative claim and still another epicycle. After one hundred years of such pseudo-solutions and pseudo-science (Conti, 1989), it is time for us to opt for something far more definitive.

* * *

We must, then, pull ourselves up by our own bootstraps. Despite our realization that we must be trapped in some sense within the unseen flaws of our own theory, we must find some way of freeing ourselves from the chains that keep us within Plato's cave where illusion and delusion are so commonplace. We need, then, a new way of organizing psychoanalytic data—of listening to and formulating the therapeutic dialogue; if nothing else, we need to experiment with new ways of listening to see if a new vision emerges—and with it, those missing puzzles we so sorely must catch hold of if the field of psychoanalysis is to move forward.

There will, I suspect, eventually be many attempts at reformulation and fresh thinking in psychoanalysis; given the humanness of its endeavours, periods of uncertainty and discontent are inevitable. In the first part of this book, I will try my hand at offering a new perspective which raises a number of significant questions that I believe cannot find satisfactory answers through current dogma. Hopefully, these arguments will prove convincing; for me, they are sufficiently strong to motivate me to use them as a justification for expanding psychoanalytic theory by offering a somewhat new and definitive means of accessing the unconscious domain and by generating an elaborate systems theory for the field. I will also propose a new model of the mind related to the means by which we process emotionally charged information and meaning. All of these fresh ventures will be cause for a new definition of psychoanalysis itself. And the entire effort will culminate in a formal critique of psychoanalysis as a science, and in the offer of the outlines and initial quantitative results of one form this science may well at last be taking.

This is likely to be a difficult journey. I will argue that in its present form the main body of psychoanalytic theory is probably not capable of spawning a Galilean/post-Galilean (modern-day) science, but that with suitable modifications such a science is possible and even likely—if not certain—to emerge. But this means that we will have to question seriously some basic psychoanalytic postulates of the very kind that are not only now accepted without question, but also part of the bedrock foundation of today's clinical practice. It asks a lot of a reader to question such fundamentals, but doing so is, I believe, the only way that the field can genuinely change and evolve. Indeed, if tolerating doubt and withholding judgement is the only way that we can experience a sufficient number of anomalies or unsolved puzzles within psychoanalysis to force us to move into the domain of modern science, then we should all be prepared to do so. By creating doubt, widening and revising existing theory, and providing a foundation for a formal science—even if we err here and there along the way—we ourselves and the field at large can only stand to gain.

Some problems in clinical practice

Though I write now as a full-time researcher and teacher of psychoanalysis, for some thirty years I shared with others the usual position of those in the field of dynamic psychotherapies—that of a practitioner. Psychoanalysis can boast of few individuals committed entirely or primarily to psychoanalytic research, however crude the undertaking. Even then such researchers as do exist show at least two problematic features, both of which are difficult to overcome. First, they tend to be extremely biased through a commitment to one particular version of psychoanalytic theory—and I myself do not claim the status of an exception. All anyone can do is to try to move as much as possible away from the values and position of an inevitably prejudiced clinician, towards that of a naturalist and open observer; we need, too, a genuine capacity to search for new paradigms, and more basically to develop and use a theory that is flexible and sound enough to reveal those aspects of nature—for us, the therapeutic interaction—that insist upon a search for new ideas. Second, psychoanalytic researchers (and practitioners) are all too slowly just beginning to absorb and utilize a working knowledge of mathematics, computer and systems science, and quantitative methods such as those used in physics and other sciences, which can provide them with the kind of multi-levelled knowledge and instrumentation necessary to create and advance a formal science of psychoanalysis. In the final chapter of this book I attempt to indicate in some preliminary way the kinds of advances that can be made with such knowledge in hand.

Actually, it appears that few, if any, researchers have adopted a major commitment to forging such a science; most are content with correlational studies that reveal gross trends that involve findings of general interest to the field. Indeed, it appears that it is mainly philosophers such as Grunbaum (1984) and psychoanalytic theoreticians such as Edelson (1984, 1989) who are concerned with the question of whether psychoanalysis can ever be a science in the sense that physics and chemistry are sciences, and if so, how this might be accomplished.

I speak of this in order to indicate again the considerable problems that stand before us if we wish to create an established science for psychoanalysis. How are we to overcome inevitable bias and acquire the tools we will need? It is accepted knowledge that it is impossible to organize—meaningfully see—nature without the lens of a sound theory, yet our situation is such that we must be able to find ways of inventing a visionary lens without the help of an available one that would make the next step easier to negotiate. We must also be capable of generating findings—clinical or research—that cast doubts on our theory and move us to question the implications of our results. Though we are all committed in principle to these attitudes, they are difficult to achieve in practice.

We are all the more hard-pressed because we lack the 'pure' theoreticians who would normally be committed without question to observing nature with a minimum of bias, and to creating a science and testing our psychoanalytic postulates in the crucible of an appropriate psychoanalytic laboratory. We are, as I said, mainly a field of practitioners—'engineers', to use the language of physics. After all, psychoanalysis was created by an 'applied' psychoanalyst, an individual who had a service to offer and a living to earn—and who remarkably enough created an elaborate theory along the way. We are yet to appreciate fully the effects of this fateful aspect of the history of the field, a deep influence that is with us to this very day.

Unfortunately, practitioners make poor scientists; they are poor observers in general. They are strongly and understandably motivated to justify their techniques and interventions, and to rationalize away anything but an overwhelming degree of evidence that there are basic flaws in the procedures that they are using—and, perhaps even more ominously, that some aspects of what they are doing may be harmful to their patients. This quite natural attitude is difficult to modify despite all good intentions. Given that psychoanalysis sees itself as a healing art and that the very nature and, at times, existence of the lives of those who offer and submit to its procedures are at stake, the clinician is likely to leave little room for doubt and uncertainty. Given the ways of human nature—both before and after personal psychotherapy or psychoanalysis—until psychoanalysis creates and supports its own fully qualified theoreticians who are at the same time deeply informed as to practice (this may well be a two-step process, with clinical practice and scientific training in the first phase, and 'pure' research in the second), the field will be extremely hard-pressed to recognize the limits of its explanatory domain (a requisite for every science) and of its healing powers. Once more, an offshoot of the falsifiability issue is before us: without falsifiable hypotheses and anomalies, the unexplained territory cannot be mapped; much that is related to adventure and growth is thereby lost.

We are faced, then, with another paradox: at the very moment that we are searching for clinical and other indications of a dire need for a science of psychoanalysis, we require that very science and its scientists to show us in clear measure that the need itself does exist. In the absence of quantified observations and data, all we can do for the moment is turn to clinical observations that might well raise some serious questions with existing ideas. If we are successful in this pursuit, we will feel justified in proposing some amendments to current theory—and practice.

* * *

Perhaps first among these anomalies—and it stands in the broader domain of psychotherapy in general—is the fact that there are today some 350 forms of psychotherapy, each a somewhat different proposed means of bringing relief to individuals who are suffering emotionally. Many of these approaches stand in near-total contradiction to each other, though many share ideas in common as well. Yet despite efforts to integrate these diversities, there is an unsettling quality to the realization that relief from emotional suffering is said to come from methods as different as deconditioning; bodily exercises; family therapy carried out by multiple therapists, at times with the use of a one-way mirror; individual, insight-oriented psychotherapy carried out in a highly private setting; the use of chemical substances and even the controlled use of electricity applied to the brain; and a seemingly endless array of other techniques. Virtually all of these practices are supported by a set of theoretical postulates—theories that in many instances are mutually contradictory as well.

This situation is reminiscent of the early centuries of medical practice, when, by today's standards, techniques now known to be of little if any value, such as the use of amulets and magical incantations, were in abundant use. Each approach had its champions in both patients and therapists. We must therefore be forewarned that qualitative impressions of favourable outcome are an unreliable guide to the validity of any theory or practice—then and now. There is far too great a human need for over-idealization of therapy and therapist, and far too much denial of detrimental consequences, for this criterion to prove illuminating (Langs, 1982a, 1985a, 1989a).

Chaos and contradictions of this sort speak quietly for serious problems in both practice and theory. There is at this time no single theory that has established clear command of the field and no single theory that in some overarching way explains this diversity and conflict of claims and ideas. In this light, it is not difficult to see the situation as cause for concern.

Without question, only a formal science of psychoanalysis will be able to change this situation. As I said, the history of science shows unmistakably that it is only with meaningful quantification and mathematical analysis that confusion and conflict of this type can be resolved (Kuhn, 1962). Left to qualitative impressions and relatively trivial measurements, each and every one of these different approaches to psychotherapy can—and does—stake a claim for some type of scientific support, much of it pseudo-scientific (Conti, 1989) at best. At the very least, then, we need a science of psychoanalysis to help us find our way through a maze of therapeutic approaches and ideas that speak for unmanageable confusion and beg for a means of bringing fresh insight that will help us to pass through this confusing epoch. Clearly, a central issue lies in finding the means to establish meaningful quantitative measures.

In arguing for science as the arbiter of clinical and theoretical disputes, we must also acknowledge the vulnerabilities of scientists and avoid an over-idealization of scientific methods and results—which at times, in the history of science, have been quite misleading. Indeed, many false theories—e.g., those of phlogistan and luminiferous ether—had considerable scientific support. The point is to realize that science—and especially dynamic science—is the best we have to go by: it is the best available means of reducing the possibility of error and false belief, and is far more efficient in this respect than qualitative impressions. Furthermore, science also provides us with the optimal means of identifying misconceptions; there is a methodology to science that insists on a continual search for false premises and conclusions and allows for the discovery of data that run counter to theory and theories that do not seem to be supported by sufficient data, or that do not seem to evolve in surprising and meaningful ways that expands our understanding.

In all fairness, it does appear that there is some variety of clinical evidence that most extant forms of psychotherapy can bring a measure of relief to at least certain select patients. But, on the other hand, each of these modes of practice appears to do so at a price—i.e., with a measure of detrimental consequence (Langs, 1982a, 1985a, 1989a). I call this the *help/hurt ratio.* There are indications that in general this price is far higher than we have been prepared to acknowledge or believe. A science of psychoanalysis could help us in time to quantify *both* the measure of relief and its cost, and thereby enable us to develop far more efficient—less costly—ways of doing psychotherapy.

There is much, I believe, to suggest that the universal dread of deep unconscious meaning and of secure frame therapy conditions—i.e., of interactionally decoded narratives and the ideal ground rules of therapy and their inevitable constraints (Langs, 1984–85, 1988a)—are major factors in the denial and overidealization that have to some extent deceived us all. These anxieties create unrecognized, unconscious needs for forms of psychotherapy that fail to arrive at deep unconscious truths and that involve loosely constructed frames as conditions for particular forms of treatment. These problems are compounded by the pervasive *unconscious sense of guilt* experienced by virtually all psychotherapy patients, a malady that prompts a search for hurtful, punitive—rather than insightful—forms of relief. This has its complementary factor within therapists who in the main appear to be motivated by strong fears of the experience of *conscious guilt* (i.e., the acknowledgement of any hurtful consequences of their interventions; Langs, 1989a). Still another factor in this state of uncertainty lies in our universal need for idols and revered parental figures whose omnipotence and omniscience help to support a similarly universal need to deny all sense of personal vulnerability and mortality. The psychotherapy situation is therefore an especially treacherous space within which to seek answers to theoretical problems or to establish its own basic techniques. There are great needs on both sides of the therapy dyad for less than ideal practices and for theories that will support these errant ways. Here, too, the resolution undoubtedly begins with science.

One final point in this connection: much has been written about Freud's (1916–17) tally argument. It was his claim that the outcome of psychoanalysis, since it produces both symptom relief and a sense that the patient's forgotten past has been faithfully reconstructed—that the patient's picture of or insight into past and present realities as interpreted by the analyst tallies with and helps to illuminate the patient's neurosis—speaks for the validity of psychoanalytic theory (see, for example, the discussions by Bucci, 1987; Edelson, 1984; Grunbaum, 1984; Wallace, 1989). On the face of it, this line of thought is specious in that it is patently circular and tautological; one wonders if it is worthy of debate.

Nonetheless, a tally argument can be garnered in some form, however subtle, in each of the existing types of psychotherapy. Advocates claim that because the treatment they offer brings relief to the patient, the theory on which the treatment is based must be accurate and sound. Clearly, however, this myriad of contradictory theories cannot conceivably all be correct and confirmed; and, just as clearly, the tally argument can therefore hold no claim as evidence for a basic theoretical position. Indeed, as systems theorists have shown, a given outcome for a system—here, the relief obtained by a patient in therapy—can come about through any number of different avenues (the systemic rule of equipotential trajectories, of different pathways to the same outcome) and therefore cannot bear testimony to the veracity of any particular approach. We very much need other criteria with which to establish the soundness of a clinical theory—including those that are offered in this book.

The debate over the tally argument has led to the issue of whether psychoanalysis can be subjected to the rigours of formal science or is justified in claiming that it must be accepted as an exception to these standards by virtue of its special and unique attributes. Rather than reviewing and discussing these arguments, I will establish as a fundamental assumption of the present book the proposition that psychoanalysis can indeed develop research techniques that will meet all of the standards of formal science. In the final chapter of the book I hope to show the reader sufficient methodology and initial results to make this position tenable even at this early date.

Defining the field of psychoanalysis

We come now to a second call for a science for psychoanalysis—the problems in defining the field itself. A well-defined domain of psychoanalysis should greatly promote the development of a science for its demarcated territory (which is always, of course, open to expansion); in turn, a science of psychoanalysis would assist us in properly defining the range, limits, boundaries, central attributes and concerns, and purview of the field.

Freud (1923b, 1925d) proposed a definition of psychoanalysis that was both clinically founded and at a high level of abstraction: a psychoanalyst was anyone who accepted in principle the concepts of unconscious mental processes, repression, infantile sexuality, and transference and resistance. By way of contrast, the definition of psychoanalysis that is proposed here as a means of paving the path to science states that *psychoanalysis* is a branch of the *science of emotional cognition.* This newly defined broad science of emotional cognition entails the systematic and properly disciplined investigation of *how human beings experience, process, and communicate emotionally charged information and meaning.* This definition is especially apt in light of Gardner's (1985) definition of *cognitive science,* which is restricted to the investigation of how we process information that lacks emotional charge. I am proposing here that a new science be formalized to investigate the emotional domain.

Psychoanalysis, then, is that branch of the science of emotional cognition for which *the concepts of unconscious mentation, experience, and communication are fundamental axioms.* With this definition established, I would propose an immediate subdivision of the science of psychoanalysis into two components, each with its own distinctive issues and methodologies: (1) d*evelopmental psychoanalysis,* which investigates the unfolding vicissitudes of emotional health and dysfunction in historical perspective, and (2) *interactional psychoanalysis,* which explores the therapeutic interaction and dialogue, including the process of cure. Though the experimental results and theories developed by each of these subdivisions will eventually require integration, it seems best to establish them as distinctive subsciences, since their areas of investigation and methods are so clearly different.

Current psychoanalytic theory may well be a precursor discipline in the sense that phlogistic chemistry—the challenging theory of a postulated chemical substance said to escape from objects when they burned—preceded modern-day chemistry. One might therefore argue for the use of a new term for the new science I am here defining for the field; my own preference is simply to allow the term *psychoanalysis* to remain and evolve its meaning. Still, psychoanalytic practice will undoubtedly require revision as this new scientific paradigm emerges and generates its own, distinctive forms of research and results.

In comparing Freud's definition of psychoanalysis with the definition proposed here, we may note that there are several differences and similarities. Freud's definition is highly conceptual and involves terms that are difficult to define empirically. For example, while gross behavioural resistances—e.g., absences, latenesses, silences—are readily identified and relatively easy to subject to consensus, more subtle and non-manifest resistance—e.g., seeming co-operation in a patient who does not improve clinically; the overuse of intellectualization as a defence; the failure to communicate meaningful material—have until now defied consensus (see, for example, Langs, 1976b, 1981b; Stone, 1973, 1975). The lack of a broad consensus in respect to each of Freud's defining terms for psychoanalysis is more than evident (see, for example, Holt, 1985).

As for the concept of transference, a subject I discuss below and again in chapter two, there is virtually no consensus on its theoretical definition or clinical referents. Definitions range from characterizing transference as the patient's entire relationship with the analyst to restricting it to a selected unconscious component of this relationship (see Bird, 1972; Gill, 1982; Langs, 1980; Sandler et al., 1969). Similar problems—as I also discuss—apply to the definition of the unconscious domain, its expressions, and the means of accessing their meanings.

The present definition of psychoanalysis shares with the classical position the acknowledgement of the need to define properly the unconscious domain, since this is the hallmark of the field. In addition, however, this delineation requires definitions of mentation, experience, and communication. Whatever the clinical and theoretical issues raised by this requisite, these terms are relatively neutral and more easily defined than those that need defining in the classical position.

Freud's definition of psychoanalysis is of the top-down, concept-driven variety, a proposal of high-level concepts that is expected to lead to a search for clinical evidence and other concrete applications. We seem better served by first establishing a definition that entails a bottom-up, data-driven approach—a statement of fundamentals that lie close to direct observation and measurement and are cast in scientific terms that lend themselves more readily to both definition and empirical research. Furthermore, the present definition could also lead to more than a single science of emotional cognition, and would allow for the development of findings that could form the basis for a variety of clinical approaches and theories, all of which could be subjected to scientific scrutiny. Classical psychoanalysis would stand as but one of several branches of the science of emotional cognition. With a fundamental theory in place, it would, then, be possible to enhance the field and its science with top-down ideas, thereby giving full room for imaginative thinking. The resultant science would, then, have a balance between inductive and deductive efforts.

Another important difference between the present definition of the field and the classical approach is that Freud's definition of psychoanalysis, as both science and process, centres on the *mind of the patient*—it is the patient's unconscious mentation (fantasies), transferences, and resistances with which he is mainly concerned (countertransference is an intermittent and secondary issue). It therefore follows that the database for this version of analysis pertains mainly to the products of the patient's mind: his or her inner thoughts and experience. Free association is conceptualized as a reflection of the patient's inner mental world, and the source of scientific observations is the introspective reports of the patient (Edelson, 1984; Kohut, 1971) and the empathy of the psychoanalyst (Kohut, 1971). In contrast, the definition proposed here addresses *communication and interaction, and therefore points to the investigation of the contents of the therapeutic dialogue.*

There is, then, a distinct difference in the type of scientific activities to which each definition of the field would lead. Indeed, a science of psychoanalysis may not be feasible through a study of introspective data that would be difficult to organize and quantify. In addition, the introspective reports from patients completely by-pass the therapeutic interaction and the inputs from the therapist; such reports are the ultimate in isolated patient products. In contrast, communicative dialogues inherently involve interaction and embody dimensions that are readily processed and measured. Overall, then, these revised definitions of psychoanalysis, which define its domain somewhat differently from classical thinking, strongly favour the development of a formal and dynamic science for the field.

Defining the unconscious domain

I have indicated a complete agreement in spirit between the two definitions of psychoanalysis in respect to the pivotal role played by the unconscious domain in defining the field—this is, indeed, its beacon light. Nonetheless, we must realize at the outset in exploring this area that there are dramatic differences between the clinical/empirical definition and use of the concept of unconscious mental processes proposed by the classical psychoanalyst and the delineation for which I argue. Here, too, the issue of deriving a science comes into play in that any basic error in conceptualizing the unconscious domain is likely to make it difficult for a science to emerge. Science is founded on observation, but observations are directed by theory—what is studied, how it is organized and seen, and how things are understood. If a theory is misleading, so, too, will be the observations that support it. In the presence of such confusion, the researcher will typically become preoccupied with ways to find support for the unwitting misconceptions drawn from confounded observations and the theory derived from them. Quite without awareness, under these conditions science is often seen less as an ally and asset, and more as a formalism that endangers the structure of this house of cards. Little ingenuity is applied to the development of scientific techniques, and the field will tend to languish. A sound theory is therefore far more likely to call forth a formal science that one that is misguided. If the errors are fundamental—as with the thesis that the earth was the centre of the universe—no viable definitive science can be developed. We will need to explore carefully the situation with psychoanalysis in order to develop a sound appraisal of the actual state of affairs in our own situation. Here, too, the challenge is to develop the means of recognizing previously unrecognized flaws in both observation and theory.

To map out the course I pursue over the ensuing chapters, I attempt to show that the clinical definition of significant unconscious expressions—in substance, of the unconscious domain—is a matter of uncertainty and debate. I define two approaches to this domain and show that empirically they are founded on rather different levels of observation and formulation. I argue, too, that these two contrasting approaches appear to involve distinctive paradigms (Kuhn, 1962) in that both their methods and the nature of evidence accepted as support for their propositions regarding unconscious mentation and communication are notably different. If I am substantially correct in my assessment of the situation, we will, then, find it necessary to consider the possible flaws in one or the other position and their effects on the search for a science for the field.

Freud (1900a, 1950a [1887–1902]; see also Ellenberger, 1970) initially viewed the unconscious domain as both a particular form of mentation (type of thinking) and a system of the mind—the UCS. In time, manifestly because of clinical evidence that seemed to contradict the proposed model, Freud abandoned the notion of an unconscious mental system (UCS), and considered the term *unconscious* to refer simply to *a quality of mental processes*. Images and thoughts could be either directly experienced in awareness, and therefore conscious, or experienced outside awareness, and therefore unconscious.

However, Freud had also developed, and then maintained, a series of ingenious propositions to the effect that *conscious* thinking has certain characteristics and follows distinctive regulatory principles—alluded to as *secondary process thinking*—that are different from those related to unconscious mentation, which follows the laws of *unconscious or primary process thinking*. Thus, secondary process thinking was seen as logical, reality-attuned, discrete, bound or non-displaced, and, overall, guided by the reality principle. On the other hand, primary process thinking was fluid or easily displaced, symbolic, out of touch with reality, wish-dominated, without a sense of time or negation, and directed towards immediate satisfaction in terms of the pleasure principle. Though subjected to later minor modifications (Basch, 1976; Holt, 1967; Noy, 1969; Pribram & Gill, 1976)—mainly the idea that unconscious thinking shows some appreciation for reality and some degree of structure—these differentiating characteristics can well form the basis for a study not only of how we think emotionally, but also of how we process emotionally charged information and meaning. Science can be served here, even if changes in these postulates prove necessary due to fresh observations and considerations (see chapter three).

Of importance to the present discussion is the realization that as soon as the concept of 'the unconscious' as a system was relegated to a non-systemic descriptive status (Arlow & Brenner, 1964; Freud, 1923a; Gill, 1963), its importance in psychoanalytic thinking and theorizing diminished greatly. Thus, certain ideas were conscious, while others were unconscious; further, there were preconscious ideas that suggested gradations of awareness to the point where there was no clear line between the two domains—conscious and unconscious. Certainly, the idea of unconscious mental processes was by no means abandoned; indeed, psychoanalysts speak today of unconscious resistances, unconscious introjects, and, on occasion, of unconscious fantasies and memories. But issues other than awareness—e.g., defining the nature of intrapsychic conflict or of internal object relations or of selfobject transferences—took centre stage; as a result, the distinction between the conscious and unconscious realms received less and less attention and diminished in importance as an explanatory concept.

For example, Arlow and Brenner (1964), psychoanalysts who have stressed the role of purported unconscious fantasy and memory formations in psychopathology and transference, afford a secondary role to the question of whether a particular fantasy is within or outside awareness at a given moment. For these structuralists, the overriding issue is that of intrapsychic conflict, and whether a patient's communications reflect id, ego, or superego functions—whether conscious or unconscious. In a similar vein, Kohut (1971) and others devoted to self psychology stress idealizing and mirroring transferences, patterns of need and expression that are outside the patient's awareness yet nonetheless are seen to be *expressed manifestly* in dreams and other communications and only rarely by means of a displaced or disguised vehicle. Then, too, those who stress object relations (e.g., Greenberg & Mitchell, 1983; Mitchell, 1988) take a similar approach communicatively and find direct and undisguised evidence in the manifest contents of their patient's communications for the configurations that they postulate to exist.

In the present context, this blurring of the boundaries between the conscious and unconscious domains takes on importance in that many psychoanalytic ideas, even when they pertain to unconscious mental processes, are supported clinically by direct, manifest, conscious communications from patients (Langs, 1981a). For example, evidence for an unconscious maternal introject is reflected in a statement from a patient that at times she feels just like her mother; support for the presence of a merger transference is seen in a patient's conscious wish to be understood by the analyst without having to speak openly. The apparent confusion reflected in the presentation of a conscious statement as evidence for an unconscious constellation is generally disregarded. Nonetheless, it would be exceedingly difficult to create a science for psychoanalysis—which must, as all have agreed, be founded on a clear and unambiguous definition of the unconscious realm—on the basis of theoretical constructs that embody a fundamental confusion as to the nature of conscious and unconscious expressions, and the related definition of psychoanalytic clinical evidence.

For many psychoanalytic thinkers, mentation is less central to the unconscious domain than *patterns* of behaviour, relationships, and being, of which the patient is unaware. These patterns—e.g., of self-destructive behaviours when under stress, of tendencies to eat when depressed, etc.—are outside the awareness of the patient and are therefore unconscious. Clinically, all that is necessary under these circumstances is to point out the unnoticed pattern to the patient who can then capture its attributes in awareness and strive consciously to alter the configuration. Along similar lines, many therapists work with the implicit definition that an unconscious mental process in a patient is any tendency or expression of which the patient is unaware and which the clinician claims to exist—whatever the evidence might be.

These approaches to the unconscious domain tend to be rather arbitrary, ill-defined, and difficult to sustain on an empirical clinical level. They are essentially confusing and confounding, so much so that it is unlikely that they would promote pre-scientific research or lead to a sound formal science; yet it is confusion of this kind in an area fundamental to the very existence of psychoanalysis that calls for scientific intervention.

* * *

What, then, is the alternative? In principle, there is a need to maintain the distinction between conscious and unconscious expressions as the beacon light for psychoanalytic vision. This would involve the revival of, and re-emphasis on, Freud's initial conception of two distinctive realms of experience, mentation, and communication—conscious and unconscious—both qualitatively and (more importantly) as formal systems of the mind capable of distinctive ways of thinking, processing information, memory, drive, and the like. On this basis, it becomes necessary to insist that psychoanalytic evidence in respect to unconscious processes be confined primarily to indirect communications that involve encoded expressions that lie outside awareness; manifest contents from a patient or therapist would therefore be excluded in this regard (they have, of course, other kinds of importance). The connection between manifest meaning and conscious thinking (which, however is not one-hundred percent) on the one hand, and latent (transformed) contents and unconscious thinking on the other, would be maintained; both theory and clarity would be well served in this way.

The issue here comes down to exactly how we define and access (decode) communications with unconscious meaning. We return to this critical problem in chapter two; here I have mainly attempted to define the issues and indicate how the uncertainties involved will probably require a formal science of psychoanalysis for their resolution.

Models and theories: interaction and systems

Psychotherapy is a serious intervention into the minds, relationships, and lives of human beings; as such, it must, as I have been arguing, in some way possess a solid—albeit scientific—foundation for its practices. What is needed, however, is far more than a scientific method: psychotherapy should also be grounded in a substantial theory with deep and meaningful models. Theory building has, of course, been of considerable concern to psychoanalysts, though insufficient attention has been paid to the problems of psychoanalytic theory formation—the unconscious factors that create pressures to develop both correct and especially incorrect formulations. Only history will be able to assess soundly the current status of psychoanalytic theory and the extent to which it is flawed or viable. Given the deforming pressures involved—especially the dread of unconscious meaning—it would not be surprising to discover basic misconceptions, some of which will concern us as we pursue our search for a foundation for a science of the field.

For the moment, we can identify certain problems in psychoanalytic thinking that again may well be antithetical to a scientific attitude. It has been stated by some writers (see the discussion by Grunbaum, 1984) that psychoanalytic theory does not fully or properly lend itself to Popper's (1959) essential criterion of formal science: that a proposition can be tested and found false—the criterion of falsifiability. Indeed, as it is presently cast, psychoanalysis is vulnerable to this criticism, especially as it applies to the single case method and to broad correlational studies. Because of this, some have claimed that falsifiability either does not apply to psychoanalysis (see the discussion by Edelson, 1984) or that the criterion itself is of little merit (Grunbaum, 1984). Nonetheless, I would argue that falsifiability is a legitimate aspect of science and that the absence of falsification methods poses serious problems for psychoanalysis, because it allows for unchecked impressionistic approaches to material and data that are thereby highly vulnerable to misinterpretation. This lack also, as noted before, makes it all but impossible to identify unsolved puzzles and to recognize the inevitable limits of psychoanalytic explanation (see also Kuhn, 1970, for a related discussion).

Still another problem stems from the general absence of scientific methodology: psychoanalytic hypotheses tend to be limited to the psychodynamic and genetic domains, with secondary supplements of all kinds; the search is for associations and correlations, relationships between entities rather than the laws that govern their behaviours. Indeed, there is little in the way of this kind of search for fundamental laws and deep structures characteristic of more formal scientific thought. In the physical sciences, one can show a correlation between the height at which an object is dropped and the depth to which it is embedded in soft ground. But this correlation says nothing of the law of gravity, which determines the speed at which the body hits the ground and which is vital in accounting for the observed result. Similarly, we may show a correlation between a strong therapeutic alliance and treatment outcome, but this association tells us nothing of the ways in which—and the laws that account for how—this is accomplished.

Psychoanalytic formulations are cast in a manner that does not lend itself to quantification and the kind of mathematical treatments through which deep laws are discovered. Analysts speak of oedipal conflicts, self-object transferences, primitive object relations, and the like; there is little here that suggests quantifiable entities. To the extent that they may be measurable, such measurements are likely to be both global and crude. In a way, then, the narrowness and impressionistic quality of psychoanalytic theory have contributed to the narrowness of its present science—a limitation that we must now seek to modify (see chapter six).

* * *

As for model-making, we are witness to an era when most sciences are extensively engaged in such endeavours. The computer revolution has favoured the use of visual two- and three-dimensional models, while current-day particle physics—such as the search for a grand unified theory (GUT)—requires larger multidimensional models with which to explore and resolve its remaining unsolved puzzles. The solution to the structure of DNA involved creating the proper model of its structure, and topological models provide solutions to many problems in biology today that had remained unanswered for years—e.g., the optimal structure of antibodies to particular antigens—through the use of formal mathematics.

Fixated on metapsychological explanations—in terms of mental economics, conflict, adaptation, and the like—psychoanalysis, on the other hand, has paid only scant attention to this important element of any theoretical structure (see, for example, Goleman, 1985). The die was cast in this regard when, as noted earlier, Freud (1923a) discarded his topographic model of the mind, a model that possessed a distinctly visual and interactional cast. Aside from largely cognitive models of memory and information processing (Peterfreund, 1971), model-making is not a common occupation of analytic theorists. As a result, an entire mode of thinking in which visual intelligence makes a notable contribution is lost to the field. In addition, the role that model-making plays in expanding the thinking of a discipline by offering unique insights and presenting special challenges to its researchers is not called into play. A void as seemingly innocuous as the absence of deep and complex, challenging and informed models actually contributes considerably to the absence of a formal science in the analytic domain.

Here, too, is a situation that needs rectification, and again an effort of this kind is presented in chapters three and four. A foundation for a science of psychoanalysis will require an array of models relative to the dyadic interaction between patient and therapist, including the infrastructure—the deeper elements—of human communication and experience. In addition, we will need models of the human mind and of the systems that process incoming information and meaning and generate output responses. Developing and working with models generally creates a special kind of play-space in which imagination is nourished, new ideas are bred, and creativity finds rich support. Eventually, model-making leads to scientific research, which tests out the insights drawn from the model, identifies flaws, and stimulates the evolution of the ideas behind the model—and with that, eventually, the emergence of fresh models is facilitated. The history of our insight into the structure of the atom is a case in point: beginning with crude raisins-in-the dough and then interplanetary models, research was fostered that has eventually led to far more complex, quantum physical models in which probability curves and exclusion principles rather than exact locations play a key role. From there, it was but a small step to the discovery of a 'particle zoo' of subatomic particles whose behaviours were eventually better understood through the use of visual mappings called Feynman diagrams. Progress in these areas would have been retarded considerably without model-making. Much the same applies, I believe, to psychoanalysis; there is no telling where our theory will go with the emergence of creative visual maps.

* * *

Related to these issues is the common criticism of psychoanalysis with respect to its view of the mind—especially that of the patient—as a closed system, or one that is only minimally influenced by outside events and communications. In spirit, this imbalance influences most of the clinical writings in the field, and this proposition is a tacit assumption in many research studies, which focus entirely on the psychotherapy patient, with virtually no attention to the therapist or the conditions under which the patient is being seen. This closed systems view is also antithetical to formal science, which ultimately must be dynamic rather than static, interactional rather than unilaterally intrapsychic, and framed in terms of all parties—observer and observed—and the conditions pertinent to the data under study.

Any tendency to isolate the mind of the patient from its surroundings, and especially from the ever-present interaction with the therapist, involves a propensity that classical analysts must forego if science is to be served. There have been a number of relatively recent attempts to modify this position by object relationship theorists (e.g., Greenberg & Mitchell, 1983; Mitchell, 1988), interactionally sensitive analysts (e.g., Loewald, 1960; Newton, 1973; Sullivan, 1953), and many others. These efforts have met with only limited success in that analysts in general have not adopted a basically interactional approach. For many, the centre point of psychoanalysis remains the mind of the patient (Edelson, 1984); all else is both secondary and peripheral. Such thinking leads to correlational studies and static forms of science, but is not likely to create a dynamic time-measured science of any kind. Again we see how theory casts the die in which science is moulded—if the theory can, indeed, produce any such die at all.

The stultifying effects on scientific thought that stem from the narrow perspective through which closed systems are defined where an interactional, open systems conception would be far more accurate and productive is seen in psychoanalysis on a larger scale as well. Psychoanalytic theory itself is, at present, a relatively closed system, which has drawn very little from other realms of science and from systems theory. This is an unfortunate state of affairs, since systems scientists have shown that all components of nature, animate and inanimate, share what system scientists refer to as *isomorphisms* (parallels or similarities), and they can therefore meaningfully borrow concepts from and enrich one another. The walling-off of psychoanalysis from the family of sciences, reinforced by the physical and formal independence of most psychoanalytic institutes (i.e., the preference for non-university settings) and by the belief and claim that the field does not even belong in this family, deprives psychoanalysis of a critical source of understanding and instrumentation for its research efforts.

Closed systems are in general and in some important sense subject to the second law of thermodynamics, and the law can meaningfully be applied to systems of thought and practice. This law indicates that, to the extent that psychoanalysis remains a relatively isolated system, it will show a gradually increasing level of entropy characterized by increasing disorder and eventual stasis and deadness. There is a distinct loss of energy and movement in these systems, and work—evolutionary change and progress—is all but impossible. There is as well little likelihood of an emergent science to alter the situation, though again, only such a science, and, with it, a new paradigm for the field, can significantly change this regressive course of events. Here, too, it is the stimulation from unsolved puzzles and anomalies that often forces closed systems to reach out to other disciplines for clues to solutions; psychoanalysis sorely needs such issues.

* * *

Another problem that has made the creation of a science for the field difficult to fulfil involves defining criteria with which to validate its clinical hypotheses. There are few papers on clinical validation (see Langs, 1976b, 1981b), and there is a tendency to intermingle evidence on a manifest communicative level with implications made by the therapist, and with efforts to identify unconscious reactions as well. Clearly, the greater the degree of confusion regarding clinical confirmation, the more difficult it is to identify anomalies—non-confirmatory results—that question or even refute a particular postulate and the greater the difficulty in experiencing a need for a formal science. All clinically derived theories are vulnerable to significant error, as are all qualitative approaches to nature. Still, the inevitable margin of error can be reduced with elaborate and clear efforts to confirm clinical ideas. We are reminded again of the many contradictory theories that claim validity in the therapeutic domain, despite the evident impossibility of developing a single theory that could logically embrace such opposing views. While quantitative methods are also open to error, these are less likely to occur and more likely to be recognized than with entirely qualitative approaches.

In this connection, we do well to realize that many fundamental psychoanalytic hypotheses, ideas, conceptions, beliefs, impressions, and the like are often treated as observed givens—as data rather than inference and abstraction. Misconception—often unrecognized—is inescapable.

To cite but one such example, let us try to take a fresh look at the psychoanalytic concept of *transference*—an element, as noted, that is fundamental to Freud's definition of a psychoanalyst and to virtually all forms of present-day psychodynamic thinking. In brief, transference was defined by Freud (1905e, 1912b; see also the discussions of Bird, 1972; Gill, 1982, Greenson, 1967; Sandler et al., 1969; as well as the critique by Langs, 1976b, 1980, 1982b—among many others) as *an unconscious constellation* within a patient, constituted as unconscious fantasies and memories that distort his or her perceptions of and reactions to the psychoanalyst. In substance, then, transference was not viewed as a manifest phenomenon, but as an inference made by the analyst from a patient's derivative (disguised or encoded) communications and behaviours (Little, 1951; Szasz, 1963).

In substance, it is proposed that it is through transferences—now practically redefined as surface reactions to the therapist—that a patient mistakenly reacts to the analyst as if he or she were a figure from the patient's early childhood. Transference is therefore believed to embody critical dimensions of the patient's psychopathology, which has arisen from the very childhood traumas that form the unconscious basis of the patient's distortions. In a few words, then, classical psychoanalytic theory postulates that the patient substantially and erroneously confuses the analyst of the present with the parents of the past. And the evidence for this conclusion—quickly accepted as 'fact'—is a mixture of direct observation and inference, much of it lacking in a full appreciation of the actual implications of a therapist's behaviours and interventions—the yardstick by which transference distortion must be measured (Langs, 1980, 1984–85; Little, 1951; Szasz, 1963).

On the face of it, the fundamental proposition that a human being enters a relationship in which he or she basically misperceives and distorts speaks for a degree of maladaptation that would prove to be virtually incompatible with survival. All animals, human beings included, possess fundamental perceptive apparati that are vital to continued existence. It is quite unlikely that the psychoanalytic relationship is a viable exception to this rule (Smith, 1991).

Much of the confusion stems from the fact that the clinical evidence for transference ranges from a patient's direct and immediate statements about the therapist (by far the most common clinical referent, one that is without an unconscious component) to displaced and disguised images, usually of a kind that allude to authority figures, which are taken as displaced mental representations of the analyst. In this respect, transference is understood to be a projection from the mind of the patient without stimulus or provocation from the psychoanalyst—in substance, an isolated product of the mind of the patient. Recently Gill (1982) took exception to this viewpoint and has suggested that here-and-now stimuli from the psychoanalyst often evoke transference distortions. What, then, is the problem with this point of view that has proven to be so convincing to so many psychotherapists and psychoanalysts—so much so that it is taken as observed fact rather than uncertain hypothesis?

In addition to the issues already addressed, there may well be a problem inherent to the theory itself. It could be argued that while there is indeed a strong genetic influence operating on the patient's relationship with the therapist (and the therapist's with the patient), this influence need not be primarily distorting or unrelated to the behaviours and interventions of the therapist. Indeed, a deep analysis of the implications of many interventions from therapists can be carried out to show that patients typically *perceive unconsciously and with great accuracy* these very meanings—which are themselves often outside the awareness of both patient and therapist—without distortion or inappropriate response. These unconscious perceptions are revealed through displaced and disguised narratives—encoded communications—embodied in the patient's free associations (and behaviours). The genetic influence involves the *selectivity* of the patient's responses: he or she responds to the multiple conscious and unconscious implications of a therapist's intervention by singling out those meanings to which he or she is especially sensitive; in this way all of the communications from a patient are interactionally determined and are a reflection of the therapeutic interaction with Janus-like meanings along the 'me/not-me interface' (Langs, 1978)—allusions that refer unconsciously to both therapist and patient. It is these selective introjected experiences and meanings that account in a major way for the patient's therapeutic experience and for the vicissitudes of his or her emotional problems and reactions to the therapist.

It is not my intention here to debate further the issue of which position is more valid: transference distortion and inappropriate reaction to the 'innocent' therapist on the one hand, or selective veridical perception and appropriate response to a therapist's implied and unconscious messages on the other (for clinically founded discussions, see Langs, 1984–85, 1988a). Neither position can be 'proven' in the clinical arena where qualitative impressions hold sway. In the main, the present discussion is mainly intended to indicate that there are serious questions about the clinical basis for the theoretical and clinical use of the concept of transference, and that viable alternatives to the prevailing line of thought exist. Much clinical work and scientific research is needed to clarify and possibly revise the concept and to make clear the observational base from which these inferences have been, and are being, made. Science cannot be served as long as therapists speak of patients' relationships with themselves as 'the transference' and assume that patients typically and repeatedly show basically unfounded and confounded responses in the therapeutic interaction. A closer look at many other psychoanalytic propositions—countertransference, therapeutic alliance, cure, etc.—will reveal a comparable degree of confusion between observation and inference. A science of psychoanalysis will emerge only when these terms are clarified and the relevant issues are resolved.

The model of the mind

Among the models needed to encourage psychoanalytic thinking as it gears up for science is a representation of *the human mind*—especially the means by which it processes emotionally charged information and meaning. It is therefore necessary for us to take a fresh look at the fate of Freud's initial model of the mind, in that I will argue that his decision to abandon his topographic approach was, despite the role this move played in advancing the structural hypothesis, a major step backwards for the field—and its hope for a science.

Freud presented his model of the mind mainly in *The Interpretation of Dreams* (Freud, 1900a). The model is commonly called the picket-fence model, in that the systems of the mind—CS, PCS, UCS—were portrayed in sequence, like the slats in a fence. To the left was an incoming stimulus that registered consciously in the system CS (a position Freud maintained despite the work of Potzl [1917] which convincingly showed the existence of subliminal or unconscious registration). This consciously registered information is then sent into the unconscious system (UCS) and in due course, and under certain conditions that allowed passage through censorship, forwarded to the preconscious system (PCS) and back into the conscious system (CS) through which both awareness and motor discharge took place.

The model was dynamic and basically interactional in that it allowed for incoming stimuli as the source of intrapsychic systemic information processing (to use today's language; see Basch 1976; Peterfreund, 1971). Still, the main focus was within the mental systems of the patient where conflict played a major role—especially that between the UCS (with its forbidden wishes and fantasies, and primary process mode of thinking) and the PCS/CS (with its concerns for reality and secondary process mode of thought). Censorships—psychic defences—blocked the direct expression of forbidden UCS impulses and extracted a measure of disguise before such wishes could be expressed in CS imagery or action.

The model, however, was inherently troublesome. As if to undermine the model's credibility, Freud (1915e) explicitly stated that he had no expectations of neurophysiological correlates. Also problematic was Freud's decision to place the system CS at each end of the model; the requisite of conscious registration of all incoming stimuli was especially questionable. Further, each of the three systems were globally and crudely drawn, and the model therefore lacked depth and specificity; there was no complexity to these potentially rich and intricate systems. Freud also failed to differentiate the means by which the results of this processing were reported out or communicated. For example, primary process thinking was defined in part as a mode in which information was processed (e.g., without regard to reality, according to the pleasure principle, etc.) and as a mode of expression (e.g., through displacement, symbolization, and condensation). This proved confusing and probably played a role in Freud's eventual abandonment of the model.

Freud took this fateful step when he realized that psychic defences, which had been attributed mainly to the CS/PCS system, were in many instances part of the UCS system (i.e., outside the awareness of the patient). With the contents being defended against and the defensive forces viewed as parts of the same (UCS) system, the power of the model to explain conflict—a central explanatory concept in psychoanalytic theory—collapsed. Freud had also placed the conscience and sense of guilt/wish for punishment in the CS/PCS system, only to discover that such needs were more typically in the UCS system, outside awareness—i.e., that unconscious guilt was a common phenomenon.

For these reasons, the model seemed unserviceable and was discarded. In choosing between conflict theory and the model of the mind, Freud opted to give up the latter. Later analysts, especially Arlow and Brenner (1964) and Gill (1963), buttressed Freud's arguments and topography (in which the systems of the mind were defined in terms of access to consciousness) fell into disfavour and was replaced by the structural theory (in which the systems of the mind were defined in terms of their functions, with little regard as to their relationship to consciousness). As a result, much was lost: a model that was interactionally founded; a systems theory, however intrapsychically focused; a chance to develop these systems into complex entities; and data-driven model-making in general. The open mind became a closed system crudely modelled as a ball with three compartments, the constructs of the new model: ego, id, and superego—a ball floating in space with a detached analyst there as a 'participant observer'. Again, a possible avenue to science had been lost.

The absence of systemic thinking

We turn now to yet another, relatively unrecognized obstacle to the development of a science for psychoanalysis: the general failure of the field to develop and embrace systemic thinking and a definitive psychoanalytic systems theory (for a notable individual exception see Newton, 1971, 1973, 1989). Since there is prima facia evidence that patient and therapist are interlocked as a system, we might ask why systemic thinking has had such difficulty in establishing a foothold into psychoanalytic thinking.

There appear to be several interrelated sources of this difficulty. First, systemic thinking immediately raises issues of the nature and functions of the ground rules or boundary conditions of a system, since all systems have boundaries and these boundaries are typically among the most powerful sources of influence on how the system functions and/or dysfunctions. There is evidence (Langs, 1984–85, 1988a) that we have resisted applying these principles to the patient/therapist (P/T) system largely because of our own secure-frame anxieties—e.g., fears of immobility, entrapment, and death. These anxieties prompt us to avoid discovering the ideal boundary conditions that patients consistently seek on the *unconscious* level, which render frame alterations—e.g., modifications of the optimal ground rules of therapy—attractive as defences for both patients and therapists. There is perhaps no other aspect of psychotherapy where therapists have maintained as naive and denial-based a position as they have with the boundary conditions of treatment; almost nothing is written on the topic, and those writings that do exist are usually dismissed out of hand. In a realm where unconscious responses are most critical, manifest thinking prevails; indeed, a proper access to (decoding of) unconscious communications renders unmistakable the central role of ground-rule conditions in the therapeutic interaction. It may well be that a major unconscious factor in our failure to reach a clear consensus on how to decode unconscious messages (see chapter two) involves this universal dread of the secure frame.

This gap in conceptualizing is also connected to the already noted absence of a *strong interactional position* within psychoanalysis (mainstream analysis may be characterized as having a *weak interactional position*: interaction with the therapist is acknowledged but not afforded the central role it requires). Still another factor in the absence of a systems theory appears to be the lack of a convincing and integrated theory of information processing for emotionally charged messages (again, for individual efforts, see Basch, 1976; Peterfreund, 1971; and Rosenblatt & Thickstun, 1984). Then, too, resistances to such a theory may have been heightened because those who advocated systemic thinking (e.g., Peterfreund, 1971) argued that a systems theory could entirely replace current psychodynamic/genetic thinking. Cognition was to replace drive theory and its later emendations. This position seems to have evoked a complete rejection of systemic ideas in those who were invested in current psychodynamic thinking. While a science of psychoanalysis may well lead to revisions in current dynamic/genetic formulations, in principle the entire situation is far better served for the moment by a dual theory—psychodynamic and systemic—than by efforts to restrict one's thinking to either side of this debate. Certainly, a systems theory for psychoanalysis would be more palatable for the clinician—and more valuable as a means of comprehending the therapeutic interaction—if it were established as a separate but interrelated domain to complement that of dynamics and genetics. There are reasons to argue for the value of this type of integrated theory as the best means of accounting for psychoanalytic phenomena and data (see chapter three).

Nonetheless, there is additional evidence of powerful resistances within psychoanalysts themselves against widening the scope of psychoanalytic thinking in these directions. This may also stem in important ways from a need to defend against an acknowledgement of the extent to which the therapist plays a role in the experiences of the patient. A systems theory holds the entire system accountable for all transactions of the dyad and requires an accounting of both patient and therapist for all vicissitudes of the experiences of either person. Systemic thinking also brings into focus a patient's interactionally triggered unconscious perceptions of the therapist, which are often quite unfavourable and disquieting. Since systemic thinking and interaction go hand-in-hand, the resistance against fully acknowledging the one is generally accompanied by resistances to acknowledging the other.

Inherent to these arguments is the call for a systems theory for psychoanalysis—to serve both its theoretical thinking and the development of a formal science. Isolating the patient from the therapist for purposes of study and thinking tends to produce a static science at best, where global descriptions of the state of the patient are seen as adequate and relatively fixed traits and processes are accepted as the properties to be investigated. On the other hand, a systemic view, with its stress on patient–therapist interaction, fosters a dynamic science that is asked to account for continuous change in the system and its subsystems—patient and therapist—from moment to moment.

The systems theory we require should be designed to supplement rather than replace the current analytic focus on psychodynamics and genetics. We need to postulate *two interacting fields of force* in the therapeutic interaction: *systems dynamic and psychodynamic.* In this theory, the fundamental entity of the therapeutic interaction is not the patient (nor the therapist), but *the patient/therapist (P/T) system,* of which *the patient (P) and therapist (T) are the most critical sub-systems.* All transactions within the therapeutic frame would therefore require an accounting of P, T, and their emergent P/T system—as well as of the frame (boundary conditions) itself.

Systems unfold over time; single descriptions of a system's state or functioning as a summary statement are inherently inadequate. Systemic thinking therefore also directs us towards studies of the therapeutic interaction over time and thereby to a dynamic science of action, change, and the like. Science is therefore served in many ways by the development of a systems theory for psychoanalysis, and I attempt to develop such a theory in some detail in chapters three and five.

Some attributes of a formal science

Those who stand deep within a particular paradigm cannot be expected to have the vision to see its flaws; only a truly innovative and new paradigm can incisively define the inconsistencies of the paradigm it deigns to replace. As I have indicated, the added fact that the present psychoanalytic paradigm gives substance to clinical practice—to a therapist's way of working, thinking, being, and consciously and unconsciously defending—makes it difficult for clinicians to arouse scepticism, let alone dire concern. The paradox, then, is that it is only through the eyes of a new paradigm that the flaws of the old paradigm can be envisioned—yet all the while the old paradigm is so self-satisfying that it requires someone who is not only innovative but also capable of tolerating high levels of isolation, uncertainty, and chaos to step outside its domain. Kuhn (1962) argues that individuals do not choose from competing paradigms based on evidence or even science or pseudo-science—

virtually every paradigm has some type of experimental support. The issue becomes one of persuasion and that of a conscious choice that nonetheless is under strong unconscious influence; acknowledgement of personal doubts and uncertainties can also play a role. To avoid arbitrary judgements on these issues, the science of psychoanalysis will be compelled to step outside the therapeutic domain and investigate this very process of developing new paradigms and how they are received.

The problem, then, is two-fold: first, as it stands, the current central psychoanalytic paradigm—by which I mean here the body of knowledge and practice each individual therapist carries within himself or herself—is one that inevitably presents difficulties in recognizing its own limitations and errors; as such, there is little motivation to develop a formal science that might otherwise be called for were the unsolved anomalies more precisely identified. Second, there is as yet no dramatic competition between psychoanalytically defined paradigms; debates between self psychologists and object relation theorists, for example, have not led to definitive research through which fundamental differences could be resolved in one direction or the other. Nor is there a clear and pressing challenge to central dogma. This lack of challenge within the field retards the development of scientific approaches. We therefore sorely need new paradigms in the field—sharply contrasting positions that also inherently suggest quantifiable means of resolving the issues raised—to stimulate debate and research and, in time, the development of a suitable science.

Stasis, states close to equilibrium and with few disturbing currents, and contentment with the field as it is presently structured—these are seldom, if ever, the conditions under which science and revolution are bred. For psychoanalysis to flourish, psychoanalysts must be capable of tolerating uncertainty and even chaos, and they must find the means to demand an evolutionary course based on the recognition of unsolved puzzles and dilemmas—and the science required for their solutions. On that basis alone, any theoretician who comes forth with a claim of having a means by which this evolution can be promoted deserves full and serious attention. So, too, with any claim for a science for the field; we must keep an open mind. We will return to these issues in chapter two.

To conclude this chapter, I will briefly outline the attributes of a formal science; we need a sense of our ultimate goal for psychoanalysis in order to assess the extent to which the foundation we are building here is likely to produce the desired results. In chicken-and-egg fashion, science stands on two pillars: observation and theory (Conti, 1989). There must of necessity be a theory that has consistency (in relation to other sciences and internally, and with existing observations and other established, related—and seemingly valid—propositions), integrity, beauty, elegance, simplicity, and vision; theory gives meaning and order to otherwise jumbled observations. The scientific attitude is informed through theory, but it is also open to the unexpected and the inexplicable, and to refutation of existing propositions; it is an attitude that is entirely committed to the discovery of observations that cannot be subjected to satisfactory explanation by its current postulates, and, therefore, to the inevitability of changes in accepted thinking and explanatory propositions. Science is basically an attitude, one that is fundamentally grounded in direct observation and data collection, with the understanding that the nature of the observed and of what constitutes meaningful data is itself bound to change—evolve—with time.

Science depends on measurement, on quantification. Formal science understands that measurement is always a systemic act that involves an interaction between the observer and the observed; both are changed by the act of measurement itself. It is the responsibility of the scientist to select *meaningful* variables for measurement and to define the means of testing his or her theory through such quantification. The results of these investigations must be non-trivial—in substance, less than obvious—and the outcome to some extent counter-intuitive and informative in new ways. Science speaks to the development of new levels of understanding, and to a distinct capability for prediction—even if, at times, this is stated entirely in terms of probabilities rather than definitive determinism. And, as so strongly stated by Popper (1959), a science must also be capable of proposing hypotheses that are both testable and falsifiable, though this need not imply that a single non-confirmatory result calls for the revision or demise of a theory—extended observation and careful reasoning are needed.

Sound science should provide unexpected answers to unsolved problems, though the answers themselves should consistently raise new and often unexpected questions. Furthermore, the quantifications involved should lend themselves to mathematical treatments and models and must as a rule, involve mathematical formulations that extend significantly beyond simple statistics. The ultimate quest of science is for dynamic results, measured in the context of a temporal dimension, that yield definable laws of nature and/or deep structures and constraints that are generalizable and expandable; there is stress on laws and dynamics rather than statics that involve global characterizations. Science, then, involves a sequence that is usually characterized by time series observation (the establishment of facts), hypothesis formation, experiment, identification of laws through the application of mathematical models and treatments, and theory-building (Conti, 1989).

Despite all claims by psychoanalysts that our field should be exempted from the requisites of science because of the unusual nature of its domain (e.g., the single case, the ineffable aspects of a patient's communications and experience, the problem in reconstructing a life history [this last is an issue for developmental rather than interactional science]), there is, I am convinced, no substantial basis on which such an exemption can be justified. I have tried to indicate in this chapter that there are many reasons other than the nature of psychoanalytic data that have retarded the entry of the field into the formal sciences—and additional reasons will unfold as we proceed. A central issue is the failure to develop a meaningful and measurable database for the scientific pursuits of the field. And, as I have already indicated, there are signs that such data are actually close at hand in the recordings of psychotherapy sessions—another topic that is pursued further. Indeed, if such data are available, and if the means of quantifying meaningful dimensions of these data—the therapeutic dialogue—are also available, and, furthermore, if mathematical techniques exist that can be applied to these data to reveal non-trivial laws and structures, then the issue of whether a science of psychoanalysis is feasible is immediately resolved: it can be done.

Whether we have reached such a juncture will be discussed in chapter seven, where I present some initial efforts in this direction. But these efforts are founded on a theory—one that may well be at variance with central analytic dogma—and on a way of observing and thinking about the therapeutic interaction. For now, then, let's continue to develop a foundation for this potential science. The next step is to consider how we go about observing the psychotherapeutic dyad and the communicative exchanges between patients and therapist—how we establish the facts we intend to measure and to subject to mathematical analysis. We can be certain that this is the most basic component of the foundation for a science of psychoanalysis. And it is to this problem that I now turn.

CHAPTER TWO

Two psychoscopes

> It follows that what we, as scientists, can perceive is always limited by threshold. That is, what is subliminal will not be grist for our mill. Knowledge at any given moment will be a function of the thresholds of our available means of perception. The invention of the microscope or the telescope or of means of measuring time to the fraction of a nanosecond or weighing quantities to millionths of a gram—all such improved devices of perception will disclose what was utterly unpredictable from levels of perception that we could achieve before that discovery.
>
> G. Bateson, *Mind and Nature*

The science we wish to establish pertains to the therapeutic interaction. The foundation for this science will depend first and foremost on how we observe that interaction and establish our facts or data. It is these findings that we must eventually classify and quantify, and then treat mathematically, if a science is to emerge. The source of these facts must, for the sake of completeness and accuracy, be recorded psychotherapy sessions; anything less fully documented can only be the basis for preliminary impressions at best. We must accept this setting as our laboratory and recognize that the effects of these conditions on measurement are considerable. Nonetheless, there are reasons to believe that this situation is much like many other laboratory settings, which, despite their artificial conditions, are capable of helping scientists ascertain basic laws, properties, and patterns. Indeed, the recorded therapy setting may be likened to a cloud chamber or cyclotron—specifically designed spaces used successfully in physics research to determine the properties of subatomic particles.

This analogy suggests an intriguing question for psychotherapy researchers: are there settings other than the recording studio (or its equivalent) that could be developed in order to extend our understanding of the therapeutic interaction? Certainly, any significant advance in methodology is likely to bring with it unprecedented perspectives and insights. Of course, all such work will of necessity be required to take into account as thoroughly as possible the influence of observer, observed, and setting on the results obtained. Psychotherapy research will profit greatly from innovative research settings.

We begin the search for a psychoanalytic science, then, with an attempt to establish the most fruitful and reliable means of observation and data collection that can be developed in light of present understanding. We are immediately faced with the already noted chicken-and-egg problem, in that the theory we use for observing the therapeutic interaction will largely dictate the data we choose to isolate and measure; however, a strong theory should also be flexible enough to change even its basic propositions on the basis of fresh results. All one can do is to establish a scientific attitude along with safeguards against self-fulfilling prophecies and blind spots, and hope for the best.

In psychotherapy, data collection involves the following steps, all of which are theory-driven (mere collections of words are unlikely to generate meaningful results):

1. *Recording observations: collecting the data*

The two *psychoscopes*—methods of observing psychoanalytic data—that we consider in this chapter are each based on a theory that leads to specific biases in this respect. The classical or Freudian method (which I will call the *F-scope*) leans towards the free associations of patients and their introspective reports, while the communicative/interactional method (which I will call the *C-scope*) prefers to utilize the entire therapeutic dialogue—the unfolding communications between patient and therapist. Clearly, the conclusions drawn from each of these approaches will be rather different, as will their sciences.

2. *Organizing the data or facts at hand*

Again, the mere collection of verbiage—and affects, behaviours, and the like—produces an unworkable morass. With data in hand, we are obligated to find ways of organizing the material. This may include classifying its contents and other properties, studying the temporal sequence and the exchange of responses, the identification of meanings and implications, and other ways of configuring and signifying the results to allow for meaningful formulation, manipulation, and conclusions. The psychoscopes we will study each have distinctive attachments for these purposes—mechanisms that again lead to sharp differences in viewpoint.

* * *

It is these collated and organized observations that are available for scientific treatment, be it research manipulation, quantification, the use of mathematical models, nontrivial predictions, and such. In addition, these efforts should lead to model-making, theory revision and testing, and the development of basic scientific propositions. The result should, ideally, be a central theory with substantial experimental support, a fringe of more tentative propositions in need of further exploration, and the identification of the anomalies that elude explanation based on the present theoretical structure. All of this leads the researcher back into the 'laboratory' in a way that guides future efforts. We see again how selecting data for observation and formulation determines whether a science will emerge—and its nature.

The supporting structure for this type of research and science lies in clinical practice. Inescapably, the ways in which the psychoanalytic clinician addresses the unconscious domain, creates and attends to—or ignores—the impact of the therapeutic space, listens to and formulates the implications and unconscious meanings of the therapeutic dialogue (choosing to include all or part of the patient's associations and behaviours and the therapist's own communications), and intervenes on the basis of these assessments are the groundwork for the research methods that are part of his or her paradigm. At bottom, then, all of psychoanalytic science is founded on the clinical method one chooses to use—one's means of listening and formulating, intervening, and validating—or, in the terms of this chapter, on the particular psychoscope one chooses to operate.

It is this process we examine in this chapter. For this purpose, I use, as noted, the metaphor of the psychoscope—a term coined by the mathematician Ralph Abraham for the broadly defined *listening processes* of the psychoanalyst. By way of contrast, we consider two versions of the psychoscope: the classical Freudian *F-scope* and the communicative/interactional *C-scope*. As the term suggests, the psychoscope is a way of observing the therapeutic dialogue in order to access and define its infrastructure or unconscious elements. This instrument, which is a representation of a set of mental operations usually engaged in by a therapist—though not infrequently by a patient as well—may also be thought of as a means of examining communication microscopically in order to discern its non-manifest structure, functions, and meaning. While the scope should be applied to all communications from both patients and therapists, it will prove fruitful for purposes of discussion to concentrate here mainly on the application of the scope to the material from the patient in psychotherapy. As a rule, it is the patient rather than the therapist from whom we receive the greatest amount of data to which the psychoscope is particularly sensitive. Given the overriding importance of the unconscious dimension for psychoanalysis, the operation of the psychoscope is perhaps the single most critical factor in the field today, clinically and scientifically.

* * *

Science advances in many ways. Among these, perhaps the most fascinating are the revolutions fuelled by new instrumentation. Both the telescope and the microscope ushered in new eras for physics and biology. Much the same may well prove to be true for the invention of a properly configured, working psychoscope. Though the use of this instrument in the clinical situation must be sensitively and individually honed, the general principles by which it is operated can be treated in a more perfunctory fashion in terms of basic mechanics and instrumentation—the approach to be used here for purposes of exposition.

Unlike Galileo's telescope and van Leeuwenhoek's microscope, the psychoscope is an intangible instrument—as noted, it is a set of mental functions or operations. Oddly enough, however, Freud's (1900a) version of the psychoscope shared attributes with these two devices, and, indeed, Freud made use of an analogy to the telescope in developing the model of the mind that came from his initial use of this device.

The psychoscope—specifically, the F-scope—was, of course, invented by Freud essentially in 1900. It was designed mainly with his theory of dream—and symptom—formation in mind. Since an analyst's conception of the nature of emotionally charged communication in general, and of the layers of meanings contained in messages in particular, shapes the blueprint from which a psychoscope is manufactured—its design, if you will—we are obliged to review Freud's conception of how a transformed or unconscious message is created. After all, if a theory has no place for disguised expressions—i.e., if it is concerned exclusively or almost entirely with the surface of messages, with manifest contents—there is no possible application of a psychoscope that is in essence a 'device' for ascertaining latent meanings—however defined. The psychoscope, then, can be used only by those who conceptualize a disguised or unconscious layer of meaning in messages, a deeper structure to be accessed and probed.

The extraction of meaning by means of a psychoscope is based on a conceptualization of how latent contents are created in the course of emotional adaptation. (Even though some theories treat latent contents in isolation, without recognizing their adaptive functions, we adhere to a more functional and interactional framework in developing this discussion.) Freud postulated the following steps in the creation of a message with unconscious meaning:

Step 1: the experience of a *day residue* (a trigger that may merely serve as a vehicle of disguise or may well be an emotionally charged stimulus);

Step 2: the evocation of *latent dream thoughts* (a type of unconscious processing);

Step 3: the arousal of unconscious memories and fantasies;

Step 4: the creation of the manifest dream that encodes the aroused images—fantasy/memory constellations—through the use of the dream mechanisms of displacement, disguise (symbolism), condensation, secondary revision, and concerns for representability.

Freud's central postulate was that day residues arouse unconscious fantasy/memory constellations that then seek *transformed* expression in manifest dreams. His psychoscope was therefore designed to undo these transformations carried out by the dream mechanisms—the primary processes—and expose the latent memory/fantasy (wish) in its raw or decoded state. This was the essence of his listening/formulating process, centred as it was on the repressed memory/fantasy formations, with all else peripheral.

The F-scope is therefore much like a translation machine. The central classical theory—to the extent that it can be defined *as it pertains to listening and formulating*—states that a patient experiences an *unconscious* mental conflict in which unconscious wishes, fantasies, and identity (self-images) play a role. The patient is under pressure to express these forbidden or anxiety-provoking needs and wishes, but can do so only if they are suitably disguised or camouflaged. The expression of this constellation, once suitably modified by censorship or defence, can then find its way into awareness—often in the form of a dream (which is the prototype of the encoded or disguised message)—though also through any other form of narrative and at times in actual behaviour. It is these forbidden wishes and needs that are also responsible for a patient's symptoms and resistances, and for his or her so-called transferences—whether narcissistic or involving distorted views of the analyst.

Mechanically, the psychoscope is, as I said, a means of observing and listening to the material from patients. It is, in essence, a set of operations through which a therapist decodes or unravels a patient's manifest or disguised material. By focusing and operating the psychoscope, a therapist transforms the input of a patient's material into an unmasked message. In substance, then, the psychoscope takes in manifest contents and outputs latent contents. However, not all latent contents are the same: some are actually decoded messages in that the surface images are treated as symbolic or disguised representations of deeper images that are themselves the output of the psychoscope; others, however, are simply the extracted or implied meanings of the observed manifest contents themselves. These are very different forms of unconscious meaning and reflect rather different underlying mental processes and theories—and psychoscopes.

The first psychoscope, the F-scope invented by Freud, had a blueprint that involved a design that enabled the machine to zero in on a manifest dream, enter its elements into the machine (along with accompanying associations), and output a decoded reading of the latent contents of the input message. Some use was made of a symbol decoder that was inserted as a template into the machine, including a guide to universal unconscious fantasies and wishes like those related to the oedipal constellation. However, in the actual manufacture of the F-scope and in its use by Freud, the machine was operated mainly as an extractor of meanings from manifest dream contents; little or no decoding was involved.

For example, to cite the dream specimen of psychoanalysis, the 'Irma dream' (Freud 1900a), Freud dreams that his patient is physically ill. He then extracts a latent, unconscious wish from this manifest image to the effect that his patient is physically rather than emotionally ill; if this were the case, then her continuing symptoms could not be blamed on a failure of his newly developed psychoanalytic methods. In this rather typical instance, Freud turned his F-scope towards his own dream and used it to extract an implied meaning from its manifest contents. Though other uses are made of the F-scope through Freud's associations to the dream, these efforts were used mainly to provide additional evidence for this central dream wish. The F-scope does, however, also decode a number of unconscious fantasies and memories connected to the dream. These outputs are based on and further support Freud's conflict theory of 'neurosis'.

The input for this phase of the F-scope's operation is both manifest dream elements and Freud's associations to the dream. The F-scope then operates to undo the effects of the mechanisms of displacement and disguise (symbolism, in Freud's term), and the output is a decoded dream. This product is understood, however, entirely as a formerly unconscious wish or fantasy—a meaning entirely within the mind of the dreamer. The F-scope lacks a mechanism through which interpersonal/interactional information can be taken in and processed, except in the crudest sense.

In the hands of classically trained psychoanalysts, the F-scope found less frequent use than intended by Freud (many analysts work mainly with undeciphered manifest contents), and, in general, the version of the scope that they used when they did so was the one designed to generate inferences from a patient's surface imagery. In addition, the F-scope was rarely applied to the analyst's own communications to the patient (therapists seldom analyse in detail the implications and encoded meanings of their interventions). The F-scope lost much of its fading power to *undo transformations* and became in most hands an *inference extractor* that *pulled out implications from manifest contents*, or simply repeated these contents with new words—a trivial type of output of a kind not intended by Freud. The main converting mechanism within the scope was its inference maker, and the focus of the machine was limited to a patient's surface communications; the scope was also relatively insensitive to boundary (ground-rule) inputs. Much of the sense of depth, complexity, imagination, and transformation was lost. It is this scope that is in common use by today's analytically oriented practitioners.

With respect to communication, the underlying thesis that directs the use of the more probing versions of the F-scope states that repressed material—defined as wishes, transferences, defences, and the like—lies embedded within or buried beneath the surface of a patient's communications. The main function of this scope is to dig up the hidden contents or to extract the buried implications of this surface material, guided by the ideas embodied in the particular sub-theory of classical thinking selected by the therapist—self-psychology, object relations, conflict theory, and such.

The F-scope has been designed with a particular model of the mind—and of both psychoanalysis and general human communication—as its guiding principles. To the extent that meaningful (non-trivial) unconscious meanings and contents—and, more rarely, processes—are considered, the basic model proposes that there are surface associations that cover over deeper and more critical information and meaning, constituted mainly as unconscious fantasies, introjects, and memories. It is these absent elements that are sought for through the F-scope, which is fashioned as a probing instrument designed to push aside defensive covers so that underlying images can emerge whole-cloth at a non-defensive moment of revelation.

The instrumentation of the F-scope is sensitized to and seeks out underlying fantasies/memory systems within the mind of the patient. That is, the objects probed are almost entirely the patient's mental contents, and as a result it is these purported contents that are uncovered. It is well to remember that a common danger in designing and using any psychoscope is that its mode and range of vision is defined by its structure; it will reveal only that which it is designed to reveal. The danger of self-fulfilling findings is ever-present—no matter which scope is used.

Even when Freud appended a decoding mechanism to his penetrating F-scope, one that undid the mechanisms of displacement and disguise (symbolism), the territory unmasked remained the inner, albeit unconscious and fantasy/memory, mental life of the patient. Because of the nature of the scope, it became quite easy for psychoanalysts to detach the decoding element and to restrict themselves to direct exploratory probes of manifest contents—and then to pronounce as previously unconscious the new material that subsequently emerges into awareness from the patient. To this was added a mechanism that identified unnoticed *patterns of defence, behaviour, symptom development, and the like, as well as unnoticed genetic connections to these patterns (and to the patient's communications to, and behaviours with, the analyst)*. And with these addenda, the basic design of the F-scope was completed.

Freud's F-scope, then, is a 'machine' that, in the main, attempts to dig deeper, to bring forth the unseen, and thereby to reveal hidden layers. Its main ancillary instrumentation involves questioning the patient and even pressing the patient for free associations—for further thoughts and fantasies, for more and more associations. The F-scope is a direct descendant of the hypnotic method, which postulates that, like the proverbial tip of an iceberg, there is much more beneath the surface of a patient's manifest dreams and associations, and that these deeper meanings can be gathered in with additional probes. This conception is reflected in another common Freudian metaphor, that of the archaeological dig (Freud, 1905e [1901])—the exploration of depths covered over by defensive surface matter and rendered visible by probing and scraping away. Additional techniques through which these postulated covering-over defences are removed include confrontations and clarifications, and the so-called interpretation of transference and other resistances. All of these measures implement the operation of the F-scope and are integrated into its utilization.

* * *

Having outlined the structure and theoretical foundation of the F-scope, let us turn now to a most critical set of questions: Is this a soundly constructed psychoscope? Are there any basic flaws to its operation? If so, can the F-scope be modified and improved in any significant way? And, most importantly for us at the moment, does the F-scope appear to be generating observations and formulations—insights—that are sufficiently valid and promising to speak for, or move us strongly towards, a science of psychoanalysis? At bottom, we must ask simply whether the F-scope appears to be a viable foundation for an analytic science. In principle, to the extent that the operation of any psychoscope is faulty, it will spin off misleading and confusing outputs that not only confound clinical precepts and practice, but also create the kind of uncertain fragmentation that is, as we have seen, inimical to the creation of a psychoanalytic science. It is likely that only a sound listening device can spawn a sound formal science.

There is, as I have already indicated in earlier discussions, considerable clinical evidence that the F-scope is a very much flawed instrument, and that these errors in design and application are an important factor in the absence of a science for the field. While the invention of the F-scope seems to have been one of Freud's most monumental achievements, basic problems in its architecture were virtually inevitable. This is so largely because the designer of a psychoscope must ideally be as free as possible of resistances and defences against the realization of valid decoding meaning. Often these raw meanings are deeply hurtful and disturbing for the decoder—largely because in therapy they typically involve incisive unconscious perceptions of a therapist's anxieties, hurtful interventions, and otherwise errant ways (in addition to the patient's encoded self-perceptions). No one is immune to the dread of unconscious meaning; all such meanings are encoded in part because of universal needs for disguise and conscious ignorance/denial. Indeed, such humanly shared issues as death anxiety, incestuous and murderous needs and wishes, and the like render the pressures for defensive disguise universal—and let the decoder of such messages beware. Given the state of his personal self-knowledge and the enormity of the pressures directed against creating a sound psychoscope, it is not surprising that Freud went astray.

What, then, are the problems? Three loom large: first, there is the prejudged (theory-insistent) definition of the target material as the patient's unconscious contents constituted mainly as fantasy/memory constellations. These constellations are relatively fixed, static, non-interactional mental (intrapsychic) entities that change little if at all over time. As such, they tend to promote non-dynamic, correlational studies (e.g., the extent to which oedipal conflicts are correlated with resistances in psychotherapy); there is little push towards dynamic, time-related investigations. As a result, a formal, dynamic science is unlikely to emerge, though a more limited static science is inevitable.

Second, there is the gnawing problem of defining the *meaningful, non-trivial* (predictively powerful, explanation strong) form of the unconscious dimension. Psychoanalysis is sorely lacking in reliable indicators of trivial as compared to strong hypotheses and explanations. As I have pointed out repeatedly, psychoanalysts are inclined to work with inferences drawn from manifest contents, manifest contents themselves, some symbols, and unwitting patterns of communication and behaviour as the main referents for unconscious expression; more rarely, they claim to have decoded an unconscious fantasy or memory. Much of this involves arbitrary judgements by the therapist (Little, 1951; Szasz, 1963). But, even more importantly, the concepts of encoding and decoding are all but lost.

There are strong clinical reasons to argue that *meaningful, dynamically powerful* unconscious information is almost always encoded or transformed (of course, we need a different type of psychoscope to validate this proposition). All other forms of communication without awareness, to the extent that they do exist, pale in the degree to which they influence our emotional lives when compared to what Freud (1908a) called derivative or transformed—truly encoded—expressions. Until we have a science that measures the predictive power of formulations made according to each psychoscope we design, we will be forced to decide which viewpoint is most valid by using other means—by trying as best we can to determine their parsimony, clinical utility and validity, sensibility, and even the extent to which the psychoscope's outputs integrate into a viable and evolving entity and science. Still, to the extent that this is a valid criticism of the F-scope—that it is lacking in a critical decoding implement—we are obliged to attempt to revise the scope to correct this defect.

A third criticism of the F-scope is that its processing mechanisms afford little importance to, and often entirely ignore, the day residues or triggers for emotionally charged communications. In psychotherapy, these are almost always constituted as the therapist's interventions, inputs with little or no place in the workings of the F-scope. This defect may eventually be corrected by the classicists, since Gill (1982) has recently stressed the importance of the here-and-now stimuli of the analyst's interventions in accounting for the 'transferences' of the patient. This neglect of triggers is another factor in the static quality of the outputs from the F-scope. On the other hand, if triggers are afforded their full role and allowed to impact on the psychoscope, and if they are seen as meaningful evocators of (conscious and) unconscious/encoded responses, then we are forced to design a psychoscope that sensitively inputs the meanings of a therapist's interventions, and outputs decoded formulations of the patient's material in light of his or her interaction with the therapist. This scope would, of necessity, be responsive to the therapist's interventions as well as the patient's associations, and it would be geared to study interactional temporal exchanges. The result is dynamic; it is a psychoscope designed to carry out trigger decoding from one moment to the next. And it is a result that is likely to call forth a formal, dynamic science as well.

I will call this revised psychoscope the *C-scope*. The theory on which its design is based is interactional, systemic, and, as noted, committed to the view that derivatives—transformed images—are the critical, driving component of unconscious experience and influence. But derivatives are activated by triggers —meaningful emotional stimuli that evoke both conscious and unconscious working-over and adaptation. These triggers shape the derivatives to which they are a response; thus, derivatives can be properly decoded only in light of the *implications of the triggers that have evoked them* (mainly, the implications of a therapist's interventions). There is much that therapists can learn about the implications of their own efforts through *trigger decoding*, as it is called. And there is much that we can learn about the unconscious systems of the mind, and unconscious experience in general, by modifying the F-scope into the C-scope (see chapter four).

If we again take dream formation as our model of the creation of an encoded emotional message, the theory on which the design for the C-scope is based would propose the following:

Step 1. the experience of an emotionally significant *trigger* situation;

Step 2. limited conscious response; profound subliminal registration in the form of *unconscious raw (undefended) images—selected unconscious perceptions*;

Step 3. the *arousal of unconscious memories and fantasies* on the one hand, but in addition, the *intelligent unconscious processing* of these unconscious perceptions—of self and other—towards insight and response;

Step 4. the *report out* of the results of these processes through *images that encode these perceptions and insights* by means of transformed messages, using mainly the mechanisms of displacement, disguise, and condensation.

It is the postulate of a *deep unconscious wisdom system* (see chapter four) for the processing of emotionally charged information and meaning, and the requisite that the output from this system be encoded, that most importantly distinguishes the theory on which the C-scope is based from that which led to the creation of the F-scope. Further, the interplay between triggers and encoded reaction—between stimulus and response makes the C-scope inherently interactional and dynamic, where the F-scope is basically intrapsychic and static. As would be expected, the C-scope is designed to undo the effects of the primary process mechanisms of transformation on the incisive, raw, unconscious perceptions that they encode. It is these perceptions that are critical to the therapeutic experience and to the vicissitudes of the patient's symptoms and resistances in psychotherapy.

* * *

How, then, is this revised psychoscope designed? And how does it operate?

The C-scope operates without a probing attachment in that it is basically a receptive instrument, allowing the patient freely to associate, without pressure of questions, confrontations, or clarifications. The field that is probed is interactional and communicative—the associations, affects, and behaviours of the patient and the behaviours and interventions of the therapist.

And the device is designed to trigger-decode the communications from both as needed.

For the patient, the decoding process is carried out on the surface communications of the patient as they stand—there is no special probing for more deeply excavated material. Of course, it is understood communicatively that as free associations unfold, different layers of surface meaning will emerge, and defences will sometimes be resolved revealing deeper layers of meaning. Nonetheless, the scope is designed in keeping with the thesis that these deeper layers emerge spontaneously and are themselves fraught with additional encoded meaning. In addition, the material that enters the C-scope is viewed interactionally, mainly as responses to how the therapist manages the ground rules of treatment, and maintains silence or becomes active with suitable (or erroneous) interventions and interpretations. In substance, then, the C-scope has been designed on the basis of a theory that states that encoded communications stand before the psychoscope, disguised in existing manifest contents, available for entry into the C-scope and for subsequent trigger decoding. Unconscious meanings are already present in manifest messages but are disguised or camouflaged within the message (rather than entirely hidden or covered over, and likely to emerge undisguised all at once).

While these distinctions may seem subtle, they are actually of profound importance. The F-scope at best provides a deceptive and inaccurate picture of nature, which is never static and lacking in interaction. The C-scope corrects this false picture, though its own failings remain to be discovered. For now, let us take a closer look at how this scope operates.

There are two steps in the use of the C-scope. The first involves inserting a template or decoding key into the scope. This template is forged from the implications and encoded meanings of the active triggers to which the material to be decoded is a response. Where the F-scope has no limit to the possible output of decoded or other meanings taken from the material on which it operates, the C-scope has a set of bounds—though an added attachment allows for the discovery of rare, unexpected decoded meanings as well. This trigger-guided template, then, defines and aligns the proper decoding channels for the material at hand, so that the main function of the scope, that of undoing transformed images, is carried out with interactional sequences in mind. The template defines the set of likely latent images; it establishes the constraints on possible latent contents, restricting their domain to those that are likely to have been dynamically activated.

As noted, in the psychotherapy situation—and therefore with psychotherapy data as constituted by the communications from both patient and therapist—this template is constituted virtually always by the respective communications of the two parties to therapy. For the patient, the template is created from the implications of the interventions of the therapist, while for the therapist the template has a configuration in keeping with the implications and encoded meanings of the patient's material. In both instances, the nature of the appropriate roles and functions of each forms part of the context for the decoding effort. In addition, the scope has a self-observing component through which the decoder can also decode his or her own messages and reactions to the other's inputs—ultimately the C-scope decodes along the me/not-me interface (Langs, 1978).

To focus further on the patient for the moment, the therapist's decoding template is made up of the conscious and especially unconscious implications and meanings of his or her own interventions—silences, active comment, affect and non-verbal behaviour, and ground-rule management efforts. With the template established and set in place, we then set the C-scope into motion. The scope receives the patient's manifest narrative or image and is designed to identify on multiple levels the *thematic contents* inherent to these surface images. Guided by the template, the scope next lifts these themes from their manifest context and sets them into the latent context—the configuration of the trigger situation. The themes are then afforded specific meaning in relation to the stimulus of the therapist's interventions, and defined as perceptive and insightful. As noted, another set of channels in the machine operates to decode the same material as self-perceptions. In both efforts, the output is that of a decoded message (Langs, 1978, 1982b, 1985b, 1988b).

Clinical illustrations

Two clinical vignettes will help us to concretize the similarities and differences between the F- and C-scopes, and enable us to have a clearer perspective on their relationship to a potential science for psychoanalysis.

* * *

The first patient is a young man, a second-year college student, who had sought therapy because of difficulties in sustaining his interest in his studies and problems in socializing with women. The session we consider is the second hour of the therapy. The therapist, also a young man, had arranged for the patient's father to pay the fee for the treatment. As a result, the second session began with the patient handing the therapist a cheque from his father for the previous one.

The patient, who was being seen face-to-face, began to free-associate. He spoke of a male cousin with whom he had been close, but whom he now despised. The cousin was too dependent on his parents, too inclined to make demands on their money, and he showed little concern over his evident greed. 'Kids our age', the patient went on, 'should go out and get a job and be responsible for their own lives. If you let your parents give you all that money, they're only going to try to control your life and make you do things you don't want to do. This is just the way my father is: he seems to feel that giving me an allowance makes me his slave. The same thing happens whenever he goes into a store. He's the customer, the guy dishing out the dough, so he thinks that that gives him the right to be demanding and abusive. I always felt that those store owners should have booted him out of their stores. But you can't talk to my father, tell him about any of this; he just won't hear what you are saying.'

At this point, the therapist intervened. He suggested that the patient felt dominated by his father and was resentful. He speculated that it was this kind of resentment against authority that made it difficult for him to study and to comply with the requests of his teachers. He suggested, too, that his problems with women stem from a fear of being a man like his father; the image of his father was after all, quite assaultive.

The patient seemed puzzled by the therapist's comment and indicated that he felt confused. He was pretty dense and stupid anyhow. He had thought of calling the therapist after the last session to tell him he wanted to quit therapy; he still wasn't sure if he wanted to continue. Somehow he was now reminded of a dinner conversation with his father the previous night. The father had tried to explain the workings of an electric eye, which opened and closed their garage door. The patient had found his father's explanation completely unintelligible and had had the feeling that his father was deliberately trying to confuse him as a way of being hurtful.

Next, the patient looked directly at the therapist and complained that the therapist seemed to be staring at him in an antagonistic way. The therapist denied that this was the case and suggested that the patient was misreading his expression because he was reacting to him as if he—the therapist—were his father. The patient then became annoyed, denied that this was the case, and argued strongly that at times his father actually did attempt to be deliberately confusing as a way of being hurtful. He was always teasing and making up little lies so he could side-step responsibility for his own actions.

Very briefly, in the following session—one that involved a shift in approach (a change of psychoscope) after a supervisory session—the issue of the father's cheque came up again when the patient once again paid the therapist for the prior session. The patient went on to tell the story of a college friend who got into a lot of trouble when he inherited some money from an uncle; the free bucks were a curse in disguise. After listening for a while, the therapist interpreted this narrative as an encoded perception of the problems being created by his acceptance of a cheque from the patient's father as payment for the psychotherapy. The patient responded with a story of a professor of psychology who was extremely perceptive and for whom the patient had the greatest admiration.

By way of discussion, we may note that in the first hour the therapist was working mainly along classical conflict-theory lines—he was using a version of the F-scope. Using this device, he took in the material from his patient—though not his own interventions—and set the mechanism in operation. The output was a number of implications drawn from the manifest contents of the patient's associations, which he eventually interpreted. For example, the idea that this patient felt dominated by his father is implied in his associations and almost manifestly stated. The proposition that the patient was misperceiving the therapist's facial expression and comments, based on traumas from his father—an interpretation of a father transference and resistance—is an output that came through the F-scope's implication extractor, which is programmed to transform surface images into distortions and transferences derived from past 'objects' (people).

The failure of the patient to validate the therapist's initial intervention and his thoughts of leaving treatment were viewed in this F-scope as resistances and as further expressions of the hostile father transference itself. The F-scope usually lacks an attachment for *encoded* validation and, in general, allows only for affirmation via direct agreement. The absence of a more intricate mechanism with which to confirm its own output renders the F-scope especially vulnerable to unchecked error. To correct this deficit, the C-scope has been designed with a mechanism for encoded confirmation, which, though also inevitably open to human error, serves as a safeguard against extremes of incorrect formulations.

Viewed through a C-scope, the trigger for this first session would involve the implications of the therapist's acceptance of his fee in the form of a cheque from the patient's father. The listening template that would then be inserted into the C-scope would be configured to include themes (implications) inherent to that intervention—e.g., those of frame violations and rule-breaking (this is a deviant frame), exploitation, admitting third parties into what should be a more private space, being controlled, used, and manipulated, excessive need and dependency, and the like. These channels would then guide the decoding process and its output, which would now be interactionally configured to reflect that interplay between patient and therapist.

Based on his own selective unconscious sensitivities, this patient unconsciously chose, in the actual session, to stress the implications of this deviation that involved being overly dependent, greedy, controlled by parents, being their slave, and being abused—to cite some highlights. These are shaped as valid unconscious perceptions of some of the actual effects of the fee arrangement; though they have important genetic roots in the patient's relationship with his father, these are not essentially distorted views—they are quite veridical. Furthermore, the C-scope could also be focused on this material as it reflects unconscious needs in the patient; on this level, the derivative material says much about needs in the patient that are comparable to those perceived in the therapist. However, in using the C-scope, it is critical to decode first in terms of the patient's unconscious perceptions of the therapist (which, in our inevitable vulnerability to these perceptions, we are prone to put aside), before decoding the same material as the patient's unconscious self-perceptions.

The C-scope has a highly valuable output channel that is lacking in the F-scope at present. Some of a patient's encoded images in response to a therapist's frame deviation are structured as *encoded models of, or directives for, rectification of the altered boundary condition.* In this situation, the patient encoded his advice to the therapist that he forego the fee arrangement so that the father would no longer be allowed to intrude into and dominate the course of the therapy—even if it meant the temporary termination of the treatment. Typically, an arrangement that the patient accepts consciously—a response that would be picked up directly by the user of the F-scope and accepted at face value, while it would be subjected to processing and decoding by the user of the C-scope—is repudiated unconsciously. This latter response would be missed by the F-scope but picked up by the C-scope because it is interactionally configured for genuine trigger decoding.

In the first session alluded to here, the therapist failed to use the C-scope and to trigger-decode this imagery so that he could offer both an interactional interpretation and a rectification of the frame—i.e., to define the patient's encoded perceptions of the implications of the fee arrangement and to point towards the rectification proposed by the patient: either to deal financially with the patient alone or to consider the termination of the therapy.

At this juncture, the F-scope continues to register transference and resistance. However, the C-scope generates a readout to the effect that the patient is responding to a missed intervention—the therapist had failed to make the intervention called-for through the C-scope. This generates fresh encoded perceptions of the therapist offered in the guise of the patient himself and the patient's father. For example, the patient speaks of quitting therapy, a theme decoded in the C-scope as reflecting an accurate perception that the therapist had abandoned the patient by failing to intervene properly. There is the further image of the patient's father's inability to hear what the other person is saying.

In principle, the lenses and mirrors of the F-scope are believed to be reflecting only the image of the patient. This is a serious misunderstanding of where the focus actually lies—i.e., on *both* the patient and the therapist (indeed, on the therapist as seen through similar structures in the patient). It is here that we touch on a major way in which F-scope outputs confound reality and are therefore not likely to be useful in creating a science for the field.

Perhaps because he unconsciously felt criticized (a common unconscious motive for an errant therapist intervention), the therapist then offered a so-called interpretation of the manifest and implied meanings of the patient's material as processed through the F-scope. The patient's direct and encoded responses to this effort were non-validating as seen through the C-scope and included disguised images that reflected his unconscious impression that the therapist was trying to confuse and hurt him—and that the therapist was himself confused and hurt.

When these perceptions spilled over into direct annoyance with the therapist, the latter invoked a so-called 'transference interpretation'—he intensified his use of the F-scope. Unconsciously, the patient saw this as a cop-out and a lie. Had this material been seen through the C-scope, there would have been no sign of distortion because of a purported father introject. Instead, the decoded output would have registered as a valid, unconscious perception and as a reaction that was selective, but appropriate to the actual implications of the therapist's efforts. Indeed, the therapist had not properly formulated this material; instead, he had unwittingly behaved on one level in a manner comparable to the behaviour of the patient's father—and to the pathological part of the patient himself as well.

Very briefly, in the second session (p. 60), the therapist changed to the C-scope and made an interactionally structured interpretation and moved towards securing the frame. In response, the patient produced an encoded narrative that embodied interpersonal validation—the story of a perceptive and wise professor. This is a rather typical encoded response to a sound interactional interpretation that would, in time, help the patient to understand ways in which the deviations in this psychotherapeutic frame involved interventions from the therapist that repeated the past pathogenic inputs of the father. Through both interpretation and actual rectification, these issues could be suitably modified so that the patient himself could resolve his inner emotional dysfunction—doing so through a combination of insight, positive unconscious introjective identification with the therapist, and the experience of a therapist capable of offering a sound holding relationship and environment.

In all, then, we can see that the two scopes produce very different pictures of the patient, the therapist, and their interaction. It would be almost impossible for both to produce correct pictures of reality, or for both to provide avenues to science. A choice must be made between the two, not only in the clinical arena, but also in respect to a therapist's basic view of the therapy situation and, more fundamentally, of the human emotional mind. There is much here that favours the C-scope, and the interactional approach on which it is based, as far more sound and compelling than the F-scope with its support in the more static classical position. Before making a final decision—one that should be left open to further evidence and available for continual reconsideration—let us look at a final vignette to see how it may help to clarify these issues.

* * *

Mr Norwood, a young married man in his late twenties, was in once-weekly psychotherapy with Dr Fletcher because of problems with premature ejaculation and repeated quarrels with his wife. Early in the therapy, at Mr Norwood's request, Dr Fletcher agreed to see, and held a session with, the patient's wife. In the hour that followed, Mr Norwood reported a dream in which his boss joined him in bed with his wife. The boss then became involved in sexual play with both of them.

The two psychoscopes would process this material rather differently. The F-scope would take in this dream imagery and generate an output related to its manifest contents and their implications as a reflection of the patient's inner mental life. In all likelihood, the scope would produce an output that would suggest that the patient was deeply involved in oedipal conflicts, struggling with latent homosexual issues, and still enmeshed in conflict with paternal and maternal introjects.

By way of contrast, the C-scope would operate with the inserted template of the implications of Mr Norwood's request and Dr Fletcher's actual session with the patient's wife—e.g., the violation of the privacy and one-to-one attributes of the psychotherapy, the instinctualization of the therapeutic experience (departures from the ideal frame are unconsciously viewed by the deep unconscious system as strongly sexual and aggressive), the therapist's fear of being alone with the patient (possibly based on his own unconscious, latent homosexual anxieties), and the modification of the ideal and acceptable framework of the therapeutic relationship. Next, the C-scope would identify the themes in this dream: being in bed with one's wife, being joined by a third party who is an authority figure, the seductive behaviour of the third party—and such. These themes would be lifted from the manifest context in the dream, which was the patient's home, and placed into the latent context of the therapeutic interaction (in this instance, the scene is changed, but two of the three characters remain the same; the only transformation in personage that needs to be undone is that from the psychotherapist to the boss). These themes are then joined to the activating trigger—the therapist's session with the wife—and read out as a selective but perceptive reading of the implications of this frame-deviant intervention: it is seen unconsciously as creating a kind of *ménage à trois*, as involving a bedroom rather than a therapeutic space, and as being highly seductive.

Finally, the scope would be trained on Mr Norwood and used to decode the implications of his request that his therapist see his wife. Here, we would need to know the prior triggers within the treatment interaction—i.e., the relevant prior interventions by the therapist—and the earlier and current history and inner state of the patient in order to trace his own needs for a deviant frame—motivated, in all likelihood, by his own secure-frame anxieties and his unconscious perception of similar anxieties in his therapist.

Mr Norwood's deep unconscious processing of the central deviant trigger—which goes undetected in the F-scope—is strikingly different from his manifest reaction. Consciously, he requested the session for his wife, and in the following hour thanked Dr Fletcher for seeing her. Yet his encoded images, properly decoded in light of their trigger, suggest an unconscious view of the meeting as one of seduction and sexual involvement. It is this type of typical contrast between conscious and unconscious processing that emerges so very clearly through the C-scope, and is seldom seen through the F-scope because of its particular premises of design.

The comparatively greater attention and responsibility afforded to the therapist by the C-scope is quite evident. Because it does not consistently decode the communications from the therapist, the F-scope tends to generate output about the patient when a more accurate reading would link the printout to the therapist first—and then to the patient as well. It is in this sense that important aspects of dynamic reality are missed or confounded by the F-scope; in the extreme, it can be argued that the F-scope's lenses are actually taking in information about the therapist but putting out results about the patient. While there is some validity to the classical print-out, it is appended to the wrong individual first—the patient rather than the therapist who cannot be excluded from consideration.

In this instance, for example, the patient has certainly expressed his own unconscious homosexual anxieties and incestuous conflicts through his request that the therapist see his wife, but the therapist's decision to do so gives him the greater loading of these images for the moment—they are quite true of him as well. The C-scope would read out this dyadic picture, whereas the F-scope would not and would stay focused entirely on the patient. Ultimately, this confusion as to who is involved in encoded messages is likely to defeat the quest for science, which, as noted, requires a sound and comprehensive grasp of reality—of facts and data—for its base.

Notice, too, that the F-scope cannot register and process the framework issue in the patient's manifest dream—having a third party in their usually private bed. The F-scope is designed to process and read out only issues related to psychodynamics and genetics. In contrast, the C-scope can identify and process frame-related imagery and the interactional issues and systemic configurations that they evoke—in addition to the psychodynamic and genetic constellations. In part, this is the result of the programming of the F-scope, which is configured primarily *in the context of conscious needs and concerns*, while the C-scope is set up *in keeping with deep unconscious needs and viewpoints*.

In critical ways, these two need systems and points of view are dramatically different. The therapist using the classical F-scope would, per accompanying instructions, ask Mr Norwood to associate to the various elements of his dream and would question, probe, and directly explore his other free associations in the course of the session. This filling in the voids or excavation work might well reveal associations to the patient's mother and father, and the memory of once having shared their bed. There might even be associations that directly connect Mr Norwood's father with Dr Fletcher. The result would then be a so-called transference interpretation to the effect that Mr. Norwood seemed to be entertaining unconscious homosexual/oedipal fantasies and wishes towards his analyst, derived primarily from earlier experiences with his parents—and with his father in particular. Mr. Norwood's impotency might then be interpreted—read out by the F-scope—as a fear of castration by the therapist/father because of the unconscious equation in the patient's mind between his wife and his mother. Mr. Norwood might then respond by feeling that the therapist was being somewhat attacking or seductive, and these feelings would be viewed as further transference distortions based on this inner constellation derived from his early life experiences.

Still, the main point for the moment is that the interpretation—and the theory derived from this way of organizing the patient's material, a theory that also guides this very organization and psychoscope—would see the patient as suffering from pathological fantasies, memories, and wishes that not only disturb his perceptions of the therapist, but also his relationship with his wife. Through the lens of the F-scope, the patient is seen as sick and dysfunctional, and the analyst as the healthy observer (even if he or she is called a participant–observer, one who is merely giving lip-service to the interactional aspect of the situation in the face of formulations that are concentrated mainly on the patient).

Of course, the C-scope would render a very different reading of the same clinical data. This scope would generate an output that suggests that the therapist, by having had a session with the wife, had in actuality, however latently, behaved in a seductive and oedipal fashion (in all likelihood, had acted out his own oedipal and incestuous wishes and needs, and his defences against homosexual anxieties as well). The therapist would be seen as having repeated a past pathogenic interaction between the patient and his parents—the occasions on which the parents took their son to bed with them. While the therapist's interview with the wife was fraught with a wide range of implications—all of them inserted into the C-scope as its immediate decoding template—this patient selectively chose to represent and react to those that were sexual. The deviant intervention, though arranged for by the patient (in part, for unconscious reasons of his own that are consistently under interactional influence—as are the behaviours of the therapist), re-enacted a pathological constellation that accounted not only for the patient's unconscious perceptions of the therapist, but also for the difficulties with the wife who (in agreement with the classical formulation) evidently represents the incestuous, oedipal mother. The latter constellation, active in both patient and therapist, appears to be the unconscious factor in both the patient's impotency and his frequent quarrels with his wife (whatever the additional elements).

The main point, then, is that the interpretation derived from the C-scope holds the therapist accountable for pathological or dysfunctional behaviours that are validly but unconsciously perceived by the patient in a highly selective manner as influenced by his pathology as well. The very constellation that was a factor in the patient's psychopathology has been unwittingly activated through a collusion between patient and therapist. A resolution of this difficulty within the patient, then, would require rectification by the therapist (at best he could, based on the patient's subsequent derivatives, assure the patient that there would be no further third-party intrusions), as well as suitable interpretation. To split off the therapeutic interaction from the patient's inner mental constellation is to deal at best with only half of reality, and to do so in a highly biased and substantially self-protective and defensive manner on the part of the therapist. This unconscious avoidance is unconsciously perceived by the patient and derails the active pursuit of insight. If these formulations are valid, there seems little possibility of paving a road to science using the F-scope.

The differences between the F-scope and C-scope are now quite evident. They constitute two very different means of listening to and formulating the material from patients—and the therapist's own interventions. They lead to very different types of interpretations and, more broadly, to rather different conceptualizations of the nature of the therapeutic interaction—and the process of cure.

It seems fair to claim that the C-scope produces outputs that are closer to direct observation, more patently data-driven, more compellingly validated, and more promising in light of the full consideration of interaction than those stemming from the F-scope. As such, the workings of the C-scope seem more apt to provide a path to a science for psychoanalysis and may well provide the kind of observations of encoded material that could form the basis for such a science—one in which the unconscious domain would receive its due attention. It is for these reasons that I use the C-scope as the basis for the considerations that unfold in the rest of the book—even as we deal with issues of concern to the field in general. And now, having argued for the greater power of the C-scope and its background theory as a foundation for a science for the field, let us turn to the two additional components we need to develop in order to complete this foundation: a systems theory and a new model of the mind.

PART TWO

SYSTEMS AND SUBSYSTEMS IN PSYCHOANALYSIS

CHAPTER THREE

A systems theory for psychoanalysis

> The emerging paradigm, by contrast, recognizes that the collective and holistic properties of physical systems can display new and unforeseen modes of behaviour that are not captured by the Newtonian and thermodynamic approaches. There arises the possibility of *self-organization*, in which systems suddenly and spontaneously leap into more elaborate forms. These forms are characterized by greater complexity, by co-operative behaviour and global coherence, by the appearance of spatial patterns and temporal rhythms, and by the general unpredictability of their final forms.
>
> Paul Davies, *The Cosmic Blueprint*

In part one, I touched upon reasons that a dynamic (interactional) science of psychoanalysis must, of necessity, be grounded in a comprehensive systems theory that both complements the existing theory of psychodynamics and genetics and takes into account and properly defines the unconscious domain. It is time now to develop these arguments further as a way of generating a sense of the deep need for such a theory and to show, too, the profound clinical—as well as research and scientific—implications of this proposal. I must stress at the outset that we require something more than a naive systemic conception; we need a theory that considers fully both the conscious and especially the unconscious functions and implications of the boundary conditions of the system and the unconscious communication and processing that takes place within these boundary conditions in the therapeutic interaction. Without a sound delineation of the unconscious component of the systemic domain, the theory could not rightfully claim to be psychoanalytic in nature.

We might ask, first of all: why is a systems theory so essential to a science of psychoanalysis? And why, then, has it been so neglected until now?

A systems theory for psychoanalysis can be based on but two fundamental axioms: (1) that the fundamental entity in the therapeutic interaction, which is the field of observation for psychoanalysis, is that of the patient/therapist (P/T) system; and (2) that unconscious mental and communicative processes are an essential component of how this P/T system functions.

The first axiom states a basic position that neither P nor T is the most fundamental entity—system—of the therapeutic interaction; this honour falls to their unique combination into a P/T system. P and T are, therefore, viewed as the most critical subsystems of the P/T system. The second axiom, to reiterate a key point, requires a sound definition of the unconscious domain—something I tried to accomplish in part one of the book. In addition, the two axioms imply a basic postulate derived from general systems theory (see Laszlo, 1987; Maturano & Varela, 1987), to the effect that *the boundary conditions of the P/T system* are critical to both how the system and its subsystems function and evolve, and the nature of the meanings being conveyed consciously and unconsciously in the communications of all concerned. In a systems theory, P and T are not viewed as fixed entities, but as ever-changing subsystems, under continuous influence from each other and the often changing boundary conditions of the system.

With this in mind, we can readily ascertain a familiar theme in a fresh cast: a systems theory for psychoanalysis speaks immediately for researching the temporally unfolding trajectory of the system, and of the interaction between its main subsystems—P and T. On the other hand, the absence of a systems theory would foster research into the functioning of P or T in isolation—most usually P, of course—as if each were a separate entity that lent itself to meaningful individual study. In contrast, a systems theory insists that if P or T is studied as a separate subsystem, this must be done interactionally, so that the influence of each on the other is accounted for.

There is yet another advantage of a systems theory for the field. Psychoanalytic science is also likely to be enriched by a search for, and the identification of, the *emergent properties*—attributes that are not seen in either the P or T subsystems, yet are characteristic of their interaction—of the P/T system, as distinguished from attributes of P or T alone. As noted before, isolated studies of P alone are likely to be limited to statistical measures in which a single number summarizes a lengthy and complex trajectory; this number could actually be generated by a multitude of time series or temporal configurations. A dynamic science, which seeks laws and deep structures, cannot be founded on such work; systems and interaction are vital to what we are seeking.

In light of systemic thinking, studies of P alone are also likely to be not only limited in scope, but also quite misleading—in respect to both findings and interpretation—even when they accurately capture a set of observations. Think of a camera fixed on only one of two tennis-players; if that individual tended to remain on the right-hand side of the court, without a systems theory we would theorize an intrapsychic and dysfunctional tendency to tilt—stay—to the right. Yet, with a full picture of the system—of the two players—and its rules or frame (the boundary conditions), we would propose, instead, an adaptive ability to stay in the part of the court where the opponent is hitting the ball. Systemic thinking produces a striking difference in how we picture nature as compared to the non-systemic view.

To extend this analogy further into considerations of the frame, without a knowledge of the rules and boundaries of the game, we would observe this player starting and stopping play in what would seem to be a chaotic fashion—such would be the nature of our observed facts. Yet with knowledge of the rules and boundary conditions, we would conclude that we are observing an orderly and comprehensible rhythm. Once again, we see the extent to which observation, inferences, and data are theory-dependent—not only as to how we listen and formulate, but also as to how we conceive of the fundamental structure of the interaction between P and T.

A systems theory supports a more data-driven and valid view of reality than non-systemic thinking (even as we acknowledge that all views are open to error). By stressing the evolution of the system, we are once again pushed towards a dynamic rather than static science—which is, as we know, a quite favourable development. Indeed, the selection of the variables and observations needed for an effective science requires systemic thinking. In addition, *systemic patterns* that are virtually unrecognizable in the non-systemic approach are exceedingly important once a systems theory is in place. Such a theory would expect each P and T to interact differently—and therefore 'exist' and 'be' distinctive yet changing entities—when in dialogue with different T's and P's. Systemic thinking captures the changeability in us all and in all of nature; it does not fix as unalterable the nature of the individuals who are interacting within the psychotherapeutic and other frames. In the words of Heraclitus, you never step into the same stream twice.

This widening comprehension is also in evidence in how systems thinking extends the purview and insights of psychoanalysis beyond its currently restricted range of dynamics and genetics (early childhood influences), into issues of stability and instability, distance from equilibrium, and other properties of individuals and dyads (and more complex relationships) that do not otherwise arise. Systemic thinking, as noted, also allows for the formulation of *two fields of force* acting on and within the P/T system—*systems dynamic* and *psychodynamic*. Such a theory helps to direct psychoanalytic research and science by allowing for non-trivial variables that are more readily quantified than those derived from psychodynamic thinking alone. All of the other necessary trappings of a science for the field that have been discussed previously—dynamics, falsifiability, the use of mathematical models, etc.—are also enhanced by a systemic approach.

Resistances against systemic thinking

With such a compelling prima facie series of arguments in favour of the need for a systems theory for psychoanalysis and its science, we must now ask why such a theory has been so long in coming to the field—and so long resisted by psychoanalysts.

The first answer to this question may well lie in the efforts of the initial proponents of systemic thinking to advocate this dimension as a substitute for, rather than a supplement to, psychodynamics. In 1971, Peterfreund offered a monograph in which he essentially proposed that we replace the existing formulations of psychoanalytic metapsychology with systemic and information-related concepts. More recently, Rosenblatt and Thickstun (1977, 1984) attempted to expand Peterfreund's proposal; they suggested a number of advantages to using systemic formulations in preference to formulations derived from psychodynamics. Where Peterfreund stressed the role played by a variety of postulated intrapsychic systems in the processing of information, concentrating his attention on patients in particular, Rosenblatt and Thickstun considered not only the role of internal hierarchies, but also the idea that patient and analyst together constitute an interpersonal or interactional system.

As noted by Wallerstein (1986), there has been a striking lack of interest among psychoanalysts in this particular line of thought. Indeed, Wallerstein himself characterized the existing efforts to move psychoanalysis towards 'the so-called natural science direction . . . [as both] brilliantly daring and yet fundamentally misplaced' (p. 419). Wallerstein also noted that these efforts were designed to replace present psychoanalytic theory with an information-theory, systemic, and cybernetic model of the mind, and he stated his belief that the usefulness of these concepts had yet to be established clinically, technically, and heuristically. Wallerstein was also mindful that these concepts have failed to achieve status within the psychoanalytic movement. Since psychoanalysts are not at all prepared to give up their dynamic ideas (which include, as noted, conflict theory, self- and ego-psychology, object relations, and many other variants that address a domain quite different from systems theory; see below), the effort to replace these fundamental concepts with systemic thinking made it relatively easy to dismiss the systemic aspect as unneeded.

A somewhat different fate was met by the extensive efforts by Newton (1971, 1973, 1989) to present the trappings of a clinically relevant systems theory to psychoanalysis in a way that supplements rather than replaces psychodynamic theory. Newton entered this arena as a dynamically oriented psychotherapist knowledgeable in social systems theory. He recognized that systemic thinking addresses boundary issues both with respect to P and T per se, and with regard to the demarcation between the therapeutic space and the outside world. He stressed such issues as the task of the system (i.e., the cure of the patient), the maintenance of clear boundary conditions, and the importance of systems differentiation (he considered P and T as basic systems that needed to be distinctive in order to function properly; there is little in his writings of the P/T system itself). Newton was also cognizant of the need for separate and distinctive roles for P and T, and of the part played by the therapist's frame management efforts through which boundary conditions suitable for the achievement of the system's goals can be established and maintained.

Newton's efforts indicate some of the ways in which systemic considerations widen the scope of psychoanalytic thinking and understanding. The fate of a psychotherapeutic experience depends not only on dynamics, but also on the proper systemic conditions; countertransferences are expressed not only through errant comments to the patient, but also through failures to manage properly the ground rules of therapy. Role differentiation is essential to the process of cure. There are many influences on the therapeutic process that extend beyond dynamic/genetic propositions.

As far as can be ascertained, Newton's work has been largely ignored by mainstream psychoanalysts. The field lacks what I term *system readiness* to incorporate such thinking into its purview. On a deeper level, however, it may well be that some of the inadequacies in the basic structure of each of these systemic theories—including Newton's, which is nonetheless the most clinically sophisticated—also contribute to their isolation.

Basically, each of these efforts, and virtually all of the systemic thinking in family systems approaches where such ideas are commonplace, *lack a proper definition of the unconscious domain.* Newton, for example, shows no conception of derivative communication and the workings of the deep unconscious wisdom system (see chapter four)—the kind of formulations generated by the C-scope. He is therefore unable to recognize that in the presence of frame deviations, patients communicate *encoded* models of rectification—correctives—which can be used by the therapist in his or her framework management efforts. Lacking this essential resource, Newton can only recommend confrontations and manipulations of the patient when frame issues arise; though such practices are typical of those therapists who address frame issues on the manifest level, his techniques may nonetheless offend the sensibilities of many practitioners. Still, it is only Newton, among users of the F-scope, who recognizes the importance of the boundary conditions of the P/T system; other writers typically omit this critical consideration.

Still another factor in the refutation of systemic thinking by psychoanalysts lies in the realization that such a theory brings the therapist, as a member of the P/T system, full-force into every aspect of the therapeutic experience—and with that, a full share of responsibility for all happenings within the system and its components—P and T. After all, the theory states that he or she is a basic subsystem of the P/T system; P cannot vary without some prior or later change in T. This measure of accountability has evoked considerable defensiveness among therapists in a variety of ways, as seen for example in their very limited view of the signs of countertransference activity and their failure to identify many aspects of their profound influence on their patients.

These defences are evident in my own early systemic writings. In 1976, I offered a bipersonal field concept of the therapeutic interaction that was distinctly systemic, even though it was cast in Kleinian terms (Langs, 1976a), but I failed to make any use of existing systemic ideas. Nonetheless, the importance of the boundary conditions of therapy was clinically documented, and all transactions within the therapeutic space were conceived of interactionally—e.g., all patient symptoms were seen as a product of the field and therefore as a result of vectors from both P and T. Though it did receive some initial attention, this presentation, which clearly placed a greater burden of responsibility on the therapist than existing dynamic postulates, has also remained cut off from mainstream thinking. For me, it required another ten years of clinical observation and the initiation of psychotherapy research to expand these fragmented beginnings of a systems theory into a well-formed, systematic set of postulates. There appears to be considerable anxiety among therapists about being given a full partnership with the patient in the therapeutic experience. Even though this does not imply equal responsibility for all occurrences within the P/T system, it does speak for a greater burden on the therapist than heretofore acknowledged.

A final factor in the resistance to systemic thinking seems to lie in the universal dread, in both P and T, of the secure frame—the ideal set of ground rules unconsciously sought by the deep unconscious system though feared by the conscious part of the mind (Langs, 1979, 1984–85, 1985a, 1988a, 1989a). As noted earlier, a definitive set of secure ground rules for psychotherapy provides an optimal hold and set of conditions for the unfolding of the patient's pathology-related and other communications on their own terms and, with that, the best possible framework for the cure of the patient. But this ideal set of conditions also evokes major anxieties of a paranoid, schizoid, and claustrophobic nature—in a sense, the basic anxieties of life and its outcome in death. Frame breaks relieve these anxieties, albeit pathologically and at considerable cost, and we tend in general consciously to favour this type of action/relief over maintaining the ideal frame and carrying out the analytic work that would be required to resolve these issues through insight—and thereby produce a therapeutic outcome with the highest possible help/hurt ratio as well.

Ignoring systems theory and its attention to the ground rules of therapy—the boundary conditions of the system—facilitates this type of defensiveness and denial, and the use of frame alterations that by-pass both secure frame issues and insight. This type of pathological avoidance is far more difficult to engage in when one is confronted with the overwhelming effects of boundary conditions on living and non-living systems—and even more so when these realizations are supplemented by using the C-scope and interactionally decoding frame-related derivatives when ground rule issues arise in psychotherapy itself. The defensive needs of the conscious system to by-pass secure frame anxieties and issues appears to be an important unconscious factor in our resistance to a systems theory for psychoanalysis.

The call for a systems theory

Although my main purpose in this chapter is to attempt to advocate and present a systems theory in a favourable and compelling light, the fact that a theory of this kind has a place in psychoanalytic thinking may, as I said, well be immediately evident. After all, by definition, both P and T are human systems whose totalities are greater than the sum of their parts. On the face of it, we can see that their interaction creates a system (P/T), whose attributes cannot be accounted for by an analysis of, and reductionistic approach to, the separate components—P or T—in isolation.

One might say, then, that there are three definable systems in the psychoanalytic situation—P/T, P, and T (as noted, these are actually subsystems of the P/T system). In general, system theorists would focus on the interaction between P and T, though some attention would be paid to discovering distinctive and emergent properties of the P/T system itself. Each of these systems has, as we know, its own boundary conditions. And, overall, it would be the goal of psychoanalytic systems theory to account for the intricate vicissitudes of this complex dimension of psychotherapy. It would seem, then, that this manifesto is self-evident and hardly open to dispute (though arguments could be made as to how important this dimension is to the therapeutic process; see below).

Since the pioneering work of Bertalanffy (1968), a large literature has brought systemic thinking to bear on every branch of science, including biology and its sub-discipline, neuroscience. Much of this work has met with resistance from the mainstream of the particular field involved, though many brilliant minds have shown the unique advantages of systemic ideas for their own discipline. There may well be some aspect of systemic thinking that is fundamentally inimical to how we prefer to think and work; in general, dissecting single entities and resorting to reductionistic thinking appears to be easier than dealing with the inherent wholeness and intricacies of systemic ideas. The human mind does seem to prefer simplicity to complexity, even when the latter is enriching.

A systems theory offers one immediate advantage of considerable value to the field of psychoanalysis. All systems share properties; these are called *isomorphisms*, and they are at the opposite pole from features distinctive to a particular system, which are called *diffeomorphisms*. Because of this general feature of systems, it is possible for psychoanalysis to begin its systemic thinking with a substantial base of concepts borrowed from systemic propositions developed in other fields—e.g., embryonic morphology, ecology, neuroscience. To these concepts —and their applicability will need testing—we can add features that are distinctive to the P/T system per se. Furthermore, the quantification of systemic dimensions of the P/T system, and their investigation over time, will provide data that is unique to systemic research where human communication has proven relatively difficult to investigate. There appear to be many broad advantages to this quest for an analytic systems theory.

In this context, it can be stressed again that an understanding of the systemic aspects of P/T, P, and T does not replace a psychodynamic analysis of their transactions, and of the vicissitudes of the patient's emotional disturbance. To clarify this point, we may consider an analogy to efforts to understand the workings of a watch. An analysis of the chemical and sub-atomic particle make-up of the components of a watch (psychodynamics) cannot conceivably explain its functioning as a time-piece (systems dynamics). But the reverse also applies: no amount of understanding of the systemic dimension of the functioning of a watch can illuminate its sub-atomic structure. Both are needed for a comprehensive description, and both are vital to understanding the driving power and total functioning of the mechanism.

By this argument, then, an investigation of psychodynamics as applied to the therapeutic interaction cannot adequately describe the state of the P/T system and its attributes—e.g., the system's distance from equilibrium, stability, attractors, degree of complexity, the nature of its trajectories, and the like. The very language that is used to characterize systemic dimensions informs us that this domain is distinctive from psychodynamics where the issues and measures relate to conflict, instinctual drives, psychosexual stages, fantasy–memory and perception formations, and similar issues. Clearly, the two realms are dissimiliar; we need only to demonstrate that knowledge of the state of the P/T system is crucial for comprehensive psychoanalytic understanding. With that established, it is but a small step to acknowledging the essential need for a systems theory for a science of psychoanalysis.

* * *

Two other interconnected reasons support the advocation of a psychoanalytic systems theory. First, a theory of this kind would inherently encourage research with high scientific standards, including the development of mathematical models that would account for the behaviours of P/T system itself. It would be incumbent upon systemically oriented researchers to measure the moment-to-moment system output as it stems from input factors and the processing capacities of its subsystems; this is in essence a dynamical systems approach. As noted, this kind of quantification and measurement is unlike the kind of global correlational studies that prevail in current psychoanalytic and psychotherapeutic research (Shulman, 1990).

The introduction of a systemic theory—and this point is also made more sceptically by Wallerstein (1986)—would also inherently move psychoanalysis towards or into the family of sciences where systemic thinking is, though controversial, a common matter for debate. Many of the issues involved in this development could well be resolved by a straightforward demonstration that scientific standards of quantification, measurability, prediction, and sensibility can be applied to psychoanalytic data derived from systemic postulates. In substance, then, we seem to need a systems theory for psychoanalysis because such a theory can lead directly to science—one virtually promises the other.

Some basic systemic propositions

Having proposed that a systems theory is essential as a foundation for a science of psychoanalysis, and having argued that such a move would be highly salutary for clinical theory and practice, it is time to buttress these ideas by defining some fundamental postulates of a psychoanalytic systemic theory. It is hoped that the sensibility and perspectives offered by these propositions will add weight to the importance of systemic thinking in the field.

I will begin by offering some basic systemic conceptions that appear to be applicable to the therapeutic interaction. These ideas are the result of an interplay between clinical observation, formal research investigation, readings of the scientific and systems theory literature, model-making, and theory formation. For purposes of exposition, however, it will be necessary to disassemble this particular totality and present its components separately.

Our task is to define some basic models of the structure and functioning of those systems that we consider to be pertinent to psychoanalytic investigation and practice. All science involves the selection of critical variables and therefore simplification for purposes of manageability and meaningful study. The goal is to propose a minimum number of critical propositions that can account for and predict the phenomenology under investigation. A supplementary goal entails the delineation through both theory and model-making of the minimum number of systems required to carry out the postulated functions and to account meaningfully for the behaviours (including symptoms) and communications of those involved. Initially, we will be concerned with macroscopic systems—P/T, P, and T—though in chapter four we will consider microscopic systems, those involved in the mental processing of emotionally charged information and meaning.

The propositions to be offered here have been developed over a two-year period during which some re-shaping and revision and a great deal of elaboration took place (for earlier models, see Langs 1986, 1987a, 1987b). Interestingly, as the systemic models became more complex in order to account more fully for input variables, processing mechanisms, and output results, they became easier to streamline—and consequently easier to comprehend. Still, for most psychotherapists, this is unfamiliar terrain, and it will require some time to become accustomed to its language and ideas; nonetheless, doing so is well worth the effort.

Let us turn now to a series of basic propositions that seem to be fundamental to a systems theory for psychoanalysis:

Proposition 1

As already noted, the most basic proposition states that *the P/T system*, as it operates or functions within a set of *psychophysical boundary conditions* (a set of ground rules or frame), is the *fundamental system in the therapeutic interaction*. Each component of this system—P, T, and boundaries—is in a continual state of slow or rapid change, and in continuous interaction. In order to understand and predict the functioning of this system, contributions from each element must at all points in time be taken into account. Thus, a patient's communications and functioning result not only from processes within his or her own mental sub-systems, but also from processes within the therapist and from the nature of the boundary conditions. Similarly, the therapist's behaviour and communications can be understood only by also considering the processes within the patient and—again—the nature of the boundary conditions. For purposes of analysis, then, it is possible to study P, T, or boundary conditions separately; however, a full comprehension of their behaviours and communications can be made only when the total system is taken into account.

Proposition 2

Unconscious experience and communication is overridingly important to understanding the vicissitudes of the P/T system in the emotional domain and in the therapeutic interaction, as well as the patient's (and therapist's) psychopathology and its resolution—or exacerbation. Furthermore, it is understood that there are many processes and dimensions of communication of which P and/or T may be unaware; however, these differ greatly in their power to influence emotional life. For example, such matters as body posture, internal organ functioning, implications of messages, encoded elements of messages, and the like all typically lie outside the awareness of a message sender and/or its receiver. It is proposed, however, that among these phenomena, *the unconscious implications of manifest messages and the encoded (transformed) levels of communicated meanings are especially critical* (see part one for clarification; see also Langs, 1985b, 1988a, 1988b, 1991, 1992).

As I have tried to emphasize, it is only with a proper conceptualization of the nature of unconscious communication and the power of derivative expressions that a profound psychoanalytic systems theory and science can be developed—one that extends beyond self-evident propositions. A systems theory grounded in manifest contents and direct meanings, and in conscious implications, is inadequate for the task of explaining the vicissitudes of the P/T system in any deep and nontrivial way. This is especially true when we consider intrapsychic information/meaning processing along with the gross processing of information and meaning by the total P/T system. In the emotional domain, the functioning of P, T, and the P/T system unfolds on both the conscious and unconscious levels, and both levels must be properly conceptualized and formulated if one is to comprehend fully the nature of both psychodynamic and systems dynamic inputs—and their consequences.

Proposition 3

The systemic properties and effects of the P/T system are distinctive from its psychodynamic properties along many significant dimensions (see Table 3.1). Each realm formulates and explores different aspects of ongoing functioning that interact and yet overlap only minimally. As noted, a full description of the therapeutic process requires a delineation of both domains.

For example, the emergence of psychodynamic sexual material will not only have different meanings under different ground-rule/boundary conditions, but will also lead to distinc-

TABLE 3.1

Some notable dimensions of systems and psychodynamic theories

Systems theory	*Psychodynamic theory*
1. holistic (whole greater than parts)	individual elements
2. causality: circular, totalistic	linear
3. self-organizing, self-regulating, etc.	synthetic function of ego
4. evolutionary	static
5. order vs. disorder	progression vs. regression
6. information, complexity vs. simplicity	attempts to apply information theory
7. energy flow	libido, aggression
8. overload	symptoms
9. readiness	psychological-minded; timing of interventions
10. stable, at or near equilibrium, vs. unstable	mature vs. regressed
11. open vs. closed	closed/isolated
12. boundaries	not considered (cf. ground rules)
13. equifinality	different modes of cure
14. bifurcations, catastrophes	crises
15. attractors-point (equilibrium), cyclical, chaotic	cycles of sexual urges
16. bonding, enmeshment	countertransference
17. organization; hierarchical	levels of ego integration
18. channels, pathways, trajectories	course of therapy
19. rigid vs. flexible	resistance vs. cooperative (therapeutic alliance)
20. input–output	response to interventions
21. patterns–sequences	course of therapy

TABLE 3.1
(continued)

Systems theory	*Psychodynamic theory*
22. conflict, competing systems vs. enhancement	intrapsychic and interpersonal conflict vs. enhancement
23. intergenerational boundaries and systems	role of early childhood (genetics)
24. self—in context of system	self—as isolated entity
25. power struggle	id, drives, sexuality, and aggression
26. efficiency (cost of operating the system)	ego and ego functions
27. observing system	superego
28. communication and metacommunication	conscious and unconscious processes
29. how systems interact—patient and therapist	transference
30. how systems interact—therapist and patient	countertransference
31. system rigid, inflexibility	resistance

tive outputs and behaviours in both P and T, depending on the state of the P/T system and its subsystems at the time the material is expressed. In general, when a P/T system is operating close to equilibrium, such material is not likely to destabilize the system, nor will its proper interpretation according to interactional principles—i.e., the use of the C-scope—be likely to propel the system towards higher levels of order and adaptation. In contrast, if the system is far from equilibrium at such a juncture, the system output is likely to be far more unstable after interpretation, and more likely to lead to either system decompensation (chaos) or constructive evolution (Davies, 1987; Laszlo, 1987; Prigogine & Stengers, 1984).

As indicated in Table 3.1, the systemic domain includes such dimensions as order versus disorder, equilibrium versus disequilibrium, complexity versus simplicity, and the use of various descriptors to identify the attributes of the unfolding trajectory of the system over time. Psychodynamics involves the more familiar dimensions of conflict, sex and aggression, self and other, ego and id and superego, therapeutic alliance and misalliance—and the like.

In general, systemic measures like the degree of informational complexity, continuity, and such lend themselves more easily to quantification and dynamic measurement in terms of time series than dynamic concepts that tend to be static and measurable only in a limited sense—degree of alliance, amount of sexuality or aggression, cohesion of self, are all concepts that suggest single over-all measures or immeasurability. These dimensions change very slowly over time, while most systemic measures are in a state of continuous flux. Paradoxically, then, systems theory speaks for dynamic measures, while psychodynamics speaks for static and statistical measures.

Despite these distinctions, however, it is likely that, as the science of psychoanalysis evolves, quantitative research will lead to mathematical models that ultimately reveal a single underlying deep structure to these two domains, which are so different on the surface. At present, we are a great distance from such unifying principles and need to be concerned for now with defining and measuring these two separate fields of force and their interactions. Unification is likely to evolve only after many years of intense study.

Proposition 4

The P/T system creates and is created by—and functions within—a framework or set of boundary conditions defined by the psycho-physical ground rules and conditions of the therapy. This frame may be well-established, damaged, complete or incomplete, fragmented, or virtually non-existent.

Whatever its state, the boundary conditions affect every dimension of the transactions of the P/T system unfolding within its confines. Roles, functioning, communicated meanings on all levels—manifest, encoded, and implied—symptoms, resistances, subjective experience, fantasies, and perceptions (and whatever else these two living subsystems may do and experience) are all under the influence of these boundary conditions. Strong testimony to the importance of the frame is found in the already-noted extreme sensitivity to boundary conditions shown by the deep unconscious system, as clearly reflected in the derivatives it emits. Because of this extraordinary centrality of the frame to unconscious perception and response, psychotherapy is essentially a ground-rule-based treatment; the patient's pathology and its genetics are affixed to framework issues through which they can be interpreted and resolved.

The P/T system—and P and T individually—has a special relationship with its boundaries conditions. This particular system is one of those autopoietic living systems that creates its own boundary configuration, conditions that then become the central 'metabolic' issue for the processes that unfold over time within the system (see Maturana & Varela, 1987, for a comparable discussion of the living cell). Based on an accumulation of unconscious life experiences, the deep unconscious sub-system of each component of the P/T system maintains an exquisite sensitivity to the boundary conditions reflected in the therapeutic contract and frame throughout a therapy. The boundary conditions are, then, the substantive issues and sources of information and meaning through which the psychopathology of the patient—and the therapist, as well as the P/T system *in toto*—can be explored, analysed, and rectified (a necessary component of analytic work with the frame)—and more effective modes of adaptation effected.

Overall, the boundary conditions are P/T generated and maintained; they are a major means of generating important conscious and unconscious messages fraught with especially powerful implications for the therapeutic experience. They are a living and active component of the P/T system, as much a part of the P and T sub-systems as external to them. In Winnicott's (1953) terms, the boundaries of therapy are a transitional element: both me and not me for both P and T. These boundary conditions establish not only a separation of the P/T system from the rest of the world, but also determine the very nature of the boundaries of the system's components, P and T, and the rules of their interaction. Overall, the cure or means of stabilization adopted by a given P/T system is highly frame dependent—as are all system dysfunctions.

In general, P/T systems are *frame-seeking*, in that they have a natural propensity to establish some measure of explicit and/or implicit ground rules for interacting. However, conscious and unconscious frame needs and quests are often quite at odds. In this respect, conscious system tendencies are generally pathologically defensive and involve the unconscious search for frame alterations that will provide pathological relatedness and gratifications; there is a strong frame-breaking propensity to conscious system needs. As a result, conscious choices by P/T systems (and P and T as the respective subsystems) with respect to the ground rules and framework of a psychotherapy are unreliable and tend to involve the search for immediate relief without regard for long-term consequences or immediate side-effects—all of which are usually quite negative but denied consciously.

In contrast, the deep unconscious wisdom system (see chapter four) shows tendencies towards establishing an ideal set of boundary conditions—a secure frame that is highly reliable and quite constructive. However, there appears to be a major flaw in the human mind in that the deep unconscious system expresses itself almost entirely through derivative communication; its encoded messages have little effect on actual behaviours and adaptations unless they are properly trigger-decoded. In contrast, the deeply unconscious pathological needs associated with traumatic introjects and memories have the ear of the conscious system, so to speak, and are the most powerful determinants of our conscious choices in this area. It can be seen, then, that the deep unconscious mind is split: there is a deep intelligence sensitive to and favouring secure frame conditions, and a deep unconscious memory system dominated by anxieties and guilt that dictate frame-related choices that are consistently deviant. The first system has a tract to encoded communication, the second to conscious decisions unconsciously driven.

Although one aspect of an ideal frame may be compared to the rules of a game, and boundary conditions may be likened to the definition of territories, such analogies are limited because of the complex sources, nature, and functions of the boundary conditions in the P/T interaction—qualities with important similarities with the frames of systems that function in everyday life such as those within families, schools, jobs, personal relationships, and the like. Indeed, because aspects of the therapeutic frame lend themselves so well to definition, delineation, and controlled investigation, the treatment setting is ideally suited for research into the nature and function of boundary conditions as they exert their powerful effects on all emotionally charged relationships and situations.

Proposition 5

Systems theory is the only means by which we can successfully identify and explore meaningful (non-trivial) *interactional patterns* and *emergent properties* of unfolding P/T systems. These interactional attributes cannot be found in studies of P or T alone. A psychodynamic/systems dynamic theory enables a far broader perspective—clinically and research-wise—than a psychodynamic theory by itself. The systemic element expands the dimensionality of our view of therapy and of the process of cure.

Implicit to this proposition is the postulate that the total functioning of the P/T system is greater than the sum of its separate parts. This is tantamount to stating that there are communications, behaviours, symptom vicissitudes, countertransferences, and the like that can be best explained as interactional products of the P/T system, rather than through a study of P or T separately. Much of this aspect of the P/T system is captured through an investigation of *systemic patterns*, which cannot be visualized or conceptualized without a basic systemic conception.

* * *

An illustration from a clinical (rather than formal) research study will give substance to these ideas. The emergence of *affect*, its nature and its functions, has been a difficult subject for psychoanalysis (see Brenner, 1974). We therefore undertook a systemic investigation of seemingly inexplicable expressions of affect by patients in dynamic psychotherapy. Easily predicted (and, in that sense, trivial) and generally expected responses—for example, depression and/or anxiety as reactions to major loss, illness, and trauma—were excluded from the study.

When we looked at affective behaviour within psychotherapy sessions in terms of the P/T system, a pattern began to emerge. Once identified, the pattern was confirmed in ten of eleven cases; the exception lead us to the recognition of a second and related pattern, which was then confirmed in five additional situations.

In searching for the pattern, three factors were considered: (1) the state of the boundary conditions; (2) the nature of the patient's unconscious or derivative communications—their tone and most probable encoded meanings; and (3) the nature of the therapist's interventions—type of frame management and the extent to which the C-scope was used.

Our analysis of pertinent sessions showed that the sequence of events that culminated in unexpected patient affect invariably began with a therapist's alteration of the boundary conditions of therapy—a frame break of some type—followed by an erroneous intervention. The patient's affective output was in all instances depressive—either as an immediate experience in the session or through the recall of a memory of a painful situation during which he or she was depressed or cried.

For example, a female therapist accepted a woman into therapy, even though the therapist was already seeing another woman who was a friend who worked in the same office. This is a boundary alteration initiated by the P and accepted by the T. Both patients knew of the situation from the outset. In an early session, the second patient reported a dream in which she and one of her four sisters are sitting on the couch in the therapist's office; they are having a joint session. The patient's associations involved considerable anger and distress, much of it because she deeply resented her sister's presence in the session.

This is typical of the pattern we found: an alteration of the ideal ground rules (which assure the patient privacy, confidentiality, and the therapist's full attention) is followed by the expression of negatively toned unconscious (transformed) perceptions of the damaging aspects of the therapist's participation in the deviant boundary condition. This dream expresses the patient's deep unconscious perception of the therapeutic conditions: someone else is present in what should be her own space.

The therapist, however, made use of an F-scope and interpreted the patient's dream in terms of its manifest contents and their implications—their evident psychodynamics. She ignored the systemic component of the situation and dream—a common error among today's practising therapists and users of the F-scope. She said that the images reflected the patient's rivalry with her sister and indicated her resistance to lying on the couch as the therapist had recommended. There was no hint that the dream had to do with boundary issues in the therapy.

The patient responded with (non-validating) images of not being understood by her mother. She went on to describe a situation that had both infuriated her and made her feel betrayed: a man in her office whom she had been dating had been having a secret affair with another woman who also worked in the office. At this juncture, the patient began to cry; she wept bitterly over her feelings of being betrayed, her concerns that she might be a lesbian because she could not hold on to a relationship with a man, and her upset over the injustices she had suffered in the course of her life. She recalled that she had experienced an injury at birth because of the incompetence of her mother's obstetrician, and she regarded the assault as fateful for her existence.

In physics and in other physical and biological systems, there are moments in the trajectory (i.e., the unfolding over time) of a system called *bifurcation points*—moments at which a fateful 'choice' must be made among significant alternatives (Prigogine & Stengers, 1984). In the sequence of events just cited, there is an important *bifurcation moment* (as I prefer to term these important junctures that often involve more than two possible branches and therefore might well be termed 'multification moments'—a term too awkward to use here). This occurs soon after the patient's dream and initial associations are reported. At this juncture there is ample and pressing material for intervention; the therapist's response will be especially fateful for the balance of this session—and possibly affect the long-term outcome of the therapy as well. An analysis of this moment suggests that the therapist's response could lead the trajectory of the P/T system into one of at least three major directions.

First, the therapist could remain silent. Clinical experience makes it extremely likely that this would have been unconsciously perceived by the patient as a missed intervention—a failure to understand and respond to her meaningful communications and need for insight. The patient's material has all of the ingredients necessary for intervening—representations of the frame-related trigger and encoded derivative perceptions related to that same stimulus. Adopting this course usually leads the patient towards the expression of encoded perceptions of the therapist's failure to understand the material—images of people who are deaf and insensitive abound—after which fresh derivatives related to the frame break are likely to emerge. Should the therapist then fail again to intervene, it is likely that the patient's encoded imagery would dry up, and a depressive reaction would set in.

Second, the therapist might interpret the patient's material in terms of its interactional unconscious meanings: as a negative unconscious perception of the implications of the therapeutic boundary conditions. It is highly likely that this intervention would obtain interpersonal and perhaps cognitive validation through responsive derivatives. The patient would understand unconsciously that the therapist was capable of pursuing unconscious truths and perhaps of rectifying deviant frames—though here, rectification is not possible without terminating one of the patients, so insight would have to prevail. A probable trajectory would include the appearance of secure-frame anxieties and then derivative material that touches deeply on the roots, meanings, and functions of the patient's psychopathology.

The third choice (and the possibilities are by no means exhausted—virtually any conceivable response from the therapist is possible, though some are more likely than others) is to offer either a non-interpretive intervention or an interpretation that is restricted to psychodynamic issues confined to the mind of the patient, without any link to the frame issue—typical outputs from the F-scope. This type of comment usually evokes non-validating communications from the patient and encoded perceptions of the therapist's need to avoid the central frame issue. The more confrontational and directive the intervention, the more likely that the patient would unconsciously perceive aggressive and seductive unconscious messages from the therapist as well. In general, this type of intervention implicitly promises the uninterpreted continuation of the deviant frame, a lack of interactional insight, and a 'cure', if it were to occur, through some uninsightful means.

The therapist, of course, chose the third pathway, offering a manifest content/implications F-scope interpretation that the patient experienced unconsciously as the therapist's failure to understand her communications. The patient then responded with even more compelling negatively toned derivatives. When the therapist again failed to interpret these images in light of the boundary-condition deviation and her subsequent erroneous intervention, the patient intensified her negative derivative responses, and depressive affect emerged.

A second bifurcation moment occurred after the therapist's first erroneous intervention—here, the choice mainly belonged to the patient. That is, in addition to the route to depressive affect, we have observed another trajectory at such junctures. In these instances, the patient responds to the erroneous intervention with *positively toned* imagery (rather than with negatively toned unconscious perceptions). Depressive affect does not follow these positive images, though in all but one case the patient proposed an additional frame break to the therapist towards the end of the session. We found, too, that the same patient may alternate between one or the other trajectory.

One hypothesis for this second type of reaction is that the patient is expressing an *unconscious over-idealization* of the overly traumatizing therapist. This suggests that the deep unconscious system is unable to tolerate extremes of hurt and trauma, whose meanings are unbearable even on the unconscious level. This type of response is typical when a patient (and P/T system) is in a state of *system overload*; denial and subsystem shutdown are typical reactions (see chapter five).

* * *

I have presented two of many potential—and actual—empirically derived systemic patterns. It is, of course, possible to forego a systemic description of these transactions and simply focus on the patient and describe the phenomenology of his or her communications, affect, and behaviour. But this would be tantamount to reducing a two-person interplay to the role of but one of the players—a most limited approach that is bound to be incomplete and often in error.

For example, based on these data one could state that patients show a pattern in which negatively toned derivatives lead to depressive affect, whereas positively toned derivatives do not—although they may lead to requests for alterations in the ground rules of treatment. However, such non-systemic descriptions, which omit all meaningful allusions to the therapist, appear trivial and lack the substance and penumbra of implications generated by a systemic summary.

In this instance, one would state in systemic terms that there appears to be an interactive pattern in which: (1) the therapist participates in an alteration of the boundary conditions of treatment; (2) the patient then responds with negative derivatives and, at times, encoded models of rectification; (3) the therapist attempts to circumvent the derivative meanings of the patient's response by offering a manifest-content/implication intervention; (4) the patient intensifies his or her negative derivative expressions; (5) the therapist once again fails to understand the activated unconscious meanings of the material; and (6) depressive affect appears in the patient (we did not study the output for these therapists). To this we would add an addendum: in Step 4 the patient may respond with positively toned derivatives; these tend to preclude depressive affect and to be followed by requests from the patient to alter the ground rules of the therapy.

These are, then, *systemic patterns*. The nature of the boundary conditions, as well as the contributions from, and the interaction between, both P and T give the account a sense of fullness and surprise. More significantly, the non-systemic description would suggest that all the therapist needs to do is to listen and then interpret the patient's depressive response to depressing themes—all of this is quite self-evident. In contrast, the systemic formulation is less apparent and calls for quite a bit more: in the situation under discussion, the therapist's recognition of the importance of maintaining the ground rules, and at some point actually doing so as much as possible in the therapy; her realization of the errors that she had made, and then conveying their rectification and interpretation to the patient; and her understanding of her own contributions to the patient's suffering. An even deeper systemic look would view all of these communications, whether from P or T, as expressions of the P/T system and would explore the system's input, processing, and output as a totality. This would provide us with an understanding of the attributes of this particular P/T system and how it functions. In all, the richness of systemic thinking seems evident.

* * *

Let us return for a moment to the systemic concept of *bifurcation moments*, a term, as noted, that identifies critical-choice points in the course of a psychotherapy session—or overall therapy. These are moments when P, T, or both (P/T) are consciously and unconsciously faced with critical choices that will prove especially fateful for the course of the treatment. Without a systems theory, psychoanalysts have had only limited ways of identifying crisis moments in therapy, restricting their thinking to situations that are obviously dangerous—e.g., a threat of suicide or of premature termination of the therapy.

The concept of bifurcation moments suggests a broader notion of critical junctures in the course of a psychotherapy. Of course, we will need adequate criteria with which we can identify such occurrences, but there is much to be gained in technique, science, and understanding through the recognition of these more quiet crisis points and their ramifications. The definition and investigation of bifurcation moments is now under way and suggests interesting ideas with regard to the trajectories or pathways that a treatment experience can take—again, pathways determined systemically by both participants to treatment and by the boundary conditions as well.

* * *

The two postulated fields of force, psychodynamic and system dynamic, that influence the unfolding of the P/T system are also in evidence in this vignette. Psychodynamically, the system is evidently being powered by latent (unconscious) issues of sibling rivalry, maternal abandonment, homosexual betrayal, and body-related trauma—all leading to depressive affect. Each of these dynamic elements also seems to have a systemic component that arises from both P and T, and from the deviant boundary conditions of the therapy. For example, clinical observation consistently reveals that alterations in the ground rules—a form of system destabilization—consistently evokes in patients intense unconscious perceptions of perversity in both their therapists and themselves. The dynamic derivative in this material involving the patient's fear that she is a lesbian is therefore empowered by both fields of force.

To elaborate: systemically, the ground-rule deviation appears to have destabilized this P/T system, which may well be operating at a significant distance from equilibrium. The patient's images suggest uncertainty and instability—betrayal and physical damage. It may well be that affect emerges more readily in unstable P/T systems as compared with those that are relatively stable or close to equilibria. So, too, with powerful derivatives, such as the patient's concerns that she might be a lesbian. System instability may well evoke strong psychodynamic images, while powerful derivatives are likely to destabilize P/T systems. There is much work to be done in exploring P/T system stability and its interaction with psychodynamics—both affect the process of cure. Much of this effort will, of necessity, be concentrated in the formal research investigation of recorded sessions, because systemic factors and variations are difficult to identify by way of general clinical observations. Indeed, this difficulty may help to account for the tendency among dynamic therapists to show relatively little appreciation for the role of systemic factors in psychotherapy.

Prigogine and Stengers (1984) have cogently presented many physical systems that enter a state of extreme disorder out of which a fresh and often more advanced and more adequately adaptive system can emerge (see, also, Davies, 1987; Laszlo, 1987). This moment of *chaos*, then, rather than existing as simple disorder and randomness, has a hidden and underlying order and structure that is difficult to ascertain. Whether such order out of chaos actually transpires in two-person therapeutic interactions is open to empirical investigation (see Dell & Goolishian, 1981, for a discussion of these issues in family therapy). There is already some evidence (see chapter seven) that P/T systems, and their individual subsystems, change very little when near to equilibrium and noticeably stable; in contrast, instability does seem to foster change—whether regressive or progressive—depending on a host of factors. Systemic thinking will alter the psychoanalytic concept of cure, extending our thinking well beyond current dynamic conceptualizations.

Proposition 6

The great majority of P/T systems have inherent curative potential and move towards some type of relief from emotional suffering for both participants to treatment. This postulate is in keeping with the general systemic principle that all living organisms are to some extent self-healing; human therapeutic systems have a complex version of this trait in all but extremely pathological and dysfunctional cases. However, all P/T systems provide relief at price—there is a critical *help/hurt ratio* to all such efforts. Some P/T systems provide their members with relatively smooth and flexible adaptations, others eventuate in relief via acting-out or through deviant frame breaks and behaviours—to cite some examples. Often, both P and T ignore the cost aspect of this ratio; denial of detrimental consequences to a therapeutic experience is commonplace.

It can be argued that the greatest healing power within the P/T system lies in the deep unconscious wisdom system of the patient; this voice is heard, however, only with disguise and by means of derivative expressions. Thus, the power to cure optimally lies in the therapist's interactional interpretation of these derivatives, and in his or her management of the boundary conditions of therapy at the behest of the encoded advice from the same source. This mode of cure clearly has the highest help/hurt ratio we can hope to achieve, given present theory and technique. (The hurt lies mainly in inevitable secure-frame anxieties and the ever-present pain caused by devastating emotional truths.)

There are, of course, other relatively unrecognized means by which P/T systems seek relief from emotional suffering (as shared by P and T, or as located in P or T alone). Systemically, relief may come from a traumatic or well-controlled destabilization of the P/T system, which restabilizes without symptomatic disturbance (Dell & Goolishian, 1982). Or relief may come through a combination of systemic and dynamic factors (indeed, both are always present), such as is seen in 'cure' through nefarious comparison (through the patient's *unconscious* realization that the therapist is more dysfunctional than he or she), or through a therapist's usually inadvertent guilt-relieving punishments, sanctions of pathological trends and behaviours, and the like (Langs, 1982a, 1985a). Still, embedded in most errant interventions by therapists—even those that are blatantly seductive and/or destructive—is some measure of healing intention. Indeed, one of the most glorious attributes of P/T systems is their healing capacities, evident even in the face of manifestly traumatic therapist interventions.

Proposition 7

The P/T system and each of its component subsystems—P and T—are endowed with special capacities for self-observation, self-awareness, self-reflection, and self-monitoring, *on both the conscious and unconscious levels* (not enough can be said of unconscious intelligence in the emotional domain). Systemically, the system shows highly complicated cybernetic properties, with both positive and negative feedback and feedforward (anticipatory) loops.

As noted, self-monitoring occurs on two distinctive levels—conscious and deeply unconscious. Each mental system has its own standards and values and arrives at its own conclusions. Each assessment (which may be conceptualized to include a variety of evaluative superego and ego ideal functions) influences the subsequent behaviour of the total system and its components. In the emotional domain, the conscious assessment, of which P and/or T are aware, is far less reliable and has far less influence than the evaluation of the deep unconscious system, of which the dyadic members are, as a rule, entirely unaware. Indeed, the conscious system often functions as a *rationalizer* for behaviours that stem mainly from deep unconscious evaluations; these unseen assessments can impose great influence on behaviour without conscious choice (Langs, 1987a, 1987b; 1988a). I have already suggested that the P/T system can remedy this situation only if one or both members turn to the C-scope and engage in interactional trigger decoding—an undoing of displaced and disguised messages in light of their evocative stimuli (Langs, 1985b, 1988a). In such instances, the knowledge and capacities of the deep unconscious system are momentarily accessible to the conscious system—and to direct adaptation.

It follows from this description that the deep unconscious system does monitor its own state and that of others—and in therapy this includes the P/T system itself. Indeed, one of the unique properties of P/T systems—and human dyadic systems in general—is their capacity to generate *a report on the state of the system*—past, present, and future (see below). This output may take the form of a conscious or transformed (unconscious) report from P or T, though here, too, direct assessments are quite unreliable while those of the deep unconscious system—voiced through derivatives—can by and large be trusted. By using the C-scope, we can tap into this great unconscious resource rather than letting its voice go unheard.

Proposition 8

The P/T system is an active and selective system, not merely a passively receptive system at the mercy of outside forces and influences. Each component—P and T—is an open system with its own boundary conditions (see below). In addition, the P/T system itself shows a curious blend of both open and closed properties. As a rule, during a psychotherapy session, the P/T system is closed to all external inputs, though it remains sensitive to certain pressures peculiar to the boundary of ground rule conditions of the therapy. Still, it is obvious that at the end of a therapy session both P and T leave the P/T system and its confines—dissolving the system in reality while maintaining the mental representation of the system in some form (this capacity to continue the trajectory of a system intra-psychically may also be unique to human systems). At this point, P and T are free to interact with others extra-therapeutically (for T, this may, of course, involve entering into another P/T system with a different patient). The system then remains unmaterialized until it is reconstituted and resumes its trajectory in the following session (or through an extra-therapeutic contact outside the therapist's office).

The two components of the P/T system—P and T—are each capable of stimulating or evoking responses in the other member of the dyad—and of processing, metabolizing, and modifying this incoming information.

Thus, neither component is a stimulus-bound system. The course of a P/T system is shaped by the internal structure of its two components and by the nature of the stimuli that activate them as individuals and as part of the P/T system as a whole.

In this regard, it is well to single out another highly distinctive feature of the components of the P/T system. Human systems in general, and P's and T's in particular, have the remarkable capacity *to choose the systems with which they will and will not interact, and often the particular boundary conditions within which this interaction is to take place.* This selectivity is, however, under the influence of powerful unconscious forces.

As for the therapist, he or she has made a choice of profession and responds selectively to incoming initial contacts from and with patients. Indeed, the choice of the profession of psychotherapist is in part, however unconsciously driven, a decision to participate in emotionally charged P/T systems and all that they imply. Preference for a particular type of therapeutic approach—e.g., contrast classical psychoanalysis with family therapy—implies special dynamic and systemic needs and anxieties in the therapist (e.g., a possible fear of crowds and open or deviant frame conditions in the analyst, and a fear of intimacy and a secure frame in the family therapist). This capacity to select systems for interaction is clearly most developed in human systems (of all kinds) and quite undeveloped, though not entirely absent, in physical systems such as those seen in chemical reactions.

The patient's tendencies in this respect are especially important. He or she is the component of the P/T system that, as a rule, actively initiates the creation of the system, doing so by seeking out a particular therapist—and often a particular therapeutic frame as well. There are dramatic paradoxical tendencies among patients that lead them unconsciously to seek out therapists and frames that will tend to sustain rather than alter their psychopathology. Thus, a patient will often seek out a therapist who can provide pathological modes of relatedness similar to the disturbed relationships that have characterized the patient's early—and presently disturbed—life. There is an unconsciously driven search for the very patterns of interaction that are a factor in the aetiology of his or her psychopathology or interpersonal difficulties. The sources of these paradoxical needs—for repetition rather than constructive change—remain a mystery. There is little evidence that the patient is seeking a new opportunity for mastery, for this seldom occurs. Nor do explanations in terms of loyalty to the traumatic and hurtful parent or needs to maintain pathological ties seem satisfactory. There is some evidence for the role of guilt and masochism—an unconscious need for punishment—in these choices, and even some signs of blind repetition of a type not unlike animal imprinting—indications that the human mind has not evolved very far from the minds of its animal ancestors. This unconscious propensity is one of the unsolved anomalies of the interactional paradigm that created the C-scope.

Observationally, then, P systems tend unconsciously to seek other systems and conditions that often resemble the very family systems—however indirectly and unconsciously constituted—within which the patient's pathology developed, systems that are compatible with a variety of defensive, punitive, and pathologically satisfying needs. This process, which is typical of both family and individual therapy though seldom recognized as such, is a product of another distinctive aspect of human dyadic P/T systems: the existence of motive forces that drive the system's behaviours, but whose nature and structure are in their most significant aspects outside awareness—often unconscious for both members of the therapy dyad.

This capacity of human systems to select other systems for interaction is supplemented by still another critical attribute:

the capacity of the system—in therapy, P or T—through conscious volition to leave the total system in which he or she is interacting (to a degree, this may be done either psychologically or physically). Although it is true that there are many unconscious needs that keep a person in an interactive system that is fundamentally harmful and ultimately self-destructive, it is also true that an individual can walk away from this type of system as well. By the same token, an individual can also leave a basically constructive and helpful system—usually, because of powerful, self-defeating unconscious needs.

It should be clear from the foregoing that the P/T system itself, and the P subsystem in particular, often generates reactions that seem paradoxical and are *unpredictable on the basis of dynamics alone or through the application of naive assessments of the state of the system, its components, and the nature of their interacting processes.* As noted, it is only by means of a sound decoding of the patient's unconscious perceptions in therapy that we can gain an incisive understanding of the status of this domain—including the nature of a therapist's interventions and the conditions of the treatment. Yet, these insights run counter to, and seem to be inexplicable in light of the patient's conscious thinking and actual behaviours. Indeed, the evident split between the conscious and unconscious systems and their assessments of reality, as well as their needs and preferences, and the division within each of these systems of the mind, are another set of distinctive characteristics of P/T—and all human—systems and their individual subsystems.

For example, there are many situations in which a patient *unconsciously and accurately* evaluates a therapist's interventions as highly seductive and destructive but responds consciously and behaviourally by increasing the number of weekly sessions. Similarly, other patients will leave therapy despite their encoded validation of the bulk of their therapists' interventions, and indications of a strong, positive introjective identification with the therapist—and even evidence of constructive inner structural, mental change in themselves. In one specific case, a patient's material conveyed a positive evaluation of two sound interventions by his therapist—one, an incisive interactional interpretation of the patient's encoded material, the other a securing of the ground rules at the behest of the patient's encoded observations and advice. Yet, the patient abandoned the psychotherapy by virtue of a nameless dread—one that was related to rather typical secure-frame, death-related anxieties but experienced as disproportionately excessive. Indeed, this dread is another distinctive attribute of human and P/T systems (see below).

Understanding these splits in the minds of P and T helps to account for many seemingly inexplicable behaviours; they are fateful for the trajectories of the P/T system. Nonetheless, despite the complexities of these systems and their interactions, it is possible to predict with a high degree of probability many systemic patterns of communication and behaviour based on combined psychodynamic/system-dynamic formulations.

Finally, it is well to mention here that many of the systemic capacities under discussion rely on complex memory structures—conscious and deep unconscious—that serve as resources for the system, as well as both known and silent influences. These memory structures are quite elaborate and more complex than those seen in non-human and in certain inorganic systems (see chapter four).

Proposition 9

The P/T system relies on *system differentiation* in order to carry out its functions and goals—overall, the 'cure' of the patient—properly and effectively. This aspect of the P/T system has been spelled out most cogently by Newton (1971, 1973, 1989), who has discussed the distinctive *role requirements* of both P and T, and the means by which the boundary conditions of a psychotherapy help to define and maintain these roles (see Langs, 1982b, 1988a, for similar discussions).

The physical boundaries and ground rules that exclude outsiders from the therapeutic space and situation create a foundation for establishing the distinctive roles assigned to the P and T subsystems of the P/T system. Fulfilling those roles enables the total P/T system to negotiate a course of therapy that generates an optimal cure for the patient. Any break in this internal/external boundary of the P/T system will, of necessity, entail alterations in these roles, which are unconsciously defined and assigned by the ground rules of therapy and validated by the patient's derivative expressions. On the unconscious level, this boundary break/role alteration will often involve role reversals—T functions as P, and P as T—and blurring of role differentiation.

Within the treatment experience, the essential boundaries between P and T are established and maintained in part by adhering to the role distinctions that are ideal for therapy, and which are well defined in the P's derivative communications (see Newton, 1971, for an analogy to the differences in role requirements of mother and child within the family system). Indeed, empirical research is suggested by the realization that certain communications are therapist-role-related, while other expressions are characteristic of patients. One can therefore study shifts in role functions by this means.

It is by adhering to his or her assigned role that the therapist functions as therapist and the patient as patient; failure to maintain this differentiation tends to shift the therapist towards becoming the functional patient (Langs, 1980; Searles, 1975), and the patient towards being the functional therapist. As a result, the work of the therapy to effect the insightful cure of the patient is diverted—usually towards the cure of the therapist. Much of this is experienced without awareness in all concerned, and the interlude may well harm rather than help the patient—who, nonetheless, may obtain some relief by means of the unconscious realization that he or she is functioning as therapist to the therapist. Indeed, *systems dedifferentiation* in general has a variety of detrimental consequences for the P/T system and its components, even though it may serve as a stimulus for communication and growth if the situation is recognized for what it is and is rectified and interpreted. In extreme cases, however, role dedifferentiation can lead to the demise of the P/T system and the end of a therapy.

In brief, the patient is distinguished from the therapist by such matters as being the individual who seeks the other's services, comes to the other's office, free associates (preferably while lying on a couch), listens to the other and learns about himself or herself, pays the other a fee, and the like. The therapist is the one who agrees to see the other, sees this other in his or her office, listens to the other and responds primarily with interpretations and frame-management responses, and receives the fee—to cite some of the main distinctive features. It is the patient, then, who is directly personally revealing, and the therapist who is not (or who is only indirectly or inadvertently revealing); the therapist speaks essentially to explain the communications of the other.

System differentiation typically breaks down in two interrelated ways: (1) when patient or therapist behaves or communicates in ways that are characteristic of social rather than therapeutic relationships; and (2) when therapist or patient adopts the role assigned to the other. The first of these involves an inter-systemic failure to maintain the differentiation between social and therapeutic roles (a common error in today's psychotherapies), while the second is an intra-systemic failure to maintain the differences between P and T. These vicissitudes are monitored by the patient's deep unconscious system (and that of the therapist as well, though little is known of this without engaging in C-scope self-analysis); the patient's derivatives wisely define the issues involved.

For example, system dedifferentiation is in evidence when a patient becomes seductive, inquires about the therapist's health or family, suggests a drink together, and seeks contact with the therapist outside the assigned sessions. Dedifferentiation is also apparent when a therapist behaves in seductive or aggressive fashion, responding to a patient as would a friend or lover—or the proverbial bartender. In all such instances the task or functions of the P/T system is derailed, and some new set of functions—usually related to the cure of the therapist, should he or she participate—takes over. On the other hand, efforts directed at dedifferentiation by the patient, if not gratified by the therapist, can lead to productive therapeutic work. Such actions constitute attempts to modify the frame of the therapy (often in response to deviations by the therapist) and are inevitable reflections of the patient's psychopathology. Proper rectification and interpretation not only produces insight for the patient, but also restores both P and T to their basic roles.

There is an important distinction between free associations that allude to role and boundary changes, and intentional wishes and efforts to accomplish such changes. There is also a close relationship between frame deviations and role dedifferentiation in which the systemic imbalance evokes dynamic responses—sexual and aggressive—as well as impairments in self-image and the like. The secure frame is the best means of inherently ensuring that the role distinctions between P and T are maintained.

These issues can be seen in a situation where a male therapist changed the time of a session for a female patient, who then responded consciously with seductive overtures, and unconsciously with efforts to cure the errant therapist. Psychodynamically, the frame alteration was unconsciously experienced as a seduction, similar to ways in which the patient's father allowed himself to be seduced by his daughter. This placed the daughter in the role of spouse, and a similar blurring of roles had occurred in the therapy. Treatment was stalled as resistances set in, until the frame change was interpreted and rectified (the patient's derivatives instructed the therapist to not change her hours in the future).

System dedifferentiation also occurs when P or T assumes the role of the other. This is seen when a patient interprets (consciously as well as unconsciously) to a therapist—or to himself or herself—or takes responsibility for the therapist's office, as in closing a blind, disposing of the towel for the patient's head while lying on the couch, etc. Or a patient may be the one to set the fee, or to change it. On the other hand, there is loss of distinctiveness when a therapist free-associates to a patient, tells one of his or her dreams, reveals his or her own problems or any aspect of his or her personal life. In all such cases, there is a shift away from the central purpose of the therapy, if only on the unconscious level—though quite often on the surface as well (e.g., the patient or therapist wants consciously to change the nature of their continuing relationship).

Because of his or her deep perceptiveness and need for cure, a patient will respond to systems dedifferentiation with powerful derivative material. Despite unconscious (encoded) protests, the pathological gratification afforded by this type of interlude often leads a patient to be consciously gratified by what has happened; a similar state is often true of the therapist as well. For these and other reasons, there has been a general failure to appreciate the dire consequences of system dedifferentiation. There is much to be learned about how differentiated and dedifferentiated systems behave and function. As we have seen so often now, these newly raised questions carry with them a call for scientific study—even as the systemic component provides a framework for such investigations.

Proposition 10

The P/T system, as suggested, is best modelled as two subsystems—P and T—within a set of boundary conditions. Three dimensions merit consideration: (1) input; (2) processing by the system and its two components (each having two mental subsystems; see chapter four); and (3) output. Each aspect of the total process is accessible for definition, measurement, quantification, and clinical and research exploration.

* * *

Input information and meaning seems best organized around the following dimensions:

1. inputs from outside the therapy session: these may be carried into the session by patient and/or therapist, or directly intrude into the system—as when a relative calls the therapist or accompanies a patient to a session;
2. inputs from the boundary conditions of the therapy (see below);
3. inputs from the communicative exchanges between P and T: here, the direct and encoded information and meanings must *both* be taken into account; the nature of the patient's associations (e.g., are they derivative in nature or not?) and the therapist's interventions (e.g., how is the frame being managed; what are the implications and validity of his or her comments and behaviours?) are critical in this regard; the data of the therapeutic interaction lend themselves to moment-to-moment quantification of these and related variables that need to be decomposed into their essential elements and studied.

* * *

As for *the P/T system* itself—and its two subsystems—we may think of its receptivity to incoming stimuli and its capacity to be stimulus-seeking. These are highly variable attributes, which are selectively attuned to conscious/manifest and unconscious/latent information and meaning. With respect to this receiving function, it is possible to measure the extent to which the P/T system and its component sub-systems are relatively open or relatively closed to various types of incoming information. A critical consideration in this regard involves the concept of *system readiness*, which defines the extent to which a given system is open to modification through receptivity to unique information and meaning, or is refractory to its incorporation and influence. The potential for inner change and growth—in both P and T—depends on such readiness.

Much of the work of psychotherapy (and, by extension, of virtually any interacting human system) involves the various means by which a system can be influenced to develop receptor sites for and openness to information and meaning to which the system has previously been impervious—often for reasons of psychological defence. The means by which system readiness is effected is open to empirical investigation, though general clinical observation once again suggests a strong influence from the boundary conditions under which the P/T system is operating; the more secure the frame, the more likely that a system will open itself to new information and meaning. Psychodynamically, the degree of anxiety and conflict evoked by the material to be taken in also plays a role.

A variety of effects on system readiness appear also to depend on the nature of the therapist's interventions and the communications of both members of the dyad. System's readiness virtually always precedes *system change*, and for P it is typically a prelude to either symptom alleviation or exacerbation—without it, symptomatic remission is likely. In chapter seven I present some surprising and somewhat inexplicable research findings in this area. In many ways, the problem of how to enhance system readiness through the creation of open receptor sites is one of the most challenging and difficult questions raised by these initial considerations of a systems theory for psychoanalysis.

* * *

With respect to the internal processing of incoming information and meaning, in general the P/T system functions best in some type of middle-range of receptivity (and information/meaning load) and does poorly at either extreme. The extremes may be thought of as a rigid, closed system on the one hand, and, on the other, a system that is so excessively open as to border on the chaotic. Every P/T system, and each of its components, has an optimal capacity for processing information and meaning. Beyond this point, a system goes into a state of *system overload* (see chapter five) and either shuts down or processes information chaotically rather than with some degree of order.

The study of the capacity of P/T systems to generate, contain, and process information and meaning is already under way (Badalamenti & Langs, 1991, 1992, in press–a, –b; Langs & Badalamenti, 1990, 1991a, 1991b, 1992, in press). Each P, T, and P/T system would appear to have a definable *capacity for information/meaning (I/M) load*. Much depends on the psychic structure of all concerned, and on how much emotionally charged information and meaning each participant carries as derived from both prior and current life experiences and therapy sessions. This capacity interacts with the total charge—burden—of the information/meaning entering into and exchanged within the P/T system. Here, such factors as the intensity of I/M, degree of complexity, amount of emotional charge, impingement on special vulnerabilities, and the like come into play.

Recognizing that every P/T system, and every P and T, has a limited and broadly definable capacity to process incoming information and meaning can foster an unprejudiced and empathic understanding of the limitations of the psychotherapeutic process—and of the P and T engaged in this process. We cannot ask a system to perform functions for which it lacks design and capability, or to perform beyond its utmost functioning—a point often missed in thinking about human systems where unconscious wishes for omnipotent power often play a role. P/T systems can be expected to process only a limited amount of trauma and stress; inputs that are especially charged with death anxiety and devastating unconscious meanings are especially difficult to metabolize. There is a fine line between somatic channels and those related to pathological action-discharge. Overall, where output is concerned, we are interested in the adaptive capacities of the P/T system and its components, and with the *cost* of these adaptations—the Help/Hurt ratio. Thus, as noted, every P/T system has some capacity for adaptation and for the resolution of conflict and dysfunction; and every such system achieves this adaptational level at some price. There are flexible and inflexible systems, and those whose options are relatively wide and others where the choice of output is relatively narrow and dysfunctional—requiring, for example, pathological modes of relatedness and defensiveness, frame deviations in therapy and in life, and the like. Clearly, the better the resolution and the lower the price, the more efficient the resultant system. It is important to define empirically these concepts, both qualitatively and quantitatively, so that eventually we can make sound comparisons of various P/T systems and what they have to offer to patients. The uncertainties, biases, and pitfalls in measuring system output and its important offshoot, therapy outcome, are such that careful, open, unbiased, and controlled research studies are very much needed.

Proposition 11

Human systems in general, and P/T systems in particular, have the well-known unique capacity to use symbolism flexibly and extensively—a capacity far in excess of the possible crude symbolic powers seen in some other mammals. Human systems, as we have seen, actually have a special capacity for expression on three levels of communication: manifest and direct; implied (as extracted from the direct message); and transformed or encoded. The latter constitutes the symbolic or metaphoric level; it entails a form of meaning that has been displaced in situations in which there is maximal bearable stress on the conscious and deep unconscious systems to a degree where creative chaos is temporarily created, and those situations where disorganized and regressive chaos takes hold.

Another consequence of this conceptualization is the recognition that there are many ways to process incoming information and meanings—perhaps as many as there are types of psychotherapy. Each method has advantages and disadvantages, and each has its own tolerance level for charged information and system instability; each is likely to be characterized by a distinctive way of stabilizing itself—and its components—as well. And because a perfect processing system is an ideal that is unachievable in the real world, each P/T system brings stability at a price—an aspect that is in great need of investigation.

* * *

Finally, the *output* from the P/T system can be measured along a number of dimensions. Whereas *empowered input* is mainly a factor of the communications from P and T, and especially their handling of the boundary conditions of therapy (inputs external to treatment are much less compelling than those within the therapeutic interaction), output needs to be measured along several lines: (1) whether a P/T system or its components are communicating with derivative or largely non-derivative expressions, (2) the nature of expressed behaviours (the distinction between adaptive action and pathological acting out is crucial here), (3) psychological symptoms and their vicissitudes, (4) resistances, (5) affects, and (6) somatic responses.

There are important interactions between these output channels. For example, high levels of derivative output from P's tend to reduce the gain from its original source and are (usually) disguised. In general, manifest contents are processed by the conscious system, and rarely by the deep unconscious system. Implications are processed either by the conscious or deep unconscious system, while encoded meanings are processed by the deep unconscious wisdom system (see chapter four). This layering of the mental structures of the P and T subsystems makes for much of the richness and complexity of the therapeutic experience—and of life itself.

Equally unique and important for P/T systems is the distinctive human capacity for *unconscious perception*—and possibly for unconscious information processing itself. Dixon's (1971, 1981) detailed reviews of the subliminal perception literature found no evidence for this capacity in non-humans. This ability renders the realm of unconscious experience especially pertinent in the functioning and understanding of human and P/T systems. Unconscious perception and information processing affects the input side of the P/T system, is pertinent to the internal mental processing that follows, and is a significant factor on the output side in regard to all output dimensions—behavioural and communicative.

Proposition 12

Another unique feature of the P/T system involves the capacity of the total system, and of its components, to *anticipate the future* to a significant degree. In its positive sense, this means that human systems have the ability to generate hypotheses—consciously and unconsciously—to test them out, and to anticipate likely trends. More grimly, human systems have the remarkable capacity to anticipate their own demise—and the demise of systems in which they participate. This capacity generates a unique level of death-related anxiety that permeates all P/T systems and exerts an enormous influence on every aspect of the therapeutic interaction.

For example, it can be shown clinically that the deep unconscious system dictates ideal ground rules for therapy. When these ground rules are in effect—secure-frame conditions—both participants experience a sense of intimacy and claustrum-like immobilization that evokes personal death-anxiety images. On the other hand, alterations in the ideal ground rules are typically experienced unconsciously as damaging; they generate persecutory forms of death anxiety. Whatever the extent of conscious awareness in this realm, there is at all times an unconscious sensitivity to anticipated endings or death that insinuates itself into the therapeutic experience. On some level, then, both the communicative interaction and attributes of the boundary conditions themselves will involve death anxiety in one way or another. The components of the P/T system will experience this in terms of their respective internal states and processes, and the P/T system as a whole will unfold in light of these effects. Indeed, the working-through of death-related issues is an essential aspect of the process of cure.

P/T systems are, then, finite rather than infinite, time-bound rather than endless. Despite this, and perhaps in response to the apprehension of mortality, P/T systems are often difficult to terminate and prone to operate beyond all apparent utility.

Proposition 13

P/T systems tend to be *evolutionary* and to search ultimately for order and defined patterns. In their capacity to evolve, P/T systems frequently move, often simultaneously, towards increasing both complexity and simplicity; they also tend to be self-regulating, self-healing, and self-stabilizing. Even as they continue to evolve, P/T systems are drawn to a variety of attractors or momentarily stable states, particularly cyclical attractors. In addition, P/T systems appear to seek out more lasting forms of both stable and chaotic states. The attributes of each of these attractors require specific definition.

There is reason to believe that P/T systems are inherently evolutionary—that is, cast in the direction of higher order and complexity. Clinical observation strongly supports the proposition that the patient who is allowed to flourish within a defined set of boundary conditions will move towards self-stabilization and self-healing efforts, along with efforts to stabilize and heal the therapist as well.

Repeated observation, however, suggests that in most instances the assignment of the role and responsibilities of therapist actually disturbs these natural healing tendencies and replaces them with relatively destructive tendencies. Therapists appear to be prone to interfering with their patients' innate healing propensities. Why this should be so is for the moment an intriguing unsolved puzzle, whose solution may well have something to do with being assigned the direct and conscious role responsibility for securing the therapy frame and making valid (interactional) interpretations of the unconscious meanings of the patient's material. The human mind is so constructed as to have little natural capacity for such work, largely because it tends to intensify death and other terrifying anxieties to a point beyond system capacity. Thus the patient is relatively safe in expressing himself or herself through derivatives, but the therapist is relatively unsafe in having to express the same issues manifestly and directly (Langs, 1984–85).

Special efforts at self-analysis are needed to enable therapists to carry out effectively their role requirements, which run so strongly counter to their usual and natural defensive posture and requisites for self-protection. It is only then that they are able to free up their own creative and evolutionary potentials within the therapeutic interaction.

Human systems are also *pattern-seeking*. They attempt to order disorder and to identify variants and regularities within seemingly complex transactions. On the whole, P/T systems seem consciously to prefer simple patterns and the reduction of complex constellations of information into extremely simple elements. While the deep unconscious wisdom system does seem to seek out and tolerate a great deal of complexity, P/T systems in general seem on the surface to be disturbed by complexity and by the absence of clearly defined patterns. These systems are also quite vulnerable to charged encoded information, no matter how simple its structure. P/T systems tend to seek stability and non-change, though under certain conditions—in need of definition—they will actively seek out chaos, disorder, instability, and disequilibrium (as noted, these are the likely preconditions for growth and constructive change).

Proposition 14

There is a complex interplay in the P/T system between the dynamics of its power sources and its capacity for processing information and meaning. In considering this area, we may ask what it is that sustains this system, and what activates or motivates this system into movement, change, work, and active adaptation?

The fundamental power capacities of the P/T system appear to be derived from survival instincts, sexual and aggressive drives, and the need for a sense of self and identity. These powers, of course, operate on all levels—conscious and unconscious. Another driving force is the inner need of P and T to create various kinds of internal and external (environmental, interpersonal) conditions. These intrapsychic tendencies shade into those types of environment and internal changes that are imposed on, and without choice activate, the P/T system.

Included here are extra-therapeutic disturbances constituted as excessive gratifications and especially as traumas (attack, seduction, deprivation, overstimulation, and the like). Alterations in the boundary conditions of the P/T relationship will also activate the system, as will any type of interpersonal tension between the component sub-systems. In general, any information loaded with sexual, aggressive, and anxiety-provoking meanings, such as those related to death anxiety and bodily damage, will also activate the P/T system, as will communicated tensions, such as disturbing affects and contradictions (double binds) on different levels—or the same level—of expression.

It can be seen, then, that environmental, interpersonal, boundary, and internal disequilibria and shifts in meaning will all activate the P/T system; that is, a wide range of stimuli will destabilize the system and move it towards efforts at stabilization. In general, *P/T systems tend to favour stabilization through the generation of non-meaning and deviations in the boundary conditions of the therapy.* Only rarely do they stabilize through the validated interpretation of unconscious meaning and the securing of the frame. These clinical observations speak strongly to the intensity of secure-frame and meaning anxieties in most P/T systems in today's psychotherapy situations.

As I have indicated, it seems most promising to conceive of two basic fields of force operating on and within the P/T system: one that is *psychodynamic* and related to the sources of power and conflict in the system; another that is *systems-dynamic*, involving issues such as stability, distance from equilibrium, and the like. These two components are best thought of as fields of force that determine the trajectory of the P/T system and its main attributes. By way of an analogy, the psychodynamic field may be thought of as the fuel that powers a train or the pressured movement of a river, while the systems-dynamic component would be the tracks and river banks, respectively. We need both components to understand the course of a system. However, these analogies break down in characterizing the systemic component as relatively fixed and inert; their main value lies in helping us to visualize dual effects on a central system—and to grasp the limitations of descriptions confined to one or the other domain.

Proposition 15

P/T systems possess a variety of additional distinctive attributes, some unique to human systems, others shared with non-human systems as well. For example, as noted, P/T systems possess emergent patterns and properties that cannot be identified by investigating the P or T sub-systems in isolation or separately while interacting. The total evolutionary trajectory of the system is one such example in that it is the result of vectors from both P and T, and is of a different order from that seen within P or T alone.

The mental/emotional domain of the P/T system appears to have the greatest degrees of freedom—the largest number of possible states—of any known human system, and therefore represents one of the most complex challenges for understanding in the domain of the biological sciences. The degree of complexity of the P/T system has made the application of dynamic science all but impossible until very recently. There is much that is unknown and uncertain about P/T systems; its properties have barely been investigated as yet. There is no other known system in the universe where problems of conceptualization, research, and science exist to the degree seen with the P/T entity (see chapter six).

Along other lines, there appears to be a general trend towards autonomy in the component systems of the P/T system. The system tends, however, to establish itself initially in terms of a pathological symbiosis—a mode of relatedness and of processing information that needs to be modified and resolved for the total system to grow and for the symptoms of the system to be constructively resolved.

Paradoxically, it appears that every factor that stabilizes the P/T system on one level destabilizes it on another level. This occurs because of the distinctive attributes and differing needs of the mental sub-systems within both P and T (see chapter four). The conscious and the deep unconscious systems require very different stabilizing factors; quite often what is stabilizing for the conscious system is destabilizing for the deep unconscious system—and vice versa.

P/T systems tend towards repetition of past patterns and adaptations, and yet are capable of new solutions as well. These systems experience affect (emotion) as a form of output, but also as a silent internal regulator of information processing. And it should be noted, finally, that P/T systems have moral and ethical values. These help to regulate the solutions chosen by a given P/T system in light of the repair or damage done to its components and to outside figures.

Some final comments

I have dwelt for some time in the systemic domain in order to afford the reader a sense of its importance and the need for psychoanalysis to add this dimension to its thinking and theorizing—and to its considerations of technique and science. In some ill-defined way, systemic thinking points to a dynamic science for psychoanalysis. There is also the intellectual and clinical stimulation that stems from ways in which systemic thinking introduces considerations long absent from psychoanalytic studies. Matters such as the stability or instability of a system not only deserve consideration, but also need to be quantified and investigated in terms of influence. Distance from equilibrium, the critical existence of cyclical systemic patterns, self-healing and self-ordering faculties—such concepts are inherently intriguing and seem likely to lead to investigations that will yield many important new elements of understanding.

It is also evident that aspects of these systemic dimensions seem difficult to measure at first look and will require much ingenuity for their development before they can be studied definitively and applied by the clinical practitioner. Nonetheless, the concepts themselves have already proven helpful in understanding many puzzling courses of events within an analysis or psychotherapy; indeed, systemic thinking facilitates the recognition of unsolved anomalies and helps to reveal better the limitations of present analytic thinking, even as it offers fresh solutions to known puzzles.

For too long now, psychoanalysts have lived in a kind of Flatland (Abbott, 1884) with its two limiting dimensions of dynamics and genetics. The real world is far more complex and multidimensional—both more difficult to comprehend and more interesting as well. By allowing the systemic universe to merge with the psychodynamic, we will have created a new territory of considerable richness and fertility—one that will have as its motto: bring science to our realm.

CHAPTER FOUR

The systems of the mind

> But if it be implied that nothing should be produced to the student, with or without warning, which cannot be understood in all its generality, I should, with deference, protest against a restriction that would tend, in my opinion, not only to give false views of what is already known, but to stop the progress of discovery. It is not true, out of geometry, that the mathematical sciences are, *in all their parts*, those models of finished accuracy which many suppose. The extreme boundaries of *analysis* have always been as imperfectly understood as the tract beyond the boundaries was absolutely unknown. But the way to enlarge the settled country has not been by keeping within it, but by making voyages of discovery, and I am perfectly convinced that the *student* should be exercised in this manner; that is, he should be taught how to examine the boundary, as well as to cultivate the interior.
>
> de Morgan

The systems theory presented to this point has involved mainly macroscopic systems. With all this outlined, a key question remains unanswered: what is going on within the so-called black box—the P/T system? This is tantamount to asking how emotionally charged information and meaning (throughout this chapter, for the sake of brevity I will use the term *information* to refer to both entities: information itself, which involves matters of complexity, and meaning, which refers to signification) are processed within the P and T subsystems? That is, how does the human *mind* process such information: what are the structures and functions involved?

In keeping with the goal of this book, the answers to these questions are essential to the development of a comprehensive and solid foundation on which to build a science for psychoanalysis. Indeed, a suitable model of the mind is likely to reward us with fresh perspectives, even as it raises research questions and provides, as well, many leads for actual investigation. Further, an imaginative model of these mental systems, one that is close and faithful to clinical observation, will in all likelihood lend itself to furthering the systems theory presented in the previous chapter, and it should also promote the development of artificial intelligence (AI) models that take into account the emotional domain that they have so long neglected. Given that we will be modelling two distinctive, but inter-related systems, there is considerable likelihood of using recently developed parallel processing neural networks for models that could add to our present thinking.

There have been few heuristically useful models of the mind in psychoanalysis. Freud (1900a) offered such a model in *The Interpretation of Dreams*, but he made little use of it in the years that followed. Then, as we saw, in 1923, he repudiated the model entirely, replacing topography with the structural theory of ego, id, and superego—structures that were so globally portrayed and ill-defined that they do not lend themselves readily to further model-making of any kind. Nonetheless, some efforts along these lines were made; most involved some concept of unconscious information processing and attempted to account for repression as well (see Basch, 1976; Peterfreund, 1971). These models were largely cognitive in nature and included a sensory filter, a recognition that the first stage in emotional information processing is in all likelihood always unconscious (Broadbent, 1958), and an understanding that the route to awareness involves considerable unconscious screening.

Briefly to review again Freud's (1900a) original model of the mind (see Part I), he postulated three systems: the unconscious system (UCS), a preconscious system (PCS), and a conscious system (CS). His delineation of these systems was relatively general, and they were not treated as highly complex configurations of structure and function. The UCS was largely the seat of repressed wishes and, later, of id urges; the PCS was a transition system with a censorship/defensive gradient at both interfaces; and the CS was the executive system that dealt with both the UCS and reality—it was seen as the locus of the conscience and the function (hypercathexis) of consciousness. 'Neurosis' was postulated to be the result of conflict between these agencies of the mind—especially between the UCS and the CS. As noted in chapter one, Freud abandoned the model when postulated CS needs and functions—especially those of conscience and defence resistance—were found to be part of the UCS system, and this version of conflict theory, which was primary and, for Freud, a *sine qua non*, all but collapsed.

Most significant to Freud's initial topographic efforts was his brilliant insight that the two basic systems, UCS and CS, have different ways of thinking. This realization can easily be expanded into the statement that the two systems of the mind process information differently and function according to distinctive rules. For Freud (1900a), the UCS systems followed the laws of primary process thinking, while the CS system followed those of the secondary processes. To reiterate briefly, Freud characterized the former as fluid, easily displaced, symbolic, under the sway of the pleasure principle and wish-fulfilment, timeless, lacking in negations, and discharge-seeking without regard for reality considerations. The latter, by way of contrast, was fixed and not displaceable, direct without the use of symbolism, under the sway of the reality principle, time-bound and with negations, and deeply concerned with reality and its issues.

Even after Freud abandoned his topographic model of the mind, these attributes of conscious and unconscious thinking have remained with us almost unchanged since Freud's first delineation. However, the term *unconscious* has been demoted from its allusion to a system of the mind to a mere descriptor of a quality of thoughts and wishes; still, whatever is unconscious is thought of (processed) according to the rules of primary process thinking. Perhaps the main addendum to Freud's original propositions is the belief that the UCS system (and, later, the id) is not entirely structureless, but does have a measure of structure and is to some extent concerned with reality issues (see, for example, Holt, 1967; Noy, 1969).

Freud's model, which was developed in regard to dream formation, was clinically derived and stems from a mixture of direct observation and clinical inference. However, it included a confusion between *the mechanisms of dream formation* and *those that are involved in processing subliminally perceived information in the unconscious part of the mind*. This confounding of the processing mechanisms and those of disguise—the means through which the unconscious mind reports out the results of its processing—may well have contributed to the abandonment of the model and the only limited use of its viable ideas. As I said earlier, this turning away from model-making is a great misfortune for the field.

I will attempt here to fill the void left by Freud and his followers by proposing a fresh and well-defined model of the mind as it relates to the processing and communication of emotionally charged information. The value of the model will be tested through its heuristic and explanatory powers and its own capacity to evolve. In creating the model, which will be data-driven, we will make considerable use of the sharp distinctions I have already developed between direct/manifest contents, implications of manifest contents, and derivative or encoded meanings in emotionally charged messages. By this means we can clearly define two systems of the mind: one that involves conscious and manifest responses to activating emotional triggers, and one that entails unconscious and nonmanifest responses. Observations have accumulated that indicate that two systems of the mind are indeed operative, and that, furthermore, they behave, function, and process information differently—though not entirely according to the rules proposed by Freud (1900a).

The stimulus for this kind of model-making was not entirely intellectual. There were a number of unsolved clinical puzzles that created pressures to generate models in the hope for unseen answers—e.g., indications of inexplicable levels of secure-frame anxiety and dread of unconscious meaning, the propensity to repeat traumas rather than resolve them, etc. The question arose: what is there about the human mind that is so vulnerable, and why are seemingly paradoxical behaviours so common? And could the model suggest dimensions for quantification and research questions that could bring us to science and fresh ideas?

Finally, there was the hope that a sufficiently data-based and sophisticated model of the mind could stimulate neuroscientific research, through which mind and brain could better be united. Where Freud did not expect brain correlates for his model of the mind, we had every reason to insist on such an eventuality—even though the first job was to forge a proper mental model and data base of sufficient force as to promote this possibility.

The basis for the construction of the model

Let us briefly review the clinical basis for the construction of the model of the mind that I will propose. I have already discussed the distinction between manifest/implied meanings in a message, and those that are encoded. Clinical observation has repeatedly shown that manifest perceptions, fantasies, and needs/wishes are quite different from those that are encoded and therefore unconscious. The consistency with which discrepancies arose in respect to goals, motives, viewpoints, experience, solutions, and the like, suggested two distinct information-processing systems—one *conscious* and the other *deeply unconscious*. Investigation of manifest/implied levels of communication and of derivative expressions fraught with latent meaning revealed a series of differentiating features and eventually suggested a complex model of the mind (see Langs, 1986, 1987a, 1987b, 1988a, for earlier versions of the model).

Once the model was in place, new lines of thought emerged, and the model seemed to grow and expand.

Cognitive research has clearly shown that all incoming information passes through what is called an unconscious filter (Goleman, 1985). We will soon see that this filter is somewhat more complex and sophisticated than had been previously thought. After all, the human brain has some 300 billion cells, each with up to 30,000 interconnections; the human mind must be at least as complex as the brain, if not more so.

Figures 4.1 to 4.3 build the model of the mind that we will consider. Let us delineate the model as a series of information processing steps:

1. The first step in processing incoming information is, of course, that of sensory reception at a *sensory receptor site (SR)*. For present purposes, I will follow an incoming message from an outside source; however, with but a few modifications, much the same would apply to messages from internal sources—mental or somatic.

There is evidence of an emotional influence on the very experience of sensation, suggesting a great complexity of feedback and feedforward linkages between each of the systems we will consider. The deep unconscious memory system (see below) is especially powerful in this respect. Furthermore, it is important to keep in mind that the use of a sensory channel as a conduit for incoming information is a process that is quite different from those processes that determine whether at any time information registers in conscious awareness or remains confined to subliminal registration and unconscious experience.

2. Information enters the unconscious part of the mind and is immediately given meaning through the operation of a *synthesizing centre (SC)*. We know that all sensory input involves raw stimuli that are given *meaning* by some mental operation. We will soon see that unconscious information processing is highly organized and intelligent, and it is postulated that meaning is afforded incoming messages immediately on entering the unconscious part of the mind. And this is done on all three levels,

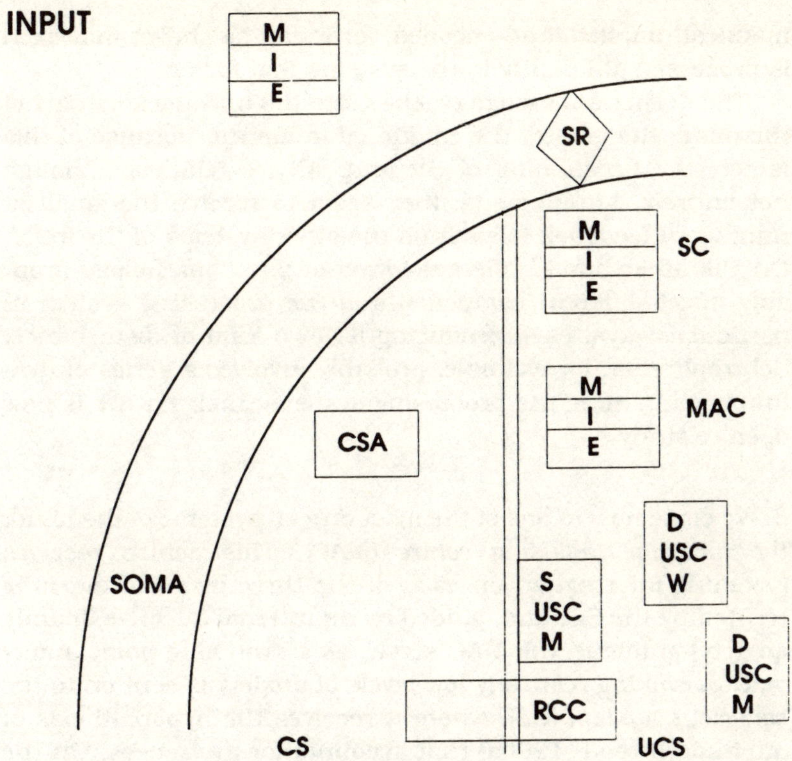

M = manifest content
I = implication of manifest content
E = encoded meaning
SR = sensory receptor
SC = sorting centre
MAC = message analysing centre
CSA = conscious system awareness
SUCS-M = superficial unconscious memory system
DUCS-W = deep unconscious wisdom system
DUCS-M = deep unconscious memory system
RCC = response control centre
CS = conscious system
UCS = unconscious system

FIGURE 4.1
The components of the model of the mind

manifest, implied, and encoded, for it can be shown that each is processed differently in the systems that follow.

The deeper a message reaches into the unconscious part of the mind, the greater the emotional influence. Because of this factor, the functioning of SR and SC are relatively, though not entirely, autonomous; they seem to receive the smallest number of feedback loops from the other systems of the mind. On the other hand, different forms of psychopathology probably affect different components of the processing system in particular ways, each producing its own kind of disturbance. Schizophrenia, for example, probably involves a series of dysfunctions in all of the processing systems; their nature is now open to study.

3. We come now to one of the most crucial systems of the mind: *the message-analysing centre* (*MAC*). This centre receives incoming information on each of the three levels of meaning created by the SC, and, guided by an internal affective (mainly anxiety) gradient, the MAC serves as a switching point. Information evoking relatively low levels of anxiety is sent on to the *conscious system* (*CS*), where it receives the hypercathexis of attention (Freud, 1900a) that accounts for awareness. On the other hand, information that evokes a relatively high level of initial anxiety is forwarded to *the deep unconscious wisdom system* where it is further silently analysed and responded to. In the first case, we are directly aware of the information we have received; in the second case there is no direct registration—and only sometimes an encoded one.

The conscious system is designed to enable survival in reality and is highly refractory to emotionally charged meanings. It is a delicate system that requires high levels of defensive protection—much of it through denial and avoidance—to ensure its smooth functioning. The MAC is sensitive to these needs and responds protectively, screening out all stimuli that might disturb or even overwhelm the CS. Indeed, the model indicates that the *fragile state of the conscious system* and the limitations this imposes on awareness is of prime importance in the pathways chosen by the MAC—and thereby in what information is processed consciously or unconsciously.

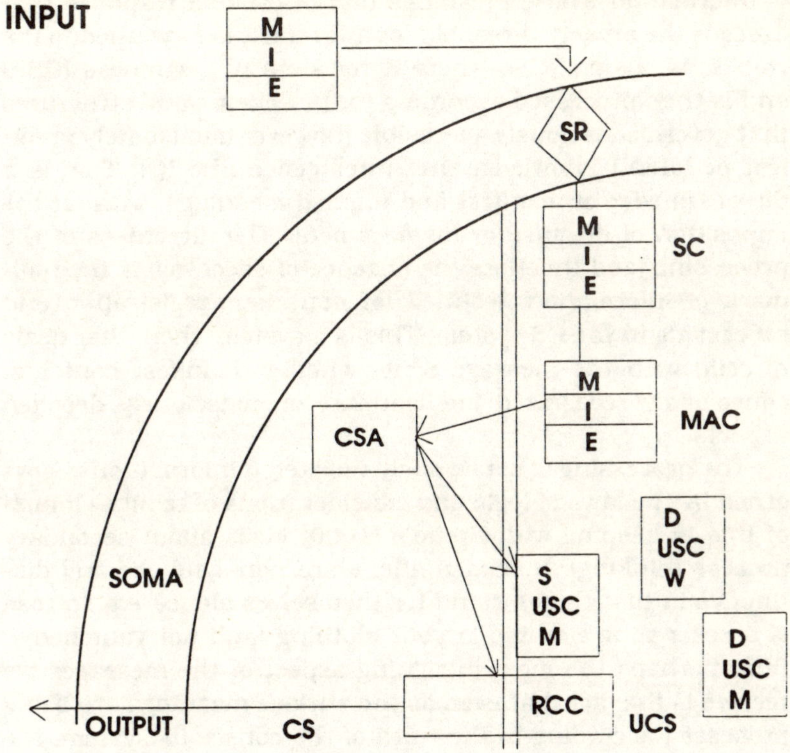

M	=	manifest content
I	=	implication of manifest content
E	=	encoded meaning
SR	=	sensory receptor
SC	=	sorting centre
MAC	=	message analysing centre
CSA	=	conscious system awareness
SUCS-M	=	superficial unconscious memory system
DUCS-W	=	deep unconscious wisdom system
DUCS-M	=	deep unconscious memory system
RCC	=	response control centre
CS	=	conscious system
UCS	=	unconscious system

FIGURE 4.2
The processing of a manifest message

4. Information whose meanings do not evoke a response that exceeds the anxiety threshold for awareness is forwarded to the *conscious system (CS)*, where it registers in awareness (CSA) and is then processed according to the schema and structures that govern consciously accessible (however immediately manifest or latent) knowledge and intelligence (the IQ). This is a direct transfer of manifest and implied meanings, without the imposition of disguise or displacement. The directness of the processing (and therefore the absence of encoding) is the hallmark of information destined for conscious registration and processing in the CS system. This is a system, then, that deals *directly* with the message sent—whether manifest contents, consciously recognized implications, or consciously decoded aspects.

The processing of consciously registered information is governed by the laws of logic and considerations of reality—(much of this in keeping with Freud's [1900] ideas about secondary process thinking). Representations are non-symbolic and distinctive in that things stand for themselves alone—e.g., a rose is a rose; your clothing is your clothing (and not your body). Still, perhaps the most intriguing aspect of the messages we receive is the fact that even as the surface meanings are being processed according to the rules of the conscious system, the latent meanings of the same message are being governed by the rules of the deep unconscious system (see below).

One of the main characteristics of the CS system that has not been sufficiently emphasized is its aforementioned high level of defensive need. This is reflected in the extent to which meaning is channelled away from awareness by the MAC, and in the degree to which the CS system denies and otherwise avoids many of the ramifications of registered emotional information. The CS system is denial- and repression-prone, and as a result, conscious thinking in the emotional domain is naive and unreliable.

The main functions of the CS system are to perceive reality directly and to facilitate immediate and long-term survival. The smooth operation of the CS system therefore relies on the denial of disturbing emotional meanings that would otherwise disrupt the functioning of the system. While, of course, many

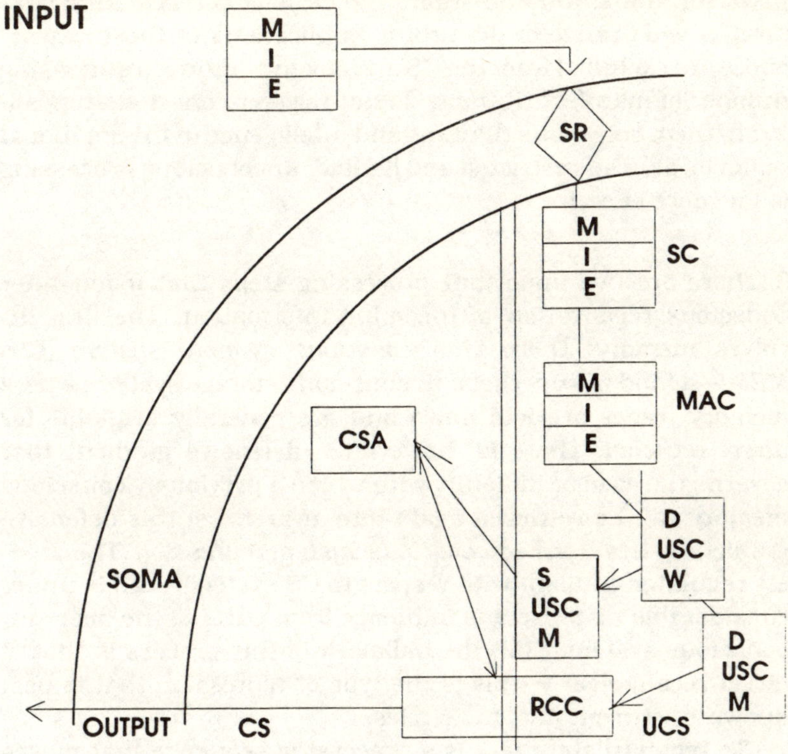

M = manifest content
I = implication of manifest content
E = encoded meaning
SR = sensory receptor
SC = sorting centre
MAC = message analysing centre
CSA = conscious system awareness
SUCS-M = superficial unconscious memory system
DUCS-W = deep unconscious wisdom system
DUCS-M = deep unconscious memory system
RCC = response control centre
CS = conscious system
UCS = unconscious system

FIGURE 4.3
The processing of an encoded message

powerful and traumatic stimuli do register directly in awareness, a wide range of disturbing implications to these experiences are excluded from the CS system; in addition, a surprising number of manifest traumas do not register consciously at all. In all, then, conscious thinking and intelligence in the emotional realm is, at best, restricted and limited; unconscious processing is far more effective.

5. There are two important processing steps that follow after conscious registration of incoming information. The first involves memory: there is a *conscious memory system (CS–MEM)*—a kind of superficial unconscious storage system, where memory traces are laid down and are generally available for *direct retrieval*. There is, however, a defensive gradient that governs the ease or difficulty with which a previously conscious memory can be retrieved again into awareness; this defensive gradient is best termed *conscious system repression*. The anxiety regulator gradient with respect to CS system recall is under considerable unconscious influence from parts of the deep unconscious system. Still, the hallmark of this process is that of direct recall; clearly, this is the type of repression that is best known in current analytic circles.

To recapitulate: there is a processing sequence that moves from the SR to the SC and is then analysed by the MAC, where the anxiety gradient is sufficiently low as to allow for the direct passage of the message and certain aspects of its meanings into the CS system. Once registered in awareness, these meanings are stored in the CS–MEM system, where they are available for direct retrieval, though re-entry into consciousness depends on another anxiety gradient—CS system repression. This is, however, but one of the two systems with which we deal with emotionally charged information—we will soon examine the second system.

Before moving on, we must recognize that we have as yet been restricting ourselves to the problem of conscious versus unconscious registration of message meanings. This constitutes but one of several output channels, once incoming messages have been processed within the mind. Thus, there are, as noted, possible behavioural, affective, symptomatic and physical, and other responses. Each of these output modes will be accompanied by either conscious or unconscious awareness—and sometimes both. We will therefore need to expand our model of the mind to account for all possible forms of output. To do this, we will later consider the *response control centre (RCC)*, the ultimate conduit for all incoming information. For the moment, however, let us continue our study of the options available to the MAC.

6. There is a different fate and mode of processing awaiting information that the MAC assesses as too disturbing for the CS system, and therefore forwards for unconscious rather than conscious processing. Such information is routed to *the deep unconscious wisdom system (D–UCS–W)*, where it is subjected to *premises* (i.e., afforded properties that influence experience) that are rather different from those applied to information channelled into the CS system. In addition, aspects of the processing, while quite logical in respect to its own view or terms, is different from that used by the CS system.

Safeguarded by the absence of immediate awareness or the possibility of later conscious registration—all reports from the D–UCS–W system are under the obligation to be disguised or encoded—this system is able to process emotional charged information readily and effectively, with virtually no defensiveness and in terms of its most raw, primitive, and compelling meanings. The D–UCS–W system is not a seething cauldron of drives and wishes (these reside in the *deep unconscious memory system* [D–UCS–M]); it is a system with considerable aptitude, wisdom, and intelligence (the UQ). The D–UCS–W system has developed over the years by means of processing subliminal perceptions and learning how to evaluate their meanings and implications; it is a system that in the emotional realm has seen more, knows more, and is far wiser than its more restricted counterpart—the CS system.

It appears, then, that when we are anxiety-free and unaware of what we are learning, we can more easily process the painful lessons we must metabolize. When we consciously think over an emotional issue, we are likely to be defensive and inept, but when we think over the same issues unconsciously—when we don't know what we're thinking—we're quite effective. Simply put, in the emotional domain, UCS learning and processing is far superior to what the CS system can accomplish. However, as we will see, it is perhaps the greatest flaw of the evolved human mind that such knowledge is imparted only through encoded messages; not only do we not know that these insights exist in our minds, but we cannot make use of this great resource—it has little direct effect on our output decisions and behaviours. This state of affairs can be changed only if the relevant encoded material is properly trigger-decoded.

The D–UCS–W system processes information in keeping with its own premises, such as parts equal wholes, possessions equal the possessor, what happened before will happen again—much of it in keeping with Freud's (1900a) ideas on primary process thinking. But the D–UCS–W system is highly sensitive to reality—in a sense, far more so than the conscious system. For example, it is the D–UCS–W system that is exquisitely in touch with boundary/frame issues which prove to be major factors in our emotional lives. In contrast, as noted before, the CS system is generally insensitive to these nuances.

Contrary to Freud's contention, there is strong derivative evidence that the D–UCS–W system also has its own negations, which are different from those in the CS system. This difference in viewpoint stems from the fact that Freud was concerned mainly with unconscious wishes, which were also positive in nature, while here we are considering information processing that is open to positive and negative effects (in the present model, the wishes are part of a different system—D–UCS–M).

For example, if you are my social friend, then you certainly can, in the CS system, be my therapist (there is no negation or contradiction there); but in the D–UCS–W system, you can never be both—you are either friend *or* therapist, but never friend *and* therapist. This is the structure of D–UCS system logic, which operates somewhat differently from the more familiar CS system logic. This means that, on the unconscious level, a therapist with whom a patient has had a social relationship is never entirely and deeply experienced as fulfilling his or her assigned role as therapist; instead, the therapist is seen as an incestuous 'object' or some other pathological figure. And, of course, these unconscious perceptions deeply affect the therapeutic process.

The D–UCS–W system assesses and evaluates reality, the image of others and ourselves, and advises us on how to respond and function. Together with the primitive drives contained in other parts of the D–UCS system, these constellations form a set of structures that could well be described as embodying id, ego, and superego functions. These structures are configured quite differently from the comparable structures that exist within the CS system. In a sense, then, we have two egos, two ids, and two superegos—each a reflection of a distinctive way of experiencing and reacting to ourselves, the world, and others.

The D–UCS system has its own storage system, *the deep unconscious memory system (D–UCS–M)*, where unconsciously experienced memories and meanings are stored and subject to *encoded* retrieval—and not direct recall. The barrier to transformed recollections may be termed *deep unconscious repression*, and this anxiety gradient is actually directed against disguised recall; it speaks for fears of the emergence of even camouflaged remembering. On the other hand, because the recall is encoded, it is extremely difficult to recognize its presence; this can be determined only through an effective use of interactional decoding.

The D–UCS–M system embodies and stores our most terrifying memories, introjects, and unconscious perceptions; it is there, too, that the incessant realization of our personal mortality is housed (a more benign version is also kept in the CS–MEM system). For reasons yet to be clarified, it is these deeply unconscious constellations that exert by far the greatest unconscious influence on the RCC—in essence, on our total emotional lives and choices (outputs). There is no overestimating the power of this subsystem of the mind—its fears and guilt.

We have yet to speak of displacement and symbolization/disguise—the means by which the encoding of D–UCS realizations takes place. There is, however, a requisite that all information and understanding processed in the D–UCS–W system is obligated to obey: none of its registrations and insights can be passed directly into the CS system and awareness. Except perhaps in instances of severe pathology (possibly only with psychotic disturbances), this requirement of *transformation before registration* is absolute; it is the essential safeguard that allows for the processing of perceived meanings that would otherwise be emotionally overwhelming and crippling to CS system functioning. The key means of transformation are the well-known mechanisms of displacement and disguise (condensation, concern for representability, and secondary revision are secondary).

The actual release of information from the D–UCS–W system is a matter of considerable interest. First, there is no obligation of the system to reveal, even in encoded form, its perceptions and how they have been understood and processed. Some individuals seldom generate such reports, doing so mainly when they experience a major frame-break or frame-securing moment—we call these individuals *non-transformers*. Others emit many encoded messages and can be identified as *transformers*. But with either type, the intelligence of the D–UCS–W system is conveyed in disguised rather than direct fashion.

How is this done? There are *mental tracts* (possibly related to brain conduits) that carry information from one system to another, while other tracts carry signals that influence the processing going on in the various components of the mind. There are two means by which the D–UCS system can impart messages that ultimately reach the CS system in encoded form. The first involves the CS–MEM system, in that these are the only memories outside awareness that can be conjured up and brought into awareness (D–UCS–M system memories are not directly accessible to consciousness).

The steps in message formation are these (I will anthropomorphize for sake of clarity):

1. The D–UCS decides to report out on an unconscious perception and how it has been worked over.
2. The system then sends a signal to the CS–MEM system. This signal is a complicated, searching directive that asks for a representational (disguise-enabling) image that is related metaphorically through *shared themes* to the D–UCS message; there is a request for a suitable encoding vehicle in the form of some recollection that at the same time can emerge into awareness with some degree of surface logic (this process is quite amazing in the course of free associa-

tion or daydreaming; it is somewhat easier in dreams where a lesser degree of sensibility is required). The signal also indicates the degree of disguise sought for, in that the unconscious process can be conveyed with little or a great deal of transformational distance.

3. a suitable vehicle is then chosen, one that meets all of the requirements conveyed by the signal. The selected item can take the form of a personal memory, a movie or story, a dream, or any other narrative that is suddenly brought into awareness—actively or passively. The messages emitted from the D–UCS system are typically narrative in form (though they may be non-narrative as well).

Notice that this process has entailed two essential steps: (1) a D–UCS processing and (2) a report on this processing through a disguised image. This latter is what we refer to when we speak of indirect or encoded communication; *unconscious communication requires two steps rather than the single step involved in direct CS expression*. It is this two-step process that enables the use of disguise. And, of course, this implies that the comprehension of the unconscious meanings of a message requires a decoding process that unmasks this two-step sequence and undoes the disguise involved in light of the evocative triggers that evoked the encoding in the first place.

A second means through which the D–UCS system can find expression involves *imagination*—the creation of images not experienced in reality. This function is carried out by a *creative centre* (CC), which can conjure up unprecedented images suitable for conveying encoded meanings at a moment's notice. Here too, the expressed images share *themes* in common with the latent meanings they represent. It is this centre that is responsible for idiosyncratic dreams filled with imaginary people, places, and things, and which stands as a special resource for human creativity and encoding.

Finally, we must consider the extent to which D–UCS–W processing is accurate and reliable. I have already indicated that the transformation-of-output requisite ensures a maximal degree of veracity and wisdom in this system's handling of emotionally charged information. There are, however, limits to this reliability, in that there are situations in which a clearly traumatic intervention by a therapist evokes a *positive encoded response* from the D–UCS–W system, rather than a devastatingly negative set of images. In these situations, the choice of representation usually lies between undisguised recall of the trauma, with no derivative—dream—expression at all, or the use of a derivative that is defensively positive (manic) in tone. Analysis of these situations suggests that these positive images are a result of D–UCS–W system overload—that is, when under undue stress, the system shuts down its veridical processing mechanisms and substitutes what appears to be self- (system-) protective positive imagery that defends against this extreme degree of unconscious emotional assault.

I have termed this type of response *deep unconscious over-idealization* (see above) and view the phenomenon as comparable to the frequently observed *conscious* over-idealization seen in the presence of less traumatic interventions from therapists—and persecutory experiences in general. The defensiveness of this type of conscious praise is belied by the finding that the directly praiseworthy manifest allusion to the therapist is immediately followed by a negative image of someone else—this, the displaced negative unconscious (derivative) perception of the consciously admired therapist. Indeed, as a rule, directly stated positive images of a therapist are characteristically followed by negative images of someone else. In the situation with unfounded positive derivative images, negatively toned derivatives tend to emerge some time after the initial defensive expressions.

7. All mental system outputs other than conscious and unconscious registration of meaning is controlled by a *response control centre (RCC)*, which orchestrates our behaviours and other modes of output/expression. This system straddles the conscious and unconscious parts of the mind; it is a system that takes in information from all sources, conscious and unconscious. The RCC has access to and controls a variety of output channels—somatic, symptom-related, action/behaviour, affect, verbalization—that are interrelated in important ways. For example, use of derivative images tends to lessen the gain (degree of openness) of the output channels for somatic response and blind action (so-called acting out).

There is considerable clinical evidence to suggest that the two most powerful influences on the RCC are those of consciously perceived reality (which defines emotional dangers as well the real possibilities of response) and the D–UCS–M system—the storehouse of our most dreaded memories, fears, guilt, and introjects. On rare occasions, the D–UCS–W system will evoke an intuitive conscious response—such as sensing the presence of a missing trigger. But, on the whole, the D–UCS–W system appears to be lacking tracts through which it might influence the RCC and thereby directly inform and affect our behaviours. This leaves the RCC, the locus of our conscious decisions and the director of our behaviours, at the mercy of the D–UCS–M system—a vulnerable position at best.

There is, then, a most powerful influence on our lives that arises from a system entirely outside our awareness—the D–UCS–M system. This results in *influence without choice*, a situation in which the CS system functions mainly as a *conscious rationalizer* for actions and ideas that are unconsciously driven via effects on the RCC, even though we often do not realize that this is the case. Many emotionally related decisions made by both patients and therapists are of this nature, and they need to be analysed with these factors in mind.

A clinical illustration

A brief clinical example will illustrate the operation of these centres and systems. A young man in therapy with a male therapist for depression was seen by his therapist on the morning of a major holiday—Labor Day. In the session, the patient began by directly questioning the therapist's seeing him on a holiday, but went on to state that he felt that the therapist was a deeply committed individual who showed great concern for his patients. The patient then thought of his mother, who could not let go of his sister, even though she was now in her early thirties; the sister seemed incapable of leaving home. For her part, his mother should be able to let go by now, too.

This material went uninterpreted, and in the following session the patient described a 'weird' incident with his girlfriend with whom he spent time after the session. She had come back to his apartment for a night-cap, and when she decided to leave, the patient became upset and insisted that she stay on. They had argued over his pressure to keep her with him, and she had begun to cry that he never listened to what she had to say. He realized that he had actually held her captive until she had run off when he looked away.

To analyse this brief vignette, let us begin with the main incoming message for the patient: the frame-deviant decision by the therapist to hold a session on a legal holiday, in violation of their original agreement that this would not be the case. This complex message was received mainly through SRs of audition and, secondarily, vision, and then given its three levels of meaning—manifest, implied, and encoded—by the SC. Next, it was forwarded to the MAC, where the manifest meaning and selected implications—e.g., that the therapist is concerned about his patient's welfare—were sent on directly (without disguise) to the CS system; once registered, these meanings were stored in the CS–MEM system. It was on this basis—plus additional information processed in the D–UCS—that the RCC brought the patient to his session. There he conveyed his conscious impressions about the matter, speaking directly on behalf of the CS system.

What, then, of the patient's D–UCS–W system; how did it process the same input in terms of those implications that were registered unconsciously rather than consciously? The answer lies in the patient's encoded output, which in this case involved both a behaviour (his actions with his girlfriend—a very real consequence of the patient's unconscious perceptions of the therapist's message) and verbalized derivative communications (his associations in each of these sessions).

To trigger-decode these associations in light of their evocative trigger, we turn to the material about the patient's mother and his sister. The *themes* involve being unable to let go of someone who should be allowed her freedom. Connecting this narrative to the trigger of the holiday session, we can see that the D–UCS–W system perceived the therapist's problem in allowing his patient his freedom and autonomy, and his need to hold on to the patient in an inappropriate way. The system shows its remarkable intelligence and processing capacities in encoding a model of rectification or corrective: let me go!

All of this was accomplished in two steps: (1) the unconscious registration and working over, and (2) the signal to the CS–MEM system that asked for a memory that would encode this entire process. The situation between the patient's mother and sister contained the necessary themes through which the D–UCS–W system could express itself in disguise. Indeed, the situation rather candidly encodes the shared pathology reflected in the therapist's offer and the patient's acceding to it. In addition, we can vividly see that the patient's unconscious view of his therapist as his mother and himself as his sister alludes to an actual re-enactment of a past pathogenic interaction (ultimately between the patient and his mother). Rather than involving any measure of distortion, this is a selective but accurate reading of implications of the therapist's frame-deviant intervention.

The therapist's failure to interpret this material interactionally is, among other matters, a reflection of system overload (see chapter five). The P/T system itself and the P then became overloaded with uninterpreted action and meaning, and it was under these conditions that the RCC directed the patient's inappropriate actions. While the patient's derivative communications were based on the inputs from his D–UCS–W system (which recognized both the therapist's pathological behaviour and his failure to listen), activation of pathogenic memories in the D–UCS–M system undoubtedly had the greatest influence on the RCC, which directed his treatment of his girlfriend. We can see, too, that the therapist's use of an action-discharge mode of expression (the deviant session) increases the gain in the patient's own action-related output conduit. Both identification with the therapist and system overload—dynamic/genetic and systemic factors—played a role in the patient's pathological output (the incident with the girlfriend).

Outside support for the model

While this model was developed almost entirely through the use of the C-scope, there is some supportive evidence from other sources for its configurations. First, there are the studies by Silverman and his associates (Silverman, Lachman, & Milich, 1982)—and others—using the stimulus, *Mommy and I are one*, for exposure to subjects either supra- or sub-liminally. By and large, these investigators found that there were profound positive effects on cognitive functioning, schizophrenic symptoms, addictive patterns, and the like *only when the stimulus was presented outside awareness*. These results speak strongly for two very different mode and means for the processing of emotionally charged information—one conscious and the other unconscious—and each with distinctive output consequences. Suggested, too, is the likelihood that subliminal (and possibly hypnotic) stimuli gain direct entry to the D–UCS system, where the effects of the unconsciously registered information are able to influence many different types of outputs from the RCC.

A second type of support comes from neuroscience and the study of split-brain patients, for whom the corpus callosum has been severed so that the two hemispheres of the brain are essentially without a communicative bridge (Gazzaniga, 1985; Sperry, 1961). Of interest here are the findings that arise when a strange situation is shown only to the right part of the mind (corresponding to the right side of the brain, which is, in the main, without language), and the individual demonstrates a patently bizarre or inexplicable response. When the left part of the mind (corresponding to the left side of the brain) is shown the situation and the patient's peculiar response, this language side of the mind confabulates marvellous rationalizations for the behaviour so blindly dictated by the right mind. These results are in keeping with the idea of two separate sites of information processing—the D–UCS, which may well be located mainly in the right hemisphere, and the CS, which may be mainly in the left. The view generated by this work supports that part of the present model of the mind that proposes that the D–UCS drives emotional decisions, while the CS is primarily designed to rationalize these deeply determined behaviours so that they seem logical in the context of reality—instead of bizarre or inappropriate.

A third and more recent piece of supporting evidence comes from the work of Shevrin and his colleagues (Shevrin, 1988; Shevrin, Williams, Marshall, Hertel, Bond, & Brakel, 1988), who have shown that emotionally charged words taken from a patient's own conflict-related images in consultation sessions evoke different *brain* responses, depending on whether they are shown supra- or sub-liminally. Indeed, supra-liminal exposure causes no transfer of information across the parietal lobes as measured by evoked potentials, while subliminal exposure causes a strong transfer of this type. These effects are not seen with generally (non-personal) negative words or with the subliminal presentation of words related to the patient's symptomatic picture. Here again we have strong support for the model, including indications that unconscious perception and processing is indeed highly selective in terms of a patient's own pathological issues—and relatively insensitive to generally hurtful words to which a patient has not shown a particular vulnerability.

Finally, in a more esoteric vein, there is the highly speculative contention made by Penrose (1989), a well-known mathematician, that consciousness—i.e., the CS system—is non-algorhythmic in that it lacks systematic processing programs, while unconscious responses are algorhythmic in that they are organized and predictable. Oddly enough, this, too, is in keeping with the model of the mind proposed here, in that conscious system responses do appear to be rather unpredictable and unreliable, while deep unconscious reactions are far more consistent and predictable—which speaks for algorhythmic functioning. At this point, definitive research related to the model is needed to provide further clarification.

Integrating the macroscopic and microscopic models

In order to develop a more defined and research-oriented, comprehensive model, it behoves us now to attempt to integrate the two models—macroscopic and microscopic—that I have proposed for the therapeutic interaction. The microscopic model can be illuminated by studies of conscious and unconscious communication, which will clarify the functioning of the postulated structures needed for information processing. The macroscopic model promotes a more careful investigation of input and output factors, which can provide clues and data related to the internal systemic processing of P, T, and P/T. Both models are pertinent to the study of the role of the boundary conditions of therapy, which is a factor at all levels of interaction. A central goal, too, is the understanding of the interplay between systemic factors as seen in ground-rule or framework considerations, and dynamic factors that arise out of the state of the frame and, in turn, influence how the frame is managed and the meanings imparted in frame-management responses.

Figure 4.4 is a model of the ongoing interaction between P and T. The system is encased in a particular environment or membrane, one that is open to some degree to outside factors, though it is primarily a creation of the P/T system. Incoming information from all sources within and outside the P/T system and its frame is processed by both P and T, leading to some form of output from each. Taken together, these outputs are the products of the P/T system, the most fundamental level with which we are concerned. These outputs are, in turn, received by P and T—and by the P/T system itself—once more, and the sequence continues from moment to moment in the course of a session.

Specifically, Figure 4.4 portrays inputs, processing by the P and T (and the totality of the P/T system), and their collective outputs. The value of this particular systematic configuration lies in its holistic approach. In general, systems function as total emergent entities; it is the tendency of observers or researchers to break them down into sub-components. In this instance, the totality is the P/T system, which we then artificially separate into a P subsystem and a T subsystem, isolating each subsystem and studying their interaction. Research studies and findings should be significantly different in isolated studies of P or T, as compared to studies in which each is treated as an interacting subsystem. At the very least, as noted

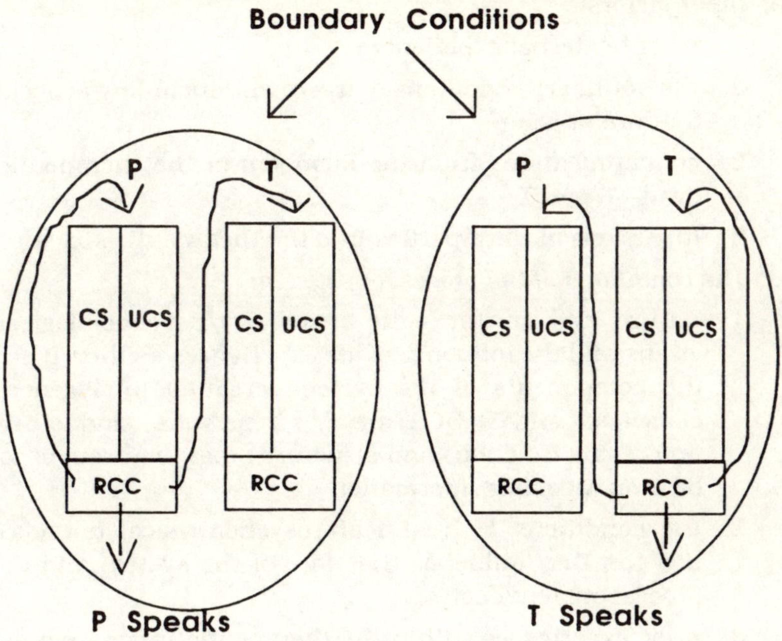

FIGURE 4.4
The P/T system as patient, then therapist, speaks

before, this particular systemic approach calls for accountability at all times by both P and T for all outputs by the total system—regardless of the person from whom the output specifically arises.

This macroscopic system diagram calls for the specific definition of input, system, and output factors. Quantification of these variables has been initiated (Langs & Badalamenti, in press; see chapter seven), and is crucial to the development of the models we need, and to the emergence of new discoveries. The following summary of the factors that appear to be pertinent to the functioning of the P/T, P, and T systems and subsystems expands on the presentation from chapter three and should help us to grasp the situation better:

A. *Input factors*

1. recent external experiences
2. the boundary conditions of treatment, including aspects that are at issue
3. communications from the members of the therapeutic dyad—P and T
4. intrusions of third parties into the therapeutic space

B. *The conditions of the processing system*

1. nature and nurture—the hereditary/psychobiological givens and the influence of life experiences as they affect the components of the system, creating intelligence, conscious and D–UCS memory reservoirs, and other processing functions and structures that are brought to bear on incoming information
2. the conditions of treatment—psychophysical boundaries—as they influence the state of the system and its processing tendencies
3. prior experiences within the therapeutic interaction as they create particular response tendencies
4. specific response tendencies, such as the preference to utilize particular channels for information processing—e.g., a preference for derivative or non-derivative communications, and biases that favour certain channels of action, affect, symptom, somatization, and the like
5. a system's capacity factor, including an I/M load factor that pertains to specific types of incoming information that the system is especially capable of handling or to which it is especially vulnerable
6. the capacity of the system to change its mode of processing based on ongoing, incoming information, and its capacity to alter both immediate processing and the nature of the internal influences brought to bear on the system and its components

C. *System output*

1. the nature of verbal and image expressions, and in particular the extent to which such communications are

derivative-loaded or relatively free of transformed (derivative) meaning

2. responsive behaviours, including facial expressions, body posture, and extended actions
3. affect
4. psychological symptoms or their alleviation
5. somatic responses

The categories described above tend to overlap. However, they apply equally to P and T, though the structure of the therapeutic interaction generally dictates a situation in which the data generated by each participant may—or may not—be skewed in particular directions. The degree of similarity and differences in P and T subsystems, and comparisons of P/T systems pairing, are now open to empirical investigation.

There are many dimensions along which these three elements—input, information processing system, and output—can be studied. Because we are considering the process of psychotherapy, one of the most important of these dimensions is the extent to which an emotionally related output is pathological or dysfunctional rather than healthy and adaptive. Furthermore, the study of attributes of immediate output from the P/T system evolves into considerations of overall treatment outcome—a most treacherous topic and one that is most difficult to handle systematically and without bias.

On the macroscopic level, it is necessary to define indications of pathological output from P, T, and P/T. As noted, in most instances, the characteristics for each are expected to be distinctive. For the patient, this involves the appearance of certain, though not all, gross behavioural resistances (overt obstacles to the progress of therapy), as well as the emergence of maladaptive behaviours (acting out, acting in, and interpersonal disturbances), pathological forms of affect, the specific appearance of emotionally founded psychological symptoms, and all forms of pathological, somatic expression. Careful research will be required to determine the distinguishing features of the healthy and pathological forms of patient outputs.

For the therapist, the indications of system dysfunction may be comparable. However, we need precise data to be in a position to learn of a therapist's somatic and emotional symptoms. In addition, we need the opportunity to study the expressions of therapist resistances to the progress of therapy, of pathological affects, and of dysfunctional interactional behaviours. Beyond such information, the interactional approach described here, by means of unconscious and derivative validation from patients, has defined the parameters of non-dysfunctional technique in a way that permits the identification of many unrecognized dysfunctional outputs from the therapist—though we require a wide range of limits here. Of special interest are a T's non-validated (erroneous) interventions and the ways in which they reflect not only the state of the T, but also much of the state of the P and the P/T system itself—including the overall boundary conditions of the therapy.

This viewpoint provides potentially measurable criteria for the dimensions of the therapist's interventions, an approach that can be supplemented by a careful examination of the patient's derivative responses—his or her unconscious perceptions of the therapist's efforts. The latter expressions are a highly reliable, though not entirely impeccable, source of valid information with respect to therapist output measures (Langs, et al., submitted).

Finally, it may well be possible to develop somewhat independent criteria of dysfunctional outputs from the P/T system itself. At the moment, it is possible to identify output dysfunctions in the P, T, and their interaction. A more holistic approach to these dysfunctions may help us to generate new insights into the therapeutic experience. The study reported in chapter three of the P/T patterns that account for the emergence of unexpected affect point in this direction (see Langs, 1989b). In that study, the therapist input clinically appeared to involve errant interventions (countertransferences). However, the patient's output was not evidently pathological—especially in those situations where unconscious over-idealization followed the errant intervention. These are clues to new ways of researching and thinking about the therapeutic interaction based on our two fundamental models—macroscopic and microscopic—a topic to which we return in chapter seven.

Both systemic thinking and an intrinsic belief in the value of model-making have enabled the interactional approach presented in this book to breathe, agitate, and grow. The systems of the mind account for its psychodynamics, and the psychodynamics empower its systems. It is this kind of synergy and interplay that seems to characterize the emotional domain and contribute to its complexity, power, limitations, and intrigue.

CHAPTER FIVE

System overload

> Chaos often breeds life, while order breeds habit.
>
> Henry Adams

There are many issues raised by systemic concepts that are unique to the field of psychoanalysis and to the challenge of its science. Among these, perhaps the most interesting and consequential is the problem of *system overload (SOL)*. By way of orientation, we can establish a basic postulate: every system and subsystem—P/T, P, and T—has a capacity to absorb and process a (to be defined) quantity of traumatic or charged information/meaning (I/M load) that falls within some finite, though flexible, limit. In substance, every system can tolerate just so much disturbing input before reaching a state of overload—a state where its processing capacities change qualitatively and can no longer handle (respond adaptively to) the incoming input. In developing this idea, we can see that the intriguing interaction between information (complexity) and meaning (signification) comes into play here, as does the means by which we can define the traumatic load of a stimulus message or situation.

It can readily be seen that this load capacity is a complex function. The power or weighting afforded to meaning is likely to be different from, and usually greater than, that given to information; in general, we would expect the two dimensions each to vary in its own distinctive way. In the psychotherapeutic situation, I/M load is dependent on the nature of the traumatic input, the conditions and boundaries of the treatment experience and relationship, the prior therapeutic experience (as incorporated into the P/T system), the history and state of the system itself (including, of course, those of P and T separately), and the status of the output channels.

All of this involves the CS and D–UCS processing systems, each with its own load capacity. Indeed, CS system overload is easily recognized by the direct experience of having too much to deal with, being fed up with a particular situation or an accumulation of issues, and simply 'having had it for now'. D–UCS overload is far more subtle and can be identified only through its tell-tale indicators, much of which have a quality of emotional disturbance or, more indirectly, of a failure to maintain assigned role functions. In one sense, virtually every emotionally based symptom is a reflection of a measure of SOL.

There is a virtual maze of interconnections between the various subsystems (and factors) that interact and combine to establish the I/M load of a particular system and its subsystems—feedback and feedforward loops abound. In simple terms, the load capacity of the T significantly effects that of the P—and vice versa.

Despite these complexities, the quantification of these factors—a most interesting search in itself—should make feasible our ability to predict significant interludes of systemic chaos and dysfunction and, more broadly, the emergence of bifurcation moments (see chapter three), those sudden qualitative shifts in systemic trajectory that are based on quantitative build-up, which are not uncommon in psychotherapy. SOL is critical to these episodes in which disequilibrium is characteristic, unless it is masked and controlled by system shutdown—the most common systemic response to excessive inputs.

Unrecognized SOL accounts for many inexplicable therapeutic experiences. The defences mobilized by overload, though sometimes blatant—e.g., frank denial, physical flight, refusing to deal with issues, and such—are often quite unconscious. For example, SOL may lead a therapist to avoid unwittingly certain areas of meaning—often death-related or involving personal areas of vulnerability—or to fail to make sound interpretations. SOL may lead a patient to terminate therapy prematurely or to engage in blatant resistance to the therapeutic process. There are many important clinical consequences to SOL; the load capacity of the P/T system fluctuates greatly and is a critical factor in the way in which a therapy unfolds.

Clinical examples of SOL

Let us consider three brief clinical vignettes in which SOL played a significant role. These vignettes illustrate some of the more common inputs that favour such overload; they also show some of the ways in which the P/T system can fail to process adequately these inputs and the type of system output phenomena that can—and do—emerge under these conditions. The fascinating complexities of this problem, and the ways in which the present systemic modelling approach helps to illuminate them, should also become clearer through these vignettes. In actual clinical practice, this particular cluster of observations has made it possible to anticipate moments of system overload and to predict the nature of the emerging dysfunctions—and to intervene preventively.

* * *

The first example involves a male patient in once-weekly psychotherapy with a male therapist. The patient began a session by informing the therapist that a former patient, a man known to both parties, had been gravely injured in a serious car accident and was probably going to die. Subsequent associations encoded unconscious perceptions of the therapist as being partially responsible for the accident. The patient alluded to problems with his father, whom he described as having been unfaithful to his mother and having neglected several serious illnesses in his children. By this means, he commented in a displaced and encoded manner on the unconscious sense that the therapist had failed this patient, in part because of the frame deviation of the therapist knowingly treating two men who were friends. This boundary condition is always perceived as deviant by the deep unconscious system.

The therapist manifestly ignored the patient's mention of the former patient, and he missed entirely the patient's responsive derivative perceptions. He intervened with a rather bland, clichéd comment, suggesting that the patient seemed to back away from encounters with his father. There was little time left in the session for the patient to respond to this intervention, and the few comments he made were flat and empty. This material was entirely lacking in derivative validation.

The patient began the next session by stating that he had had an anxiety attack while engaged in cross-country skiing. His mind had begun to race, he had become terrified of thinking, felt fearful of going crazy, and feared being overwhelmed and dying. He had collapsed in a faint, terrified of possessing a single thought.

In analysing this situation, we may propose that the news of the serious accident of the former patient—an issue of meaning more than informational complexity—created a degree of system overload in both the patient and the therapist, in their interaction, and in their shared P/T system. The patient was able to process the trauma with a small measure of derivative communication, though much of the initial session was ruminative and devoid of unconscious meaning; the incident had greatly reduced the output from his D–UCS–W system—extreme trauma tends to lead to mental subsystem shutdown on all levels.

The therapist shared the non-meaning, defensive aspect of the patient's communications. Indeed, the patient had incorporated this attitude from the therapist based on earlier sessions, in which the therapist tended to avoid working with unconscious derivatives, which evidently overloaded his own mental processing systems (a common problem in all humans, including psychotherapists—and patients). In this particular instance, the therapist intervened with a clichéd comment designed to avoid and even destroy both the manifest and the latent—conscious and unconscious—meanings in the traumatic messages from the patient. In short, because of SOL, an effort was made—more by the therapist than by the patient but, on the whole, by this P/T system—to mobilize non-meaning defences against the conscious and unconscious ramifications of the traumatic incident. Unfortunately, these defences, though typical of efforts to cope with SOL, are seldom adequate to prevent untoward output responses.

There is no report of acute symptoms in the therapist—though something of its kind may well have taken place. On the other hand, this patient's anxiety attack and collapse can be understood as a consequence of the system overload and the dysfunction of all four levels of macroscopic system—P, T, P–T interaction, and P/T. It would seem that the patient experienced both an introject of the therapist's anxieties and dread of meaning and an evasive, non-thinking reaction to his own sense of overload. In this light, the patient's symptom appears to represent the dysfunction of both participants to treatment—and of the P/T system in particular. In other words, a traumatic input that led to SOL resulted in a symptomatic response in the patient (as representative of the P/T system). A proper clinical interpretation of this situation would require an appreciation of this systemic analysis and would be an apt way to reduce some of the meaning overload in this P/T system and restore the system to an adequate level of I/M processing.

* * *

The second example of SOL involves a male patient in psychotherapy with a male therapist for episodes of depression. The patient's sessions were held at the end of the therapist's day. One evening, on his way out, the patient overheard a conversation between a cleaning woman and another woman, evidently a therapist. This apparent therapist was telling the cleaning woman that she was about to use the office and that cleaning should take place two hours later.

The woman was, in fact, a therapist and the wife of the therapist who normally used the office during the day. She was a psychologist who used her husband's office to see an occasional patient in the evening. She had arrived an hour before her scheduled appointment and had thus been seen inadvertently by one of her husband's patients. Her husband learned of the encounter when his wife came into his consultation room and told him of the incident that had just taken place.

In the following session, the patient did not mention this incident directly. After speaking in general about his concerns as to how well the therapy was going, he spent most of the hour talking about his plans to attend a professional meeting related to his source of income. In the past, he had gone to this annual meeting alone, so that he could spend his time with potential clients and professional contacts. This time, he said, for some inexplicable reason, he had invited his wife to join him. It was an absolutely crazy thing to do, the patient declared, and he wished now that he could undo it.

The patient's material in this session clearly encoded derivatives related to the patient's unconscious perception of the incident of the previous week. The therapist, however, who had entirely forgotten it (CS system repression operating under strong D–UCS–M influence), was thereby unable to insert the proper template into his C-scope and trigger-decode this material interactionally, and he failed to intervene. He repressed/suppressed the memory for two additional weeks, until a supervisory session jarred his memory loose.

In this instance, there are clear signs of SOL in both patient and therapist. The therapist consciously obliterated his knowledge of the incident between the patient and his wife, as did the patient—who failed to refer to the episode in the following session. The patient also unconsciously acted out a dramatized version of the blatant break in the ground rules of his therapy, in which he had been an unwitting participant (the behavioural consequences for the therapist, which probably were significant, were not reported; these are matters for self-analysis).

We might well view the patient's avoidance of any direct allusion to this incident as a sign of pathological resistance. Yet, on the other hand, the patient produced clear derivatives through which interpretation and rectification would have been feasible, even though the incident had actually been partially enacted. The therapist's overload was manifested in the lapse through which he both forgot the incident and failed to intervene in the presence of meaningful communication. Here, the P/T system was clearly taxed beyond its capacity to process or metabolize emotionally traumatic information and meaning.

SOL and the output dysfunctions it causes are often manifested as lapses on the part of the psychotherapist. In many instances, the lapse involves a failure to intervene or a decision to intervene in a way that completely avoids the traumatic trigger. Often, the dysfunction takes the form of an alteration in the ideal ground rules or framework of treatment.

In the present vignette, the initial lapse involved the therapist's permission to his wife to use his office, though her early arrival was clearly a lapse of her own. In this situation, a probable dysfunction of a marital system—possibly one that involved SOL—created an external-to-therapy input that encroached upon a therapeutic dyadic system, producing a P/T system overload. The initial lapse in which a frame break took place was then followed by a second lapse, constituted by a pathological form of CS system repression (note, too, the resemblance to denial) and a consequent failure to intervene.

This material suggests that frame rectification and proper interactional interpretations are probably the best means to process and metabolize the excessive I/M load within a P/T system and restore its capacity to process adaptively both information and meaning. Indeed, frame deviations tend to overtax P/T systems and to create conditions under which I/M loads tend to create SOL more easily while frame-securing interventions enhance the capacity of P/T systems to metabolize I/M loads with higher thresholds for overload. This clinical finding does not contradict another series of observations, which indicate that pathological efforts to reduce I/M load are often enacted through frame deviations, whereas frame-securing efforts place a potentially constructive and metabolizable I/M load on P/T systems—even as they enhance their processing capabilities (see below).

* * *

The third vignette produced SOL under rather different conditions; it followed a valid interpretation of meaning and the securing of a deviant ground rule to treatment. The example involves a female patient in therapy with a female therapist, who allowed the patient to cancel sessions with 24-hour notice. Following one such cancellation, the therapist was able to secure this ground rule—i.e., to establish the patient's responsibility for all sessions attended by the therapist—doing so at the behest of the patient's derivatives, which informed her in displaced and disguised fashion that she was being overly permissive in a destructive fashion reminiscent of the patient's mother. The patient had then validated this corrective with several positive interpersonal images and other supporting material. There followed an effort by the patient to change the time of her session, which the therapist interpreted from the patient's material as destructive to the therapy; on that basis, the time was not changed, and derivative validation again followed.

In the following session, the patient spoke of a trip she had taken to the West Coast of the United States, during which she spent time with her extended family. She described in some detail interactions with her mother, sisters, aunts, and uncles, and especially her father, with whom there was considerable tension. Quite unexpectedly (to both herself and the patient), the therapist remarked that it sounded like a Eugene O'Neill play. The patient commented back that it was more like Edward Albee. She then indicated that the therapist's remark had distracted her. She went on to say that her father seemed to have no control over what he said, that he was enormously provocative and overtly seductive, and that both she and her father had virtually lost control during one particular argument.

In this instance, system overload for both patient and therapist was evoked by the securing of the frame. The patient's effort to change the time of her session is a common sign of patient overload—signalled by an effort to modify the ground rules or boundary conditions of the therapy. Unconscious meanings are often especially terrifying under secure-frame conditions. They are processed differently under deviant conditions. Frame alterations are a common, though pathological means, by which both patients and therapists attempt to reduce SOL; paradoxically, this may be successful on one level, while I/M load increases on another level after the alteration has been made.

Here, with the P/T system overloaded with secure-frame anxieties, there is an effort by the patient to deviate, and an inadvertent, overly personal, and clearly inappropriate intervention by the therapist—a therapist lapse and deviation. The ramifications of the lapse are unconsciously perceived by the patient and communicated in her responsive derivatives. These latter efforts may be seen as part of the patient's endeavour to restore the P/T system to an adequate level of functioning. Success in this effort requires an appropriate response from the therapist—again, via both frame-restoring and interpretive interventions.

Factors in system overload

Repeated observation indicates that the single most common systemic response to overload is that of *system shutdown*—the system stops carrying out its usual functions and tends either to close itself off from incoming stimuli or to provide a protective denial-based cover for its discontinued operation. Typically, there are extremes of CS system repression at work, and derivative outputs tend to be greatly reduced. Included, too, is a cessation of effective functioning in the subsystems of the mind, though some information processing does continue at a low level. The specific configurations taken by system shutdown are only now beginning to be studied.

In reviewing the factors that play a role in system shutdown, we will be developing—among other quests—a fresh way to conceptualize stress response syndromes (Horowitz, 1976). The human system mobilizes special resources and defences, not only in the presence of gross and major acute traumas, but also in reaction to more chronic and low-level types of stress that need not involve an acute loss or other type of blatant hurt. Indeed, we will find it necessary to modify the definition of significant stress and to take into account the locus of the overload—CS or D-UCS—once we have explored this territory.

To begin with a fresh elementary proposition, we can state as self-evident that the syndrome of SOL is the result of two factors: the nature of the I/M input and the capacities of the processing systems. Matters become more intricate when we attempt to define these two dimensions.

For present purposes we need to define two types of traumatic situations: those that are physically harmful (and thereby inevitably psychologically harmful as well) and those that are confined to psychological injury. It appears that human beings process these two classes of trauma differently, though extremes of psychological trauma tend to be experienced in ways comparable to physical damage (see, for example, Shengold, 1989). The point here is that physical trauma tends to be far more loaded in stress valence than emotional trauma per se, and is more likely to overload the structures used to process emotionally charged information and meaning.

This emphasis on the role of unconscious communication in the therapeutic interaction and in the development of psychopathological symptoms prepares us for a fresh way of measuring the traumatic valence of a particular experience or stimulus situation—that is, we must afford considerable attention to the *extent to which a traumatic message embodies encoded or derivative meaning* (or is lacking in such valences). The greater the degree of encoding, the greater the resultant stress on the internal D–UCS processing system—and the more likely the development of SOL. The CS system may well be overloaded by gross trauma and excessively complex manifest information. But, in the main, emotional dysfunctions are far more likely to eventuate when the overload extends into the D–UCS system, especially when the system is itself vulnerable to the meanings involved by virtue of its prior history—memories stored in the D–UCS–M system. This system does, of course, have more work to do with strongly encoded messages as compared to those that are relatively confined to manifest contents and their implications.

For a patient in psychotherapy—and for a therapist as well—the *source* of the incoming trauma is another important factor in its valence. Speaking in comparative terms, traumas that arise in situations outside therapy tend, as a rule, to be relatively less charged than those that pertain to the therapy—and to patient and therapist. This dimension has a strong load factor in determining the possibility of SOL and is added to the measure of direct trauma and to the other components that make up the total I/M load on the P and T systems. By this reasoning, an encoded, frame-deviant message from a therapist to a patient—for example, telling a patient an incident from the therapist's personal life—is especially laden with traumatic power. This type of intervention involves a strong derivative expression from the therapist that would reflect his or her own SOL and tax the patient's processing systems as well. It is by means such as these that SOL in one member of the therapeutic dyad overloads the systems of the other member of the dyad.

Frame breaks per se—in everyday life and even more so in therapy—are another element that adds considerably to the traumatic valence of a hurtful situation. For example, a physical attack by a child's mother is a far more traumatic experience than a similar assault from a stranger, while hurtful deviations by the therapist, such as increasing a fee or changing the time of a session or seeing a relative of a patient are, as noted, always strongly traumatic. While this area needs quantification and scientific analysis, it is still possible on a clinical basis to develop a rough estimate of trauma power—a measure that helps to predict the occurrence of SOL.

To summarize: both life stresses—physical and/or emotional—and stresses from within a therapy contribute to SOL. Particular forms of stress have strong traumatic valences: these include physical attack or illness, frame breaks of any kind, and frame-securing moments that, though inherently curative and non-traumatic on one level, are universally stressful on another—mobilizing death, entrapment, and similar anxieties. Still, in general, the trauma load from such interludes is low; the stress on the processing systems involves inevitable life/death anxieties that are more readily processed under secure frame conditions. Nonetheless, for certain vulnerable patients who harbour traumatic memories in their D–UCS–M systems, secure frame moments are paradoxically dreaded because of the terrible images they conjure up—most of them related to premature and over-intense exposure to death-related issues that the system deeply feels unprepared to process (Langs, 1988a). There is much to be studied regarding the potential for SOL under secure and deviant frame conditions.

Derivative messages from therapists and reactions in patients that are inappropriate to the therapeutic relationship and its assigned roles also tend to load heavily on I/M weightings. The issue of metabolizing high loads of I/M exists for both patients and therapists, though each is subjected to special types of stress less often experienced by the other. Thus, a patient's direct attack, threat to break the frame, efforts to secure the frame, decision to terminate therapy prematurely, symptomatic regression—especially serious symptoms such as psychotic disturbances, suicide attempts, and the like—and even clinical progress all create strong I/M loads for the therapist's processing systems and increase the risk of SOL. Therapists are also especially taxed by their patient's derivatives, as shown in a preliminary research study of consultation and therapy sessions in which a build-up of encoded imagery by a patient typically led to therapist interventions that reduced the prior derivative power.

Patients, on the other hand, suffer from high I/M loads with therapists who alter the frame or use non-interpretive—controlling and manipulative—interventions. The load factor on the patient is high wherever a therapist acts rather than speaks—a quality inherent in all ground rule deviations. Self-revelations and other errant comments and behaviours by therapists also create high loading for their patients.

There are a number of relatively unnoticed factors in SOL. For example, a therapist who does not decode the messages from the patient functions as an uninformed processor of the patient's derivative meanings; that is, he or she processes encoded meanings in the D–UCS–W system rather than through conscious recognition. This absence of conscious understanding overtaxes the D–UCS system of both patient and therapist and increases the trauma potential of the patient's messages for both. Indeed, trigger decoding and conscious understanding and mastery considerably reduces the stress load on the entire P/T processing system. This proposition is true in general and is a systemic way of portraying the role of genuine (trigger-decoded) conscious insight in the process of adaptation and therapeutic cure.

In the examples given above, SOL followed the traumatic news of the near death of a friend of the patient who was also a former patient of the therapist; the intrusion of a therapist's wife into his office time (and space); and a secure frame moment. These are typical of the kinds of issues that, when improperly or inadequately metabolized, are likely to lead to SOL. The resultant pathological outputs ranged from physical symptoms to inadvertent actions and acting out—the shift to relatively maladaptive output channels. Smoothly functioning systems tend to operate mainly in the verbal–affective mode and to not show spillage into emotional symptoms, physical dysfunctions, and action discharge.

Notice, too, that related traumas tend to be additive and produce SOL more quickly than situations in which the nature of the stress is varied. We need a well-constructed way of charting input trauma potentials and their additive influence. Every system has a threshold band for maximum bearable load before the system shifts from its usual functioning to SOL functioning—with the use of pathological defences, system and subsystem shutdown, and the increase in the gain of pathological output channels. The threshold for SOL is sensitive to the total degree of trauma but also selectively oversensitive to special forms of trauma relevant to the individual's past history—and current vulnerabilities.

The mental systems in overload

Let us now consider the systems of the mind as they operate under usual and SOL conditions. What can be said on this point based on clinical experience?

Smooth functioning of the mental processing system leads to an optimal degree of awareness (one that is, of course, never total) and may even involve conscious efforts at decoding incoming messages. The MAC is flexible—both protective of awareness and yet open enough to allow important meanings to register consciously. Ideally, too, the CS–MEM system is relatively open and accessible, and the greater share of responsibility for system output falls to the CS system rather than to the

D–UCS system. D–UCS processing continues to take place, but it does not lead to dysfunctional outputs. In particular, there is a tendency for the RCC to close the gain on blind action (acting out) and somatic output channels and to favour the use of manifest information and derivative expressions.

When the input I/M load is excessive, however, the entire mental processing system begins to function at less than optimal levels. While the SR system and SC show only minimal dysfunction, the MAC will tend under these conditions to reduce the gain in the tracts that lead to awareness—except for information necessary for direct emergency coping; meaning, and especially encoded meaning, tends to be barred from awareness. The D–UCS–W system will be hypersensitive to the implications of the trauma at hand, whose most compelling meanings register mainly unconsciously; the system will pass on to the D–UCS–M system very powerful images and meanings that will activate deeply repressed and extremely painful UCS memories. These activated recollections then exert an especially strong effect on the other processing systems and the RCC. A vicious cycle is initiated in which more and more of the I/M load is processed by the D–UCS–W and M systems, and less and less of importance enters conscious awareness. The RCC soon shifts to greater use of pathological output channels such as blind action and somatization, and symptom formation in general. This is a vicious cycle that is difficult to break; much depends on the therapist's ability to secure the frame and engage in interactional interpretations.

SOL also tends to intensify the operation of CS system repression: recollection of directly registered memories can be greatly impaired. This finding speaks to the strong influence of these subsystems on each other, though it is the D–UCS–M system that appears to exert the greatest influence everywhere—including the functioning of the MAC. In addition, these subsystems show special strengths and sensitivities on the one hand, and vulnerability to dysfunction on the other. The history of each individual has the often elusive (unconsciously communicated) clues to these problems.

There are many complex reactions (outputs) from patient and therapist when in a state of SOL. The patient's output may be directed to a variety of symptomatic reactions, as well as to a shut-down of derivative expressions (with a later rebound, as a rule, into strong derivative expression). If the I/M load (trauma) has been excessive, this shut-down is often buttressed with derivative (D–UCS) over-idealization—the insertion of overly positive images in place of devastatingly negative ones. Also common are attempts to break the frame (which may temporarily reduce the SOL state, only, as a rule, to increase the I/M load later on) and the use of CS system denial—an attempt to reduce impingements of all kinds (see Horowitz, 1976).

The therapist's output under SOL tends to involve errant interventions, unconsciously designed to move the patient away from the direct and especially encoded impingements that the therapist is having difficulty processing. Trivial comments, side remarks, attention to clichéd dynamics, avoidance of loaded material—and more—are common. Frame breaks, one of the most common forms taken by pathological efforts to reduce SOL, are legion. The therapist may also experience intrusive thoughts or fantasies and symptomatic reactions, or may resort to blind action under SOL conditions. It is here that *conscious vigilance* and a sensitivity to the indicators of SOL play an important role. Without conscious realization of the state of the P, T, and P/T systems and the unconscious implications of his or her interventions, the therapist in a state of SOL is likely to interact with the patient in ways driven by his or her own D–UCS–M system. The therapist should therefore strive to control pathological tendencies deviantly to seek relief from SOL and should, instead, attempt self-analytic and insightful resolution of the problems that have lead to this condition. This is facilitated by interpreting the underlying issues to the patient while maintaining a secure frame—indeed, the ideal means of reducing I/M load and restoring processing systems to optimal levels of functioning appears to be the same in most situations.

One final point: *system readiness* for new information and meaning, and for establishing the sites for new ways of functioning and coping, is at its highest level when the I/M load is not excessive. Surely, a state of SOL will be inimical to opening new receptor sites—the system is too taxed by its present I/M load to have the energy to move forward into new territories and it is too busy trying to reorder its forces, which are scattered in retreat. A state of SOL reduces system adaptability in a variety of ways.

* * *

In organizing the data of the communicative exchanges between P and T in terms of input, processing systems, and output, we have a framework receptive to scientific thinking and to the translation of clinical models and ideas into experimental design. While there is much more to be said of this model of the mind and the dysfunctions of its subsystems—especially the nature of the disruptions seen in psychotic syndromes—the present discussion has hopefully shown the promise of the model and its potential to promote a science for psychoanalysis.

It is time now to shift gears and to take a direct look at the issues raised historically and in the present in our difficult search for a formal science of psychoanalysis.

PART THREE

PSYCHOANALYSIS AND SCIENCE

CHAPTER SIX

Psychoanalysis as an Aristotelian science

> The *leitmotif* which I recognize in Galileo's work is the passionate fight against any kind of dogma based on authority. Only experience and careful reflection are accepted by him as criteria of truth. Nowadays it is hard for us to grasp how sinister and revolutionary such an attitude appeared at Galileo's time, when merely to doubt the truth of opinions which had no basis but authority was considered a capital crime punished accordingly. Actually, we are by no means so far removed from such a situation even today as many of us would like to flatter ourselves; but in theory, at least, the principle of unbiased thought has won out, and most people are willing to pay lip-service to this principle.
>
> Albert Einstein

Until now, we have been steeped in clinical observations and theory, trying to find our way towards a science for psychoanalysis. We have concentrated on clinical issues that have made this science elusive, and I have tried to suggest possible avenues by which we might resolve the obstacles that we have come upon. I have offered, as well, two theoretical constructs that I believe will help us forge the science for which we are searching: a systems theory and a new model of the mind. With all of this in place, it is time to enter the hallowed halls of science itself—to examine its chambers and to see where psychoanalysis now sits, and why it has so long delayed passing through these portals. It is time, then, to consider the existing science of psychoanalysis in order to establish both its strengths and weaknesses—and their remedy.

I will announce one of my main themes by claiming that psychoanalysis is in principle and in large measure—though, of course, not entirely—an Aristotelian science. As such, it is primarily naturalistic, based on common-sense observation and the statistical norm, static rather than dynamic, concerned with the 'essential nature' of the psyche's presumed elements, and intent on classifying those elements in terms of their apparent attributes and predetermined course of development. It is my intention to present arguments designed to reveal the Aristotelian spirit and philosophy at the heart of psychotherapeutic and psychoanalytic endeavours both in theory and in practice. Because the history of science indicates unmistakably that the Aristotelian approach is essentially incapable of producing a modern-day science characterized by measurement, quantification, effective prediction, and universal laws —it is strongly anti-mathematical—psychoanalysis, if it is to become a strong science, must shift from its current conceptual framework to one that will permit legitimate research to take place. We see, then, that we are embarking on another type of voyage that will wend its way through the pitfalls of present-day psychoanalytic science towards a more adequate position.

I have established my vantage point for this critique of current psychoanalytic research in the earlier parts of this book. And I would stress again that it is only by stepping outside current thinking that a meaningful critique can be made. In substance, I am speaking again of the shift from the F-scope to the C-scope as the basic means of observing and organizing the data of the psychoanalytic situation. Indeed, as long as mainstream ideas seem adequate to explain recognized phenomena—the view through the F-scope—there can only be minor criticisms of the theory and its research. Yet, oddly enough, once a new paradigm is established, it is able to mount a critique that seems outlandish to those adhering to the prevailing viewpoint, for so much that is awry suddenly appears as if by magic.

Yet this organized and reasoned critique serves many functions: it adds to the validity of the new paradigm in its logic and vision; it casts fresh doubts on the prevailing view; and it encourages research—though usually only by those invested in the new line of thought—that will pit one approach against the other as a way of proving the superiority of the new (at least, that is the agenda of the maverick researcher). Yet, if this last goal is reached, both the field and science are served in that bona fide research findings of any kind can advance our understanding of nature, regardless of the underlying motives—though these usually must involve integrity, sincerity, and a love for the field (spite work seldom advances anything but the temperature of the opponents).

Let us recall my position that the moment-to-moment communicative exchange is the critical therapeutic event, and that the P/T system is the basic interpersonal entity of the therapeutic situation. Communication involves both manifest meanings fraught with implications and, on another level, trigger-encoded meanings; and the view of the therapeutic interaction through the C-scope is multi-levelled and affords much attention to unconscious expressions and processes. Patient and therapist are united as a living system that is constantly in the process of change. To paraphrase writers as different as Bateson (1972, 1979) and Prigogine (1980), it is not in the being but in the becoming that all that is meaningful resides.

As I have tried to show, this view of the therapeutic experience and its components has led to a theory of the therapeutic process that departs considerably from present classical thinking. For one thing, the resultant focus is consistently on the individual situation, the unique entity created by a particular patient and therapist in interaction. In contrast, though the individual is recognized, classical psychoanalytic thought depends on the construction of developmental schemes—concentrating on the average person in an average situation and positing odds for and against reaching certain culturally valued human goals. The therapist is understood to preside over a line of natural development that has somehow been thwarted and to facilitate the righting of its natural course (see, for example, Freud 1916–17; Weiss & Sampson, 1986). This classical philosophy is what I am terming 'Aristotelian'.

Modern science no longer traffics in the medieval notion of averages; a law that is valid is valid even if the event in question occurs only once. Indeed, a law must account for all such incidents, not simply for frequent occurrences. By concentrating on the P/T system as a unique entity, we have fortuitously set up clinical parameters that can serve as a basis for quantitative research into the moment-to-moment transactions between patients and therapists. Temporal quantification of these data may well lead to the discovery of the very kinds of laws that are the hallmark of scientific discovery. Modern science developed when Galileo stopped making assumptions about objects and began, instead, to observe how objects actually function over time in controlled situations. Indeed, his remarkably simple discovery (simple in retrospect only) that a pendulum could be used to mark off units of time is one of those disarming revelations on which the entire history of science depends. In order to appreciate the ramifications of this discovery and Galileo's contribution, let us pursue further this contrast between psychoanalysis as an Aristotelian science and psychoanalysis as the Galilean and post-Galilean science it must become.

* * *

I am mindful at the outset that the contrast I am offering is itself characteristic of Aristotelian thought, which depends on polar distinctions. I am using this dichotomy for purposes of discourse and debate, with the understanding that gradations between Aristotelian and Galilean science certainly exist. I am also using the terms loosely, in the manner of Kurt Lewin (1931), to indicate a particular school of thought that dominated scientific thinking until AD 1600, and to represent the terms of the scientific revolution that Galileo's work helped to set in motion. Clearly, to use Newton's metaphor, Galileo stood on the shoulders of such men as Ticho Brahe and Johannes Kepler, much as Newton who followed him stood on the shoulders of both Galileo and Descartes.

The main issue with which we are concerned here is the transition from a limited and arbitrary form of science to a specific and particularized approach. Thus, I will say little about Newtonian mechanics, nor say much about subsequent developments in thermodynamics, relativity, and quantum physics, some of whose foundational concepts do require a modified 'Aristotelian' line of thought. I will also omit consideration here of systems science and of the systems theory for psychoanalysis that I presented in chapter three. In all these cases, certain teleological aspects of Aristotelian thinking are pertinent to some of the prevailing ideas and even to their scientific methods. However, in most instances, the science aspect of the discipline is distinctly Galilean rather than Aristotelian; to miss this point is to fail to recognize the limitations of the remnants of Aristotelian science in these areas. Psychoanalysis is so limited by its Aristotelian leanings that it is important for the moment to say little of those ways in which these ideas may have an iota of validity—the detrimental aspects of the situation far outweigh the constructive side.

It was in the course of my reading on the history of science and on the position of Aristotle in particular that I began to realize the extent to which psychoanalysis is still embedded in the Aristotelian paradigm. It was towards the end of this reading that Kurt Lewin's 1931 paper was recommended to me, proving once again that there is nothing truly new under the sun—only new syntheses and new applications. Lewin argued convincingly that psychology, including the investigation of instincts or drives and emotions, is an Aristotelian science in need of a Galilean approach. He also attempted to define how this shift might take place, including as a possible vehicle his own gestalt and field theory endeavours—a point that suggests that field theorists in general tend to see the need for this kind of change; the systems theory offered earlier in this book, and the bipersonal field concept that preceded it (Langs, 1976a), are strongly invested in field theory ideas.

Alluding to Freud only once, Lewin characterized his theory as Galilean because of Freud's shift from a dichotomy that pitted mental health against psychopathology to an appreciation of a continuum along which these two extremes lie. On the other hand, Lewin was sharply critical of drive theory; he demonstrated its tautological nature in that maternal behaviour is defined through the identification of mothering acts, which are, then, in turn the basis for the concept of a maternal instinct. Lewin did not, however, specifically explore the psychoanalytic theory of drives—though it seems evident that his overall criticisms would amply apply. Several of Lewin's major points have been incorporated into the present line of thought.

Parallels between Aristotelian and psychoanalytic thinking

There are many ways in which the similarities between psychoanalytic and Aristotelian approaches, thinking, and science can be documented. I will proceed by listing those that seem most important and by briefly discussing the evidence pointing to the similarities between the two positions. In so doing, I emphasize again that no attempt is being made to deprecate Aristotle's contribution to the evolution of science. Although the stress here is on those aspects of Aristotelian thinking that have kept psychoanalysis outside the domain of modern science, I again want to acknowledge that many Aristotelian concepts have of late proven to be pertinent to the thinking that characterizes quantum theory and the thermodynamic theory of irreversible processes in which historic factors and matters of becoming play a significant role. Nonetheless, the main point remains: on the whole, as a fundamental, practical, philosophical, and theoretical approach to science, Aristotelian concepts eventually contributed to a long period of stasis not unlike the situation in which psychoanalysis now finds itself.

The following series of interrelated attributes of Aristotelian thinking also seems in important ways to fairly characterize major tendencies in the psychoanalytic movement:

1. Aristotle's approach to the universe that he attempted to understand was naturalistic, based almost entirely on ordinary appearances and the use of common sense (Butterfield, 1957). Psychoanalysis is, in its origins and at present, a naturalistic rather than experimental science.

The scientific method based on Aristotelian thought results in observations that are not only inexact (Lewin, 1931) but tend to emphasize and even to reify the central qualities observed, elevating these to simply derived concepts (Kuhn, 1962). The stress, then, is on reality as presented to the senses, and the resultant impression—as well as the theories derived from them—is broad and sweeping.

Common-sense observations are, of course, open to enormous degrees of error, in no small part because they are unwittingly anthropomorphic. For example, Aristotle believed that heavier objects fall more quickly than lighter objects, because he assumed that 'heaviness' indicated the 'attempt' of an object to move downward, and 'lightness' the 'attempt' of an object to move upward. He also assumed that the laws governing the earth were different from the laws governing the heavens, because supra-lunar movement appeared to be perfectly circular or rectilinear and sub-lunar movement to be correspondingly inferior.

The naturalistic approach tends to be strikingly deductive, in that naive observations are the basis for extensive mental elaborations. Furthermore, once a system of this kind is established, it reflects the unspecified world view of its adherents, and it is therefore difficult to refute. Instead, exceptions are easily disregarded or explained away. One can see this tendency very dramatically in the case of astronomy: the Aristotelian belief that the ideal trajectory is circular led to a series of modifications in theory, known as epicycles, such that anomalous observations could be acknowledged without threatening the circular ideal.

Another attribute of the naturalistic approach is the tendency for its experimental methodology to solidify as an explanation for 'how things are'. This is because the objects observed become reference points for the prevailing cultural mythology. Thus, methodology certifies what is already believed, and experimentation proceeds according to tacit assumptions that remain unquestioned.

To clarify the distinction I am making between an Aristotelian and a Galilean approach to research, naturalism seeks to define what things are; modern science attempts to find out how processes function and change over time. Therefore, in the Galilean approach, passive observation is replaced by active experimentation (Prigogine & Stengers, 1984). One assumes nothing about what a heavy object 'intends' as it falls; one simply measures how quickly the object moves from its point of origin to a particular point under specified conditions (frames). These data are used to generate laws, almost always mathematically founded, which can be extended to other moving objects. Exceptions and anomalies then become the basis for new experiments, pending theoretical revision. A Galilean approach, therefore, would encompass the constant refinement of instrumental measurement and the relevant mathematical techniques—such as the creation by Newton and Leibniz of the calculus, the means by which Newton's laws of motion were defined. The Galilean approach is essentially inductive, deriving its principles from experimentation rather than from inner conceptions.

Turning now to the development of psychoanalytic theory, it can readily be seen that its base is naturalistic (as are those of most sciences at the time of their origins): its tenets are derived from the observations of nature (as seen naively and with some prejudice through the F-scope and by other means such as direct infant observation and the like) and from common-sense conclusions about the psychology of human behaviour. In the language of physics, as I noted earlier, Freud and his followers are best thought of an engineers, developers of a service—i.e., a therapeutic technique—to be offered to the consumer and to be tested out in the market-place rather than in the laboratory. By and large, these analysts were neither pure scientists and theoreticians nor active experimentalists. Certainly, psychoanalysis has been constrained as a science, in part, because it was initially developed as a therapeutic measure and form of cure. Nonetheless, psychoanalysts have been striking slow to produce methods of pure experimentation and pure experimentalists and theoreticians who would be different from and complement the work of the active clinicians.

As I have argued before, this naturalist approach by Freud led to the development of basic theoretical conceptions that are easily open to error or misapplication. Indeed, I wish to stress here that such distortions and falsification are an inevitable consequence of the naturalistic/Aristotelian approach. I have already challenged several such basic conceptions of Freudian theory in this regard. Here, I will add to my discussion of transference (see part one) by characterizing Freud's understanding of transference as a kind of originary myth operating unconsciously in the individual, in terms of which the patient is always orienting his or her present experience of the world. Freud believed that interpretation would help patients to make conscious the founding events that had established this myth and to measure their present experience with the analyst against the mythological pattern they had unconsciously been living out. This is exactly what the Greeks attempted to do when their myths lost their claim to being epic history and were measured against human experience by way of drama. The problem with this approach is that what appears to be a factual life history is itself affected by the context in which it is told; every moment contains its own 'founding event', as it were, which determines the shape of the patient's subsequent self-reflection.

The prevalence of dogma and authoritarianism in psychoanalysis is well known. This, too, is an Aristotelian trait, which was challenged by Whitehead in a quotation cited by Kuhn (1962) to the effect that: 'A science that hesitates to forget its founders is lost.' Thus, the vulnerabilities of psychoanalysis as a science are perpetuated.

As a naturalistic science, psychoanalysis is maintained in the face of exceptions and anomalies by the addition of epicycles; often, an exception is explained in terms of unexpected difficulties deriving from the patient's psychopathology. Documentation is thin, and disputes are readily generated, since common-sense impressions are easily debated—though usually without resolution. It is this naturalistic approach that also accounts for the frequency with which a group of psychoanalysts will generate entirely different and even contradictory formulations of the same material.

2. The very cornerstone of Aristotelian thought was definition by classification of particulars. As Lewin (1931) pointed out, classification by observed elements is an arbitrary system of reference at best, and it leads to distinct classes of objects that actually have much in common functionally. Conversely, genuine functional distinctions are obscured, because certain objects appear to be materially alike.

Classical psychoanalytic thought has defined a multitude of phenomena as 'unconscious'—body posture, internal organ functioning, perception, mentation, unregistered implications of communications, isolated fantasies and metaphors, the desire for illicit gratification of wishes. A Galilean approach would streamline these categories functionally as adaptive responses to stimuli (Langs, 1992). On the other hand, psychoanalysis has grouped together, as one category of unconscious content, mental processes that actually function quite differently. For example, Freud made no distinction between *implications* of manifest contents, which function outside immediate awareness but are consciously accessible as such, and *transformed images*, which function entirely unconsciously and reach conscious awareness only symbolically. By not distinguishing between these phenomena functionally, psychoanalysis has retained a poorly defined conception of unconscious functioning, which is reflected in the popular idea of conscious and unconscious as realms in which various mental objects reside.

3. An Aristotelian theory is essentially qualitative. The theory assumes that an object is led by its essential nature to a particular end, which is its ultimate perfection in time and space. Thus, emphasis is placed on classifying objects according to their apparent commonality not only of innate attributes, but of purpose. Certain objects, in this point of view, may be said to achieve 'higher' states of perfection than others, because their innate tendency to perfection is more fully realized, unimpeded by chance and unforeseen circumstance.

For Aristotle, objects owe their existence to varying combinations of four principles: hot, cold, dry, and moist. Four basic combinations of these elements are possible and, depending on the dominant principle, they characterize the four basic elements of the universe: fire, air, earth, and water, respectively. Transformation from one state to another, such as that from a solid to a liquid, is understood as a qualitative change, which alters an element's essence (Kline, 1985). In general, Aristotle tended to dichotomize qualities, such as contrasting cold versus warm, dry versus moist. The basic principles were seen to be under pressure to combine as a result of an attraction (identified with love) or to separate because of repulsion (connected with hate; Kline, 1985). A central notion for Aristotle was the goal or final resting place towards which a body was inevitably moving.

As noted by Lewin (1931), the psychoanalytic conception of instinctual drives involves the Aristotelian concept of essences seeking the goal of satisfaction—their ultimate fate. Indeed, Freud's basic conception of the drives of love and hate seems to borrow a page from Aristotle's writings. For example, Freud (1905d) emphasizes the quality of the drives, including those attributed to psychosexual stages (defined tautologically in terms of their phenomenology—e.g., the oral stage being a stage in which orality plays a significant role, etc.), with only a minimal degree of quantitative consideration—the latter taking the form of vague notions of drive intensity and the concept of neutralization. The problems in Freudian thinking in respect to qualitative versus quantitative considerations have been noted by Galatzer-Levy (1978).

The Aristotelian nature of Freud's thinking can be taken even further: like Aristotle's four principles, the psychic elements of the oral, anal, phallic, and genital phases are understood to generate certain constellations of behaviour. Just as medieval thought regarded earth, air, fire, and water as eternal reference points, psychoanalytic thought regards the psychic experience of the bodily orifices as a human constant. And such experience is understood in terms of its essential properties—goals assumed to be 'natural' to the psyche–soma at a certain phase of development. Occult systems of thought that were formalized during the nineteenth century, at the same time that psychoanalytic metapsychology was being developed, function in much the same way—astrology with its earth, air, fire, and water signs, the Tarot with its suits of cups, wands, swords, and coins. Like an occult system of thought, psychoanalytic methodology has become a symbol system that serves to anchor a cultural ideology; this may be understandable, but it is not science.

Although ego-psychology and self-psychology have modified classical Freudian theory, the basic conceptual pattern of Freudian metapsychology has not changed, insofar as its Aristotelian character is concerned. The concept of self-realization, for example, and the search for so-called mirroring and idealizing transferences clearly depend on an assumption of essential selfhood striving towards its perfect unfolding in time and space, and either impeded or facilitated towards that end. Similar considerations apply to recent attempts to modify Freudian theory along ego-psychological lines by Weiss and Sampson (1986). These authors believe that

> the analytic patient, unless pressed off course by the analyst, will work persistently during any given period of his analysis in a particular direction, that is, towards changing certain pathogenic beliefs and thereby attaining certain goals. . . . [The] patient's reactions [to the analyst] depend on whether he can use the analyst's responses (including the analyst's interpretations) in his struggle to move towards his immediate goals, or whether he feels impeded by them in his efforts to move toward these goals. [pp. 142–43].

Weiss and Sampson have tested this idea by seeing whether independent clinicians will agree on the essential features of a patient's unconscious plan.

In the same way, just as Aristotelian thought values certain types of motion over others, psychoanalytic thought defines certain types of drives as uncivilized, whereas others, such as the so-called maternal drive, are idealized. Resistances, notwithstanding their functionality, are understood to impede the therapeutic goal, whereas a strong therapeutic alliance is held to facilitate it.

Finally, classification by common material attribute is much more likely in psychoanalytic research than are investigations of process, functions, interactions, and relationships.

One result is the prevalence of either/or polarizations: the patient is either in a state of resistance or is not, shows transference or does not, seeks self-realization or does not, etc. Whatever their value, these considerations are highly qualitative and do not lend themselves to quantification and measurement.

* * *

Both Aristotle and Galileo studied, to a large extent, the same phenomena. But whereas Aristotle was concerned with the final goal of a moving object, Galileo concerned himself with the distance that a body had moved away from its point of origin. This particular theoretical difference had profound ramifications for the development of mechanics and for latter-day forms of modern science. The difference in their thinking is well illustrated by their respective views of the motion of a pendulum (Butterfield, 1957; Kuhn, 1962). For Aristotle, the primary consideration was the stone—his assumption was that the stone's inner nature dictated its perfect end as stasis at the centre of the earth, and that the string was constraining the stone's attempts to move towards that goal. Galileo, on the other hand, dispensed with the assumed purpose of the stone and looked at the process of motion itself: under certain circumstances, a moving body functions in a particular way. Once these circumstances have been determined, the laws generated can be extended to other moving bodies. Where Aristotle saw the stone, Galileo saw the pendulum. In the same way, psychoanalysis concentrates on the presumed striving of the psyche for satisfaction and conflict resolution, rather than on the immediate functions of the patient and therapist under the specific circumstances of the therapeutic interaction. Again, Aristotle was looking at the same elements that Galileo saw, but his preconceptions defined the way he interpreted their meaning.

Aside from the notion of transference (defined as an intrapsychically based projection and distortion of the patient's view of the therapist, unrelated to the behaviour of the latter), perhaps the most compelling reflection of the qualitative/essences attribute of psychoanalytic thinking is in the central role it accords to intrapsychic conflict and unconscious fantasy formation in both pathology and the patient's contribution to the treatment experience. Modifications by Sullivan and object relationship theorists have been addressed to this well-known conception of the patient as a closed (fantasy) system, to the extent that these writers understand the therapist as a participant/observer in the therapeutic interaction. This point of view is clearly one of the developments in psychoanalysis that could foster a shift from Aristotelian to Galilean thinking; however, in all versions it has as yet failed to recognize the influence of the unconscious dimension of the therapeutic interaction and does not give a full account of the contributions of the therapist or analyst.

4. The Aristotelian position concentrated on the object as a distinct unit, separate from its environment; an object was either moving or at rest, and its immediate environment either encouraged or hindered that state. To the extent that force and direction were measured, they were held to reside within the object itself.

We have already noted the psychoanalytic concept of the patient as an isolated system, expressing inner psychic conflict while the analyst observes and comments and interprets. This separation of therapist and patient is complemented in all psychoanalytic theories by the idea that both participants to treatment are separated from the conditions of therapy—the ground rules, physical setting, and other attributes of the environment or situation. Indeed, the prevailing view is that the ground rules of treatment fade into the background and come to the fore only on rare occasions.

Lewin's (1931) model of Galilean thinking provides a good analogy to the actual patient–therapist interaction, as acknowledged by the systems approach that I have been advocating. For Galileo, the ball placed on an incline has a trajectory that arises not only from properties of the object, but also from properties of the plane—in particular, the angle of the plane and the extent to which the plane creates friction and resistance. The prediction of this trajectory, then, requires a full knowledge and appreciation of both the object and its situation, and the two are inseparable. In the psychoanalytic situation, there are *two* interacting objects under the influence of the conditions of treatment. The result is a far more complex system, but a system nonetheless. Aristotelian thinking precludes conceptions of this kind.

5. Aristotelian thinking sacrifices the understanding of processes and dynamics for statics and classifications. Although Aristotelian science possesses a crude theory of dynamics, the idea that each object has an essential nature that predestines its trajectory—and the belief that relationships are linear (simple and one-to-one: Bochner, 1966)—precludes the quantification of interactional processes, the use of linear and non-linear dynamics, and the development of mathematical laws that pertain to such unfoldings. This disdain for quantification and mathematics—or the inability to feel a need for and develop these techniques—is characteristic of psychoanalytic thinking and research as well.

To a degree, these limitations in Aristotelian thinking are characteristic of the time and place of its development, in that the Greek manner of conceptualization circa fourth century BCE was concrete—that is, concepts could be extended to only one level of abstraction. Generalizations were more likely than symbols. Thus, the Greeks could conceive of quantities, but not of abstract real numbers (Bochner, 1966). And the Aristotelian could develop one-step abstractions from reality, but could proceed no further. The culture was unable to develop a mathematics for higher-level abstractions, nor could it relate qualitative change to quantitative shifts. Aristotle was able to conceive of average velocities but entertained no notion of acceleration. Thus, Aristotelian thinking is characterized by the use of statistics, of other types of static measures, and of averages, rather than an investigation of moment-to-moment trajectories and the definition of instantaneous velocity—the realm of the calculus. This is why Aristotelian thought tends towards the conception of general trends and not towards research into individual situations and moment-to-moment transactions (Lewin, 1931). Moreover, Aristotelian thinking is largely discontinuous, whereas Galilean thinking involves lawful continuities.

Here, too, there are many additional parallels to psychoanalytic thinking. Up to this point, psychotherapy research has mainly utilized the statistical approach characteristic of Aristotelian thinking. Even the use of Markovian methods that introduce state transition probabilities in lieu of linear statistics account for an entire session with a single set of numbers. Much information is lost thereby: a single correlation can be accomplished by a large number of possible individual or systemic trajectories. Indeed, Lewin's (1931) warning has gone unheard. Thus, average measures are developed for the therapeutic alliance and other factors in outcome. Statistical correlations are applied to various measures, but a dynamic consideration of changes in variables from moment to moment in the process of the treatment experience—measures that also include quantitatively defined factors related to the therapeutic setting—are strikingly absent from these efforts. The result is an impression of average trends and an absence of mathematical consideration and the possibility of identifying the mathematical laws of the therapeutic—and human—interaction.

Similar attitudes are evident in clinical psychoanalytic thinking. Transference is present until it is supposedly interpreted and modified or removed. So, too, with resistance. Personality tendencies in the patient are relatively constant, and conceived of in isolation, rather than as part of an ongoing and changing process, an evolving interaction between patient and analyst in a particular setting. And despite the efforts noted in chapter three to develop a conception of information processing (Peterfreund, 1971; Rosenblatt & Thickstun, 1977, 1984) and a measure of systems theory (see also Goleman, 1985), psychoanalysis has, as we have seen, clearly lacked a definitive or emerging systems theory. Indeed, the Aristotelian approach is incapable of producing suitable models that lend themselves to theory building and point towards definitive experimentation. In contrast, the Galilean effort fosters such conceptions.

This static, global, impressionistic Aristotelian approach characteristic of clinical psychoanalytic thinking and therapy creates serious limits at the level both of research and of practice. It hampers the generation of abstractions, such as models, integrated theories, and extractions from data, and it keeps interpretation from moving beyond the concrete and the self-evident. The basic Aristotelian philosophy behind psychoanalysis has, in effect, created a paradox, in that the theory values metaphoric, symbolic, or encoded/transformed imagery as indicative of unconscious expressions, but it promotes a listening and formulating process that abstracts from a patient's material meaning that is often constricted, self-evident, and immediately discernible. As a result, the clinical psychoanalytic literature reveals that most psychoanalytic so-called interpretations are simply reorganized restatements of the patient's manifest material or presentations of self-evident implications directly extracted from such material (Langs, 1981a, 1982a, 1985a).

The interactional approach described earlier supports a two-step extraction of meaning: the identification of stimuli for the patient's communications (these stimuli are virtually always constituted by the interventions of the therapist or analyst), along with an understanding of the implications of these stimuli and the recognition of these implications in displaced or disguised form in the patient's responsive material.

In substance, then, readings from patients' manifest material, including their direct implications, tend to be static and impressionistic, whereas interactional decoding tends to be dynamic, in a state of constant change, complex in nature, and highly abstract. The latter appears to be a fundamentally Galilean mode of interpretation, and communicative formulations may well have a sound, empirically validatable foundation.

6. Aristotelian and Galilean sciences are distinctive paradigms (Kuhn, 1962), and, as such, they constitute highly disparate and very different philosophical attitudes: the experimental approaches, the very definition of science, and the laws that are discovered are dramatically different for Aristotelian and Galilean/post-Galilean science. Indeed, the Galilean approach leads to levels of understanding and to the discovery of regularities impossible to arrive at through Aristotelian science (Bochner, 1966). For Aristotle, the fundamental question had to do with *why* a particular phenomenon existed or took place—a search for causes and for qualities of objects. For Galileo, the question was *how*—the detailed search for the phenomenological data that would describe the object or event. Where the Aristotelian would attempt to investigate and explain everything, thereby rendering it difficult to be definitive or specific, Brahe, Kepler, and Galileo were highly selective. Each had a deep and abiding faith in specific and detailed measurement, departing from the Aristotelian approach of general impression, intermittent mea-

surement, and the acceptance of an incomplete and uncertain database—phenomena strongly characteristic of present-day psychoanalytic clinical presentations and, in addition, present-day psychotherapy research.

The Galileans immersed themselves in the details of data. Equally important was Galileo's ability to identify and select basic phenomena for measurement, phenomena through which fundamental laws could be discovered. Intuitively, he chose such variables as space, time, weight, velocity, acceleration, inertia, force, and momentum for intensive consideration. And Galileo chose wisely; he was able to generate specific and universal laws from this intense but selective observational base. And, indeed, these laws were inconceivable for an Aristotelian science, no matter how refined.

For Aristotle, mathematics ended where nature began. For Galileo, as for Plato long before him, nature was organized in terms of mathematical laws, formulae, relationships, and interactions. Qualitative change depended upon quantitative variations. Mathematics was the language of nature and was the means by which its fundamental principles could be embodied. Furthermore, where Aristotelian laws were restricted to particular classes and essences, the Galilean laws were all-embracing, homogeneous, isomorphic, and capable of application across objects, classes, and disciplines.

As noted, Aristotelian investigations concentrated on the search for group characteristics. Lawfulness depended on frequency, and individual differences were considered an affair of chance. According to Lewin (1931), much time was spent trying to determine whether a specific attribute was lawful or fortuitous, because chance events lay outside the concept of law. In substance, the Aristotelian approach strove to identify averages, statistical correlations, and generalizations that would permit a wider latitude of individual exceptions. Methodologically, it would take many such anomalies or exceptions to challenge the law.

In contrast, Galileo's work called for specificity, quantification, and mathematization, and the general validity of laws were such that individual events could be studied carefully for their lawfulness. Furthermore, anomalies or exceptions immediately challenged a particular law and suggested that revision might well be called for. In summary, then, where Aristotle seldom measured, Galileo immersed himself in measurement. Where Aristotle virtually never quantified and applied mathematical formulae, Galileo did so intensely. Where Aristotle tried to study all components of the universe, Galileo wisely selected those variables pertinent to the universal laws of nature, variables that would lend themselves to mathematical abstraction, model-making, and theory testing. The averages of Aristotle became the specific, individual details of the moment, object, and setting of Galileo. These contrasting positions suggest a great deal to those in search of guidelines for modern-day psychoanalytic research.

* * *

Another paradox of the psychoanalytic value system is its deep investment in the investigation of the individual and his or her psychopathology, combined with an approach that seeks out common properties, general impressions, and statistical correlations. Studies (e.g., Alexander & Luborsky, 1986; Marmar et al., 1986) have shown, for example, that, on the average a patient's favourable attitude towards a therapist, formulated as a positive therapeutic alliance, has a favourable influence on the outcome of treatment. In essence, then, such studies show that an absence of hostility and negativism towards a therapist facilitates symptom alleviation. The common-sense aspects of such a finding have been largely overlooked, along with the failure to discover any comparable correlation of favourable outcome with the therapist's positive attitude. Also unexplained is a failure to find any meaningful correlation between the nature of a therapist's interventions and the outcome of treatment. These negative findings are either entirely ignored or subjected to subsidiary explanation through ill-defined conceptions, such as the non-specific influence of a favourable relationship as the major factor in cure. Yet even if more positive findings were reported with this type of approach—and certainly there are many such reports—they can in no way lead to a meaningful understanding of the laws of the therapeutic interaction and the lawful attributes of communicated psychopathology.

Fundamentally lacking from psychoanalytic clinical approaches and from psychotherapeutic research is a consideration of the phenomenology of the therapeutic experience. The comparison between Aristotle and Galileo shows clearly that there can be no unique lawfulness discovered without detailed quantification, temporal consideration of trajectories and systems interacting from moment-to-moment in a particular setting, and extended measurement of truly critical variables.

* * *

Based on this and earlier discussions we may now summarize and state the requirements that must be met by psychoanalysis and psychotherapy for the transition from an Aristotelian to a Galilean and post-Galilean science:

1. A new paradigm will have to be constituted, one that would embody a new philosophical approach to psychoanalytic data, as well as a new scientific view of the psychotherapeutic process.
2. The paradigm will have to be data-driven and founded on the detailed consideration of quantities and time. The approach would have to involve detailed measurement, with a full consideration of moment-to-moment transactions. Creative theorizing would be subjected to rigorous 'experimental' validation.
3. Quantification will lead to the search for mathematical laws that pertain to the therapeutic interaction, psychopathological adaptations, the process of cure, and such.
4. However broad, researchers will have to develop the means whereby they can select those variables that are most pertinent to the lawfulness and regularity that pertain to the processing of emotionally charged information. Such variables will have to relate in meaningful fashion to unconscious processes and lead in turn, to a sound and validatable definition of unconscious transactions.
5. Such research will have to be developed initially through the use of crude models, theories, and system considerations. In turn, the research will lead to refinement of these models in which both continuities and discontinuities, as well as

dynamical interactions, play a major role. Meaningful abstractions from the data and discovery of new laws are to be expected.

6. Finally, we would expect that this entire new constellation of a Galilean science will be capable of discovering the mutual influence of patient, therapist, and setting in terms of its fundamental ramifications. The development of a macroscopic principle of uncertainty, of definitive and probabilistic theories, and, ultimately, of new therapeutic techniques would be expected to follow.

* * *

In its present state, psychoanalysis is pervaded by 'why' questions and attempts at answers that are qualitative and global. Is the patient in a state of transference and if so, why? What are the sources of the patient's resistances? What is the nature of the patient's intrapsychic or interpersonal conflicts? Is the therapeutic alliance flourishing or in difficulty, and what is the nature of the narcissistic component of the transference? The history of science suggests that we should be asking, rather, 'what' and 'how'. What are the components of the communications from patient and therapist? How are they interacting, and how are they influenced by the conditions of treatment? What are the dimensions of these communications, and how do they vary from moment to moment—for example, at five- or ten-second intervals? What is the nature of these trajectories and the definition of their underlying lawfulness? How can information and meaning variables be quantified and measured?

As noted by Kline (1985), Bochner (1966), Kuhn (1962), and others, there is a sense of the miraculous in observing the extent to which the Galilean attempt to measure, quantify, and extract laws produced abstractions, laws, and realizations far beyond anything imaginable within the Aristotelian system. Perhaps most importantly, it was these efforts that introduced the modern age of science. One can only imagine the consequences of such a shift for psychoanalysis.

In the context of these fresh ideas, it seems apt to comment further very briefly on the already noted debate (see chapter one) as to the status of psychoanalysis as a science by such writers as Edleson (1984), Grunbaum (1984), Wallerstein (1986), and

Wallace (1989). A review of this literature indicates that the writers have failed to consider the main point of the present chapter: namely, that psychoanalysis has been created as an Aristotelian theory, and that present-day scientific standards require a Galilean approach—one that is simply not feasible without a paradigm shift and a fundamental change in direction. Some of these writers have called for the introduction of quantification, though by and large they did not distinguish between the correlational/averaging statistical approach of the Aristotelian method and the time-related, quantified moment-to-moment approach of Galileo. The debate remains confined to the Aristotelian domain, where, as I have argued and perhaps shown, no satisfactory resolution and movement towards accepted science can occur. The Galilean approach and its modern-day elaborations, on the other hand, could well provide the means for dismantling the debate since the use of that particular mode of science and its integration into a new psychoanalytic paradigm is likely to give all concerned the science they either do or do not believe at the moment to be possible for the field.

Factors mitigating against psychoanalysis as science

Different aspects of this discussion imply without answering a most interesting question: why is it that psychoanalysis has not made—or at best, is just beginning to make—this much-needed transition to a Galilean science? Is this just a matter of the relatively late arrival of psychoanalysis as an exploratory discipline in the nineteenth century? Is it something inherent to the investigation of human emotions? Or are there signs of additional distinctive factors in this regressive tendency of the field? In concluding this chapter, I will try to offer some tentative answers to these questions.

Psychoanalysis, as I have been suggesting, has been traditionally defined from the standpoint of the practitioner—as a method of treatment based on a particular theory of psychic functioning. This definition has led to the idea that psychoanalysis is as much an art as it is a science, and, as such, the means of its therapeutic efficacy are largely unspecifiable. This state of affairs is roughly equivalent to defining medical science from the standpoint of a surgeon. The surgeon is clearly an artist as well as a technician. But the labours of a surgeon do not constitute the definition of medical science, nor does a ground-breaking surgical technique constitute the whole of medical research.

I want to discuss from a fresh vantage point my belief that psychoanalysis has been slow to develop as a scientific discipline because its theory is so firmly wedded to practice that uncontaminated research is virtually precluded. That is, psychoanalytic research functions almost exclusively—as I have tried to illustrate—as the observation of therapeutic practice from the standpoint of psychoanalytic theory. We may recall, for example, psychoanalytic research projects that are seeking to determine whether a good therapeutic alliance leads to a good therapeutic outcome (Alexander & Luborsky, 1986; Marmar et al., 1986); other studies entail investigations of purported unconscious plans for self-revelation in the patient (Weiss & Sampson, 1986). The theoretical concepts of alliance and plan are assumed from the outset, and certain behaviours on the part of the patient are designated as evidence that these conditions are present in the therapy under observation. Thus, the results of the research merely confirm assumptions already held, without subjecting them either to analysis or to possible refutation.

I have already proposed (see chapter one) that we redefine psychoanalysis very broadly from the standpoint of scientific research—not as a form of therapy or as a means of understanding psychopathology, but as an investigation of how human beings process emotionally charged information and meaning. On that basis we can now pursue some fresh reasons for the lag of psychoanalysis behind the other sciences.

* * *

The present ambiguous status of psychoanalysis—as a social science, as one of the humanities, as an interpretive art, as a method of treatment—is largely an artefact of its origins in the hands of a practising physician. To some extent, it has always been a science—albeit an Aristotelian science—whose shape reflects these very origins. After all, psychoanalysis has always encompassed an investigation of the disorders or dysfunctions of a particular type of information processing and has classified a wide variety of manifest forms of emotional disorder—psychosis, depression, psychosomatic illness, borderline personality, and so forth. Furthermore, one of the goals of psychoanalysis is to develop the specific components of a particular mode of therapy designed to modify or alleviate these dysfunctions.

Psychoanalysis, then, can by no means be a matter of faith and hermeneutics. Other branches of psychology and medicine charged with such endeavours are asked to meet the criteria of scientific methodology—to list them briefly again, those of reliability, validity, measurability, experimentation, replicability of results, extension of understanding, predictability, falsifiability, and the like. There can be no sound reason to make an exception for psychoanalysis. Psychoanalysis as a scientific discipline must be pried apart from the assumptions dictated by its clinical origins. What, then, has made this such a difficult step to accomplish?

* * *

The psychoanalysis that Freud created in 1895 and 1900 through two landmark volumes—*Studies on Hysteria*, written with Josef Breuer, and *The Interpretation of Dreams*—was, despite its Newtonian cast, almost entirely, as I have argued, Aristotelian in its philosophy, methodology, and theorizing. Although it is true that all of the sciences—physics, chemistry, astronomy, and so forth—went through an extended Aristotelian phase before the year AD 1600, psychoanalysis did not crystallize as an historical phenomenon until the beginning of the twentieth century. The basic study of the human mind seems, then, to be far more difficult than the investigation of other aspects of living beings and that of inanimate nature. Ironically, too, the year 1900 was a major transition point in the shift that occurred within Galilean science (especially physics)—from the mechanistic phase, in which Newton's propositions on gravity and motion are central, to a non-mechanistic phase developed through the investigations of thermodynamic systems, irreversible processes, quantum physics, and relativity (Prigogine & Stengers, 1984). Given this limited and relatively recent entry of psychoanalysis into the scientific arena, it would appear that we are only now at the beginning of a shift from Aristotelian to Galilean science—one that is occurring some 350 to 400 years after all or most of the other sciences have made this transition.

Direct resistance to this shift within the field is only part of the reason for the difficulty. I believe there are other reasons—both sociological and psychological. Basing my thoughts on a study of the history of science, the history of psychoanalysis itself, and on my understanding of patients and therapists through the use of the C-scope, I turn now to some of the specific reasons that, I believe, help to account for this particular problem. The sequence in which these factors are presented is more a matter of developing a logical series of arguments than an indication of their relative importance.

1. *The universal dread of the inner mental world*

Science, of course, proceeds by virtue of empirical proof and consensual replicability, and its arena is restricted accordingly to natural phenomena whose material attributes can be observed and measured for change under experimental circumstances. Throughout its young history, Galilean science has concerned itself with non-mental and non-human objects—with forms of 'external' reality—so that even the science of medicine, the study of the human body, was relatively slow to develop as compared with the fields of chemistry, physics, and astronomy. Galen's erroneous ideas about circulation prevailed for over a thousand years before Harvey laid the foundations for an accurate conception of that human system.

The reluctance to tamper with human emotions and 'inner reality' has, of course, been influenced by religious ideas about the body as house to the soul. The science of astronomy proceeded only as the material elements of planetary and stellar existence were gradually pried from their cultural function as ideological reference points. I believe that the science of human cognition has lagged far behind the study of the human body—and the science of emotional cognition even further—because these fields have in some respects absorbed the ideological functions once served by metaphysical systems of thought. That is, psychology in general, and psychoanalysis in particular, functions to support and perpetuate so many of our cultural assumptions and values—moral, religious, civic, gender-related—that we resist prising the basic elements of human behaviour and emotional experience from the cultural ideology that gives them their current meaning.

As such, psychoanalysis has come to serve us, among other things, as the kind of defence against powerful and terrifying existential realities that Freud was trying to penetrate—albeit reluctantly. Genuine investigations of the inner mind, and especially of unconscious mentation, tend ultimately to touch upon our existential beings and on the finiteness of our lives—as opposed to the seemingly infinite or near-infinite existence of the universe and of material reality and its sub-atomic particles. Medicine at least offers the promise of 'cheating' death, overcoming disease, 'adding years' to one's life. But looking inward ultimately brings a scientist face-to-face with his or her own mortality, his or her utter helplessness in the face of the inevitability of death, and with the direct and derivative (unconscious) experience of his or her own death-anxiety issues. Many of our defences are in fact necessary to the health of the psyche; an acceptable 'delusion' of immortality is especially important, and if not used to extreme, is usually personally adaptive. But the need to deny death would also guide the pursuits of individual scientists away from investigations into death-related emotional experience and unconscious meaning; and such motivations have proven costly to science as a whole.

The D–UCS–M system is sensitive to our inescapable mortality; there are both secure and deviant frame sources of these inevitable feelings of persecution which unconsciously move scientists away from the pursuit of emotional truths. The information that we receive in the D–UCS–W system for silent processing and subsequent storage in the D–UCS–M system tends to be enormously anxiety-provoking and even terrifying for other reasons as well: within both ourselves and others there dwell impulses, meanings of behaviours, and fantasies that are awful to behold.

In essence, then, for scientists to look inward, they would have to deal with that which is most terrifying with respect to fundamental human existence, as well as with regard to human, interpersonal interaction. Although there is compensation for such an inner searching, especially as it relates to the unconscious domain, the potential terror of the inner experience evidently far outweighs the rewards of contemplating the enormous creativity and giftedness so revealed. Indeed, it is within the deep unconscious realm that we are at our most creative, inventive, and perceptive; there, too, we are at our highest level of emotionally related intelligence and show our greatest capacity for processing emotionally charged information.

Yet, despite these positive attributes, it can be shown again and again that both patients and therapists are wary of unconscious meaning and invoke many types of defensive and avoidance mechanisms to preclude the derivative (disguised) expression of such meaning and, even more so, its conscious realization. Indeed, it can be argued that psychoanalysis itself is often used as a way of pretending to arrive at such realizations while in actual, validatable fact not doing so at all (Langs, 1982a, 1985a). Thus, it is my belief that not only scientists in general have avoided a proper explanation of the processing of emotionally charged information, but also psychoanalysts themselves. The enormity of this dread of unconscious information helps to explain the evident existence of fundamental errors in the definition of the therapeutic relationship and unconscious expression discussed earlier, as well as the departure of many schools of psychotherapy from any consideration of unconscious processes whatsoever.

One thinks of Marie Curie, an unwitting victim of her own profound discoveries, having exposed herself to the harmful effects of the radiation she was investigating. On a deep unconscious level it appears that scientists dread psychic annihilation in the course of the proper investigation of the unconscious domain. In this connection, it is easy to recognize why it has been difficult for psychoanalysts to develop a proper psychoscope (see chapter two); the revelations are quite unbearable at times.

In all, then, it would seem that contemplating the material universe creates a state of awe and reassures us of immortality by allowing for identification with a seemingly eternal universe (though perhaps not; still, there are billions of years before us) and indestructible subatomic particles, whereas contemplating the inner universe generates an unconscious state of terror, vulnerability, and limitation. This profound existential anxiety has retarded the development of psychoanalysis as a member of the family of sciences. One might say that it is the human mind—not brain—that has an awareness of death.

2. *The origins of psychoanalysis as a mode of therapy, rather than as a fundamental theory*

I have pointed to this theme earlier, but return to it now for a more complete look. In every scientific discipline, there are both theoreticians and engineers. By and large, the theoreticians carry out research by means of carefully designed experiments; the engineers design products and services for mass consumption. Engineering also involves a form of research, of course; but this kind of investigation is not geared towards the discovery of fundamental truths—it is geared towards pragmatics: What are the structural implications of the original research? How can a product be made more economically? To what problems can new discoveries be applied?

There have been many discussions of Freud as scientist or humanist (see, for example, Holt, 1972; Young, 1986). In terms of the dichotomy that I have just introduced, Freud was more engineer than he was theoretician—that is, a humanist far more than a scientist, and clearly a practitioner more than a researcher. Nonetheless, Freud was consciously attempting to create a science, believing that psychoanalysis was a tool by which he could learn about human psychic functioning. This is part of what links psychoanalysis with other Aristotelian sciences—this twofold aspect of the discipline. In its Aristotelian phase, astronomy was linked to astrology, the latter functioning as a way to interpret an individual's place in the cosmic wheel. Freud was not just 'learning' about psychic functioning; he was 'interpreting' an individual's place in civilized development and attempting to use his theories therapeutically. This is a lot like learning to play the piano 'by ear'. You may well become a highly original and creative piano player; but the theories you derive about music from your experience are unlikely to be universally valid.

In considering this aspect of psychoanalysis, let us add here the previously noted realization that until 25 years ago, virtually all the psychoanalysts who contributed to its theory were, like Freud, practitioners. And although there is today a breed of psychotherapy researcher being developed, very few of these men and women are trained both in psychoanalysis and science. Thus, the systematic investigation of therapy from a psychoanalytic vantage point has largely been geared towards pragmatics—how can therapy best serve the client? The type and aims of the research conducted from an engineering standpoint are fundamentally different from those of theoretical experimentation. In fact, a pragmatic, delivery-of-services preoccupation is in many ways antithetical to untainted discovery and scientific development on a fundamental level.

Psychoanalysis, by way of the *Studies on Hysteria* (Freud, 1895d) had its origins as a mode of cure, a technique for treating 'hysterics' (considered now to have been a mixture of patients with schizophrenia, borderline syndromes, and other pathological entities). The theoretical propositions of psychoanalysis, such as Freud's invention of transference (Chertok, 1968; Langs, 1981b), were secondary to clinical description—indeed, transference is virtually a postscript to this work.

The Interpretation of Dreams (Freud, 1900a) is a hybrid that attempts to define the practicalities of dream interpretation while offering a rather impressionistic theory of the human mind—one that is concerned not only with how the mind functions, but with the basic freedom of humankind from enslavement by cultural structures—that freedom ensured by the relentless clamour of the biological drives. The very desire to free a patient's psyche from the partial gratifictions of 'neurotic substitutes' for the sake of a more creative use of 'drive energy' is clearly ideological and patently not geared towards fundamental research. This point of view kept Freud from seeing the interactional nature of any human exchange and from considering the fact that a patient's psyche is not only adapting to the larger cultural standards, but to the immediate environment of the therapeutic setting. Psychoanalysis was known mainly as a debated mode of cure, and it was built only slowly into a theory of emotionally founded human functioning—one that, understandably, was designed mainly to justify the techniques of its growing number of practitioners.

In many ways, this theory has not changed fundamentally from the propositions first developed by Freud—now nearly 100 years ago. The evolutionary trajectory of the field is as yet remarkably flat for a science, though it is not unlike the early phase of other sciences. Without neutral and devoted theoreticians, psychoanalysis has not been able to move substantially beyond the position of its founder and his genius, nor has it been able to progress in its efforts to mature as a scientific endeavour.

When issues of technique and the delivery of services are the overriding concern of a scientific community, resistance to the development of fundamentally new theories is naturally very strong (see Kuhn 1962). Imagine a group of engineers who have designed and are operating a hydro-electric plant, who are then told by a group of theoreticians that the basic design of the plant is significantly flawed. Typically, the first reaction of the plant operators will be indifference; the second reaction will be an attempt to claim that the plant works fine the way it is and that the theoreticians are idealists and don't understand the problems 'in the field'. If nothing else, a practitioner is busy trying to make a living with a therapeutic approach that has attracted and helped clients, established his or her profession, and afforded both pleasure and compensation. Why throw it all out the window because some theorist has decided to count the number of times a therapist says 'uh–huh'?

Unquestionably, those of us who offer the public a highly sophisticated service are defensive about its particulars. A century of experience has fashioned psychoanalysis in a way that not only satisfies clients, but also attends to the needs of its practitioners—both materially and psychologically, including needs with a strong pathological (defensive, inappropriately gratifying, etc.) bent. In addition, the psychoanalyst is competing with other types of treatment modalities. The temporary turmoil in the field that is inevitable with the introduction of a new paradigm would probably lead to a temporary loss of public confidence and a consequent problem in the marketplace. The fundamental structure of the psychoanalytic movement, geared as it is to the delivery of services, strongly mitigates against the entry of psychoanalysis into the family of sciences.

3. *The complexity of the human mind and of human interactions and the existence of dramatic paradoxical— seemingly unpredictable—sequences of behaviour*

A scientist does not generally address a research problem unless he or she has some sense that the work will prove successful, or at least informative. The human psyche is perhaps the most complex, difficult, and elusive system to which science has turned its attention. Small wonder that cognitive scientists agreed to set aside emotional issues in order to develop their field—though the limitations this may well impose upon their work remain to be seen (Gardner 1985). Patterns of human emotional behaviour not only seem chaotic, but appear repeatedly to be anomalous, unpredictable, and/or paradoxical. Even when human behavioural patterns are restricted to the arena of the therapeutic exchange, predictable reference points are difficult to establish. It is commonplace to observe a patient who has been verbally or sometimes physically abused by a psychotherapist continue in treatment or, even more unexpectedly, ask to increase sessions when the abuse intensifies (Langs, 1985a). Traditional psychoanalysis makes assumptions about such a patient's masochism or the patient's need to repeat a pattern of relationship established in childhood. And the Aristotelian nature of our discipline will suggest a statistical correlation, where patients who have admittedly remained in an abusive therapy are asked whether they had abusive parents.

One simply cannot get at the fundamentals of human emotional functioning in this way. Psychoanalytic researchers need to understand the human psychic system *as a system*. The therapist is also a psychic system. Their interaction is complicated and apparently chaotic. But there are laws underlying their exchange nonetheless—laws that can be expressed in mathematical terms and be extended to many forms of behaviour that now seem superficially unrelated or have been classified erroneously according to superficial resemblance.

4. *The difficulties in creating an experimental method for psychoanalysis*

Every science has, of course, its methodological problems and limitations. Nonetheless, the issues that pertain to psychoanalysis in this regard are extraordinary.

First, psychoanalysis shares with disciplines like astronomy an imposed restriction that limits its central area of observation to actual therapeutic experiences. Although secondary laboratory experiments are possible, these can never approximate the natural conditions of patient and therapist interacting within a defined (or ill-defined) therapeutic space. And whereas issues such as the nature of psychopathology and other aspects of human intrapsychic and interpersonal functioning can be examined in the laboratory (as for example, in the extensive subliminal experiments carried out by Silverman, Lachman, and Milich, 1982), these projects tend to be of limited value and seldom generate profound new insights.

There are special problems, however, in attempting to use the natural therapeutic setting for scientifically acceptable research efforts. I do not agree with the position taken by Grunbaum (1984) that clinical psychoanalytic research is relatively unfeasible; nor do I agree with the suggestions of Edelson (1984) and Wallerstein (1986) as to the means by which these difficulties can suitably be resolved. In all instances, as I suggested earlier in this chapter, it seems to me that the discussants debating the issue of psychoanalysis as a science have not recognized the problems inherent in the prevailing Aristotelian approach. None of these writers has suggested that the hallmarks of modern science—such as the quantification of selected variables, the search for mathematical models and laws, etc.—can be applied to and achieved by psychoanalysis; at best, some small degree of success in this direction is sought for. A full science seems inconceivable. And there is a failure to recognize that a quantitative approach is possible if research efforts are concentrated on the communicative therapeutic interaction. While we may not yet have arrived full-force at this point, we have made clear strides in this direction (see chapter seven)—sufficient at the very least to establish the promise that a full dynamic science will be with us someday.

My own collaborative research already demonstrates that quantification of the therapeutic interaction is feasible (chapter seven). I am not unaware, however, of the problems presented by attempting to describe mathematically the vicissitudes of the therapeutic interaction and psychopathology. It has become a popular cliché to say that the experimental observer disturbs the objects observed. Quantum physics has also given us an appreciation of the continuous influence of the setting within which such observations and experiments take place. These effects have contributed to the sub-atomic uncertainty principle, which states, essentially, that measuring a system reveals information along one dimension while rendering inaccessible, for the moment, information along others—that is, that certain coupled attributes can never be precisely measured at the same instant. (Actually, the deep meaning of this principle is that the two attributes simply do not coexist meaningfully at any time.) The relevance of this principle to the macroscopic world is, however, a matter of debate, though a comparable principle on this level has been suggested by Prigogine and Stengers (1984); the relevance of these ideas for the therapeutic interaction is far from defined.

Beyond these constraints, there is the specific confounding factor that an unrecorded psychotherapeutic or psychoanalytic session—the therapeutic interaction in its natural state—cannot be measured or replicated. The very recording of a psychotherapeutic session changes one of the three fundamental components of the therapeutic experience—that is, the nature of the setting. As a result, the total system—patient, therapist, and setting—generates a configuration that is in principle different from the natural therapeutic experience. And although it seems very likely that fundamental general laws can nonetheless be derived from this type of experimental situation—a position regarding which many still hold strong objections—certain exceptions or idiosyncrasies are likely to be overlooked or difficult to identify. It is, then, this exquisite influence of setting and experimentation on patient and therapist that creates special problems for psychoanalysis as a developing science.

To add briefly to my prior comments (see above and chapter one), on an empirical level my own initial investigation of recorded sessions encourages me to believe that the problem is less a matter of the vectors produced by settings in which sessions are tape-recorded than it is a matter of selecting those variables that are most likely to generate psychodynamic laws in a setting whose parameters are fully taken into account. The recorded therapy session/space may well, as I argued earlier, analogize to the cloud chamber and cyclotron—artificial situations used so successfully in physics to explore the subatomic world. Still, the answer to this question will come mainly from hard data of the type that is presented in chapter seven; only sound quantification and efforts at mathematical treatment can settle such issues.

5. *The isolation of psychoanalysis from other sciences and other pertinent problems*

Finally, I wish to allude briefly to several other factors that help to account for the retardation of psychoanalysis as a science. Psychoanalysts have traditionally isolated themselves from universities and from interaction with other scientists, and this attitude prevails in psychoanalytic training institutes, among the staff of psychoanalytic journals, and among the members of larger psychoanalytic organizations. Psychoanalysts have shown little interest in the history of science and have not encouraged training in the area of experimental research. There is no interface between psychoanalytic research and the sciences that proceed by way of mathematical models and controlled experimentation. Were this otherwise, the degree suggested earlier in the science of psychoanalysis, with training in mathematics, physics, computer science, and the scientific method, would long have been in place.

I would suggest that the psychoanalytic movement needs to find a way of developing and nurturing its own theoreticians—psychoanalytic scientists. These individuals will require a knowledge of general psychology, classical psychoanalytic theory and its offshoots, as well as the history of science, physics, astronomy, and, especially, mathematics. Although they must obtain psychoanalytic training and engage in psychoanalytic practice—or insight-oriented psychotherapy—these individuals must also be free to limit their therapeutic endeavours eventually to research patients and to immerse themselves in psychoanalytic data and the search for methods of quantification. The quest for mathematical lawfulness must become a major preoccupation of these theoreticians—and of great concern to the psychoanalytic practitioner as well. Affiliations between psychoanalytic institutes and universities seem necessary to fulfil this goal.

In keeping with points made earlier, psychoanalysis is one of those sciences in which the observer is as much a part of the system under study as any other element. Certainly, the psychoanalytic researcher can remove himself from the immediate therapeutic interaction under investigation. This is, indeed, one way to approach psychoanalytic data so that the assessor of the observations is relatively unbiased. And yet, despite the clear advantages to this type of methodology, we must allow room for a more contaminated approach as well. I believe that both intuition and innovation are served by having the same researcher experience directly the very situation and transactions that he or she hopes to explore. This particular type of effort, which is so likely to prejudice and blind the researcher, is another unique and difficult challenge that psychoanalysis, perhaps more than any other science, must meet in order to grow and develop.

There are, at the present time, two sciences of psychoanalysis, one that has prevailed for the first hundred years, and one that is now in its dawning stages. If psychoanalysts and psychotherapists will recognize the importance of fostering this transition, we will soon be in the midst of a scientific revolution of our own: the applications of new methods, the appearance of new and competing paradigms, and an era of liveliness, not unlike the earliest years with Freud. And, above all, the beneficiary of this inevitable struggle will be not only the science of psychoanalysis, but the psychoanalytic method—its practitioners and their patients.

* * *

From several vantage points I have tried constructively to show the weaknesses of the psychoanalytic position vis-à-vis the scientific community, the difficulties with its existing efforts at establishing a scientific attitude, and the avenues that might guide us towards a major shift in methodology and thinking. It is time now to introduce one possible specific means by which this can be accomplished. To do this, I will present an overview of the results of some initial applications of quantitative methods to real psychotherapy data.

CHAPTER SEVEN

Clinical implications of an interactional science of psychoanalysis

> Psycho-analysis, in my opinion, is incapable of creating a *Weltanschauung* of its own. It does not need one; it is part of science and can adhere to the scientific *Weltanschauung*. This, however, scarcely deserves such a grandiloquent title, for it is not all-comprehensive, it is too incomplete and makes no claim to being self-contained and to the construction of systems. Scientific thought is still very young among human beings; there are too many of the great problems which it has not yet been able to solve. A *Weltanschauung* erected upon science has, apart from its emphasis on the real external world, mainly negative traits, such as submission to the truth and rejection of illusions. Any of our fellow-men who is dissatisfied with this state of things, who calls for more than this for his momentary consolation, may look for it where he can find it. We shall not grudge it him, we cannot help him, but nor can we on his account think differently.
>
> Sigmund Freud, 1933a

We have until now been exploring a mixture of familiar and unfamiliar territories, trying to widen the scope of our clinical thinking and to critique existing efforts to afford a scientific cast for psychoanalysis. We come now to a related yet different issue: the specific delineation of a formal science for the field.

There is an important distinction between a *scientific attitude and spirit*, in which science is respected and seen broadly as a constraint and ideal (witness the quotation from Freud, 1933a, cited at the outset of this chapter), and a *formal science*, in which the requisites of hard science are fully and precisely met. The science that we will present here is both obligated and designed to meet all of the criteria of a formal science that have been discussed earlier—the use of quantification and time-series observations; a foundation in *mathematical* (rather than statistical; see Langs & Badalamenti, 1991b, in press) treatments; the search for fundamental patterns, constraints, and laws; a capacity for prediction; falsifiability; internal consistency and consistency with the results from other sciences; economy of explanation—and the like.

Given these requisites and the present status of psychoanalysis, we would expect a science of this kind to bring us into unfamiliar and uncharted waters—and such, indeed, is the case. Still, we hope that this sense of alien territory will not be off-putting but will, instead, invite your curiosity and mobilize your sense of adventure. For our part, we will try to link these unprecedented techniques to clinical observation as much as possible, though we ask your forbearance since so much of this is new and quite strange to us as well. In particular, we will stress the ways in which this particular science has produced findings that have powerful and unforeseen clinical implications. And we will conclude the chapter with a discussion of how this work can help to establish a scientific definition of countertransference—a specific bridge from the mathematical results to the clinical realm (for a more comprehensive presentation of this work, see Langs & Badalamenti, in press).

* * *

At this juncture, we see no substantial means by which we can foretell the future of a true science for psychoanalysis. In time, there may be many such sciences or but two—one for development and the other for interaction. The science that we will describe is *emotionally interactional* in nature; it pertains to all forms of therapeutic interaction and to charged interactions and monologues from everyday life as well. It is, in substance, a particular form of *the science of emotional cognition*.

In approaching this science, perhaps the first question to answer is how or why the communicative approach and the thinking reflected in this book have produced a science for the field. To answer briefly, we can see at least two broad and intricate sets of reasons for this development:

1. *Dissatisfaction with existing theory and practice*

As discussed earlier, contentment with prevailing concepts and clinical practices deprives a field and its practitioners of the motivation both for change and for science. Given the absence of an accepted and credible scientific methodology, the malcontents tend to adopt or create an alternative theory, rather than formally challenge existing beliefs through systematic means. Those who stay with the dominant theory continue to adhere to existing dogma and to envision and experience the purported realities defined by the prevailing ideology; very little of significance is deeply doubted and called into question. And since psychotherapy is almost entirely populated by practitioners, as long as patients continue to materialize and most *seem* to do well, there are no overbearing unsettled issues and no significant unsolved puzzles—and no substantial science.

The psychoscope used with the communicative approach presented its practitioners and theorists with a wealth of observations that did not appear to fit with generally accepted conceptions. In addition, in the clinical realm, many commonly used practices and interventions were found to be both negatively perceived unconsciously by the patients towards whom they were directed and to cause unrecognized harm.

More importantly, the approach itself was confronted with its own inexplicable anomalies. Among these, the most serious was the finding that many patients who unconsciously validated secure-frame interventions by their therapists nonetheless fled the safety and sound holding of that setting because of overwhelming death anxiety and other unconscious issues that could not be resolved with the best interpretations and frame-management responses available.

The communicative approach was also under considerable pressure to defend its postulates and clinical precepts to its many sceptics. There was, as a result, a strong need to find irrefutable evidence and support for its tenets and techniques. Overall, then, there was considerable agitation from both within and outside the approach. Something was desperately needed to resolve the tensions this caused and to establish the validity of the communicative position.

In turning to science for this balm, another fortuitous ingredient played a crucial role: a deep and abiding faith in the resiliency and soundness of communicative ideas. This faith was not explicitly articulated but was a silent force that shaped the quest for validation. Since widening the scope of clinical observation and extending clinical theory had not brought forth a solution to these dilemmas, stronger medicine was needed. Despite a lack of definition, science seemed to promise the cure.

2. *A theory that lent itself well to the creation of a formal science*

Though this was not part of a deliberate plan, the communicative approach proves to be far more compatible with and capable of providing a basis for a science of psychoanalysis than the classical approach and its many variants. The latter concentrates on the mind of the patient, affords interaction a secondary role, and stresses the vicissitudes of meaning and psychodynamics. Given that quantification requires scales on which a single dimension can be measured through continuous observations from one moment to the next, working scientifically with the vagaries of subjective reports or with the vicissitudes of different types of meaning is difficult to envision, if not impossible to achieve.

The same obstacles arise in trying to use concepts like transference, resistance, therapeutic alliance, and the like as a basis both for quantification and for moment-to-moment measurement. The absence of consistent interactional and systemic thinking also places classical theorists in a poor position to generate a formal science, since ultimately the patient/therapist system must be fully investigated and taken into consideration in order to account scientifically for the deep and compelling experiences of either party to the dialogue. Since the immediate interaction with the therapist is a vital part of the observational field on which a science can and must be founded, neglecting or downplaying this component all but precludes the movement towards formal science. Without a full consideration of the bilateral interaction between patient and therapist, we are in a position similar to a chemist who mixes two chemicals together and tries to account for the results through a study of one of the reagents alone.

In contrast, the communicative approach evolved in a way that coincidentally offered a compelling foundation for a possible science. For example, the viewpoint that the patient/therapist system is the fundamental unit of psychotherapy inevitably leads to an insistence that both parties to therapy be an ever-present part of the observational field. Similarly, the interactional grounding of the approach demands that the P/T system be in focus at all times and also asks that time sequences be fully honoured and moment-to-moment observations to be taken throughout a session; the creation of time-series data is a *sine qua non* for a formal science.

Still, all of this would have come to nought, were it not for the fact that the communicative approach focuses on *communication itself.* Communication can be recorded and measured. But beyond that salutary aspect of the situation, there is the communicative tenet that the vicissitudes of unconscious communication—the use of encoded (symbolic) and unencoded (non-symbolic) images and messages—are of overriding importance within all emotionally charged dialogues. This principle directed communicatively founded research towards efforts to identify quantifiable variables that cogently represent these vicissitudes—a choice that is inconceivable with present mainline psychoanalytic thinking. Since these shifts are readily quantified and are ever-present (we are always either encoding or not encoding), second-by-second measurement is possible.

The natural interests of the communicative approach were therefore highly congenial to the requirements of science.

While some of these ideas and realizations were evident to us during the early stages of our quest, many of these insights became clear only in retrospect. As the work unfolded, we simply allowed communicative theory and our informed hunches to guide us, and, remarkably enough (to us, at least), a science began to emerge. Though we knew not exactly where we were heading when we started out, nor what we would find when we got there, we are today, some three years after this research was initiated, in a position to present some key results that come together as a science of human emotional communication—of the human mind, if you will.

Before we delve into this science, it is well to offer some final perspectives. As we indicated, we are convinced that the work we have carried forth meets the criteria of scientific rigour discussed in chapter six. This in itself is likely to be the source of considerable anxiety among both psychotherapy researchers, for whom such work is rather unprecedented, and practising therapists, for whom the fear of being strictly measured is likely, at first, to be seen as more threatening than promising.

There is also little to prepare the reader for these results, despite earlier efforts that in small ways nudged the field towards science by means of process research and attempts to use advanced statistical techniques, Markovian (probabilistic) models, and similar methods of exploring psychotherapy transactions (Edelson, 1984, 1989; Greenberg & Pinsof, 1986). In addition to these empirical studies, there have been a handful of writers who have advocated the use of mathematical methods borrowed from physics and other material sciences in researching psychotherapy data; however, these writings lacked any grounding in real data and tended to be too abstract and uncertain to be useful here (see Langs, 1988c, Langs & Badalamenti, 1991b, in press).

We are, then, about to enter a quite unfamiliar domain, a realm we call *deeper nature*—aspects of human experience that lie beyond both conscious and unconscious experience and communication. It is a realm that is accessible only through the *lens of mathematical models*—a *mathoscope*, if you will. Yet it is a realm that deeply informs the process of psychotherapy and has the potential to offer entirely new perspectives and insights into the therapeutic interaction in particular, and human emotional communication in general.

An analogy may help to prepare the way. We can all see an apple fall from a tree, but none of us can see the laws of gravity; these laws can be articulated only through the mathematical treatment of time-series data that quantify the velocity-to-time relation of the falling missile. The laws that govern the deeper nature of human communication are similarly invisible. But to confound matters further, their observed effects are more difficult to detect than is the fall of an apple—trends in human communication are often far from evident and quite convoluted.

Still another kind of preparatory act will help one to enter this domain with an open mind. To do so, one must be prepared to surrender the highly defensive myth that the human mind and its expression through communication lie beyond the laws of nature. One must also be ready to give up the all too self-serving belief that psychotherapy is an elusive, highly individual and distinctive experience that defies measurement and lawfulness—in essence, formal science. After all, we ourselves are unique individuals in many ways, but this does not mean that there are no universal laws that we unwittingly obey. Our bodies and brains would be a jumble, were it not for the physical laws that govern the chemistry and physiology of human existence.

So, in the spirit of informed adventure, with faith that all of us are in countless ways governed in every sphere of our lives and behaviour by the laws of nature—whatever our additional individuality—we now present some high points of the work that we have done.

The database

This chapter is focused on six psychotherapy consultation sessions through which we first developed our methodology, though it should be understood that our methods have been applied successfully to ten additional consultation sessions, two ongoing psychotherapy contacts (three sessions from one, and all six sessions of another), three emotionally charged dialogues outside therapy, and two emotional monologues. The basic findings that we describe have held up across cases that have been approached through a wide variety of therapeutic modalities (Langs et al., 1992a).

Despite these successes, there are, of course, many issues one could take with the measures and methods we used and the results we obtained—and their implications. However, dealing with these technicalities would clutter this presentation beyond readability; they must, then, be by-passed here in favour of stressing the positive findings and clinical pertinence of this work (for a full discussion, see Langs & Badalamenti, in press).

* * *

The sample on which we concentrate involves two women patients in their late forties, both diagnosed as having characterological disturbances, each of whom saw three well-known psychoanalysts in consultation. Each woman was in a stalemated psychotherapy and was seeking help to resolve the problem. They had agreed to be interviewed and videotaped in the hope that the analyst–interviewer might assist them in resolving the impasse. The analysts were asked to try to do just that and to conduct the consultation in a way that would reflect their usual way of working with patients. All concerned were told that the taped sessions would be shown to professional audiences as part of a series of seminars on how analysts work.

There were one female and five male analysts. Patient A saw the woman analyst first, myself second (by request from the analysts, we cannot identify the others), and a male self-psychologist third; the interviews were all separated by 6 months. Patient B saw the man we call the international interpersonalist first, the American interpersonalist second (both on the same day), and the man we identify as the unstable analyst last—some six months later. Aside from my communicative orientation and the self-psychologists' Kohutian commitment, all of the analysts were oriented towards object relations theory, classical interactional concepts, and interpersonal effects; all except myself were focused entirely on conflicts within and issues of the patient.

The transcribed dialogues were reliably scored (Bryant, 1990) for speaker duration (in sequence) and five dimensions selected to represent critical aspects of these communicative exchanges. Four of the items were chosen to reflect different aspects of the vicissitudes of unconscious or encoded expression, while the fifth (continuity; see below) was selected to represent a systemic factor. Together, they were treated as a *five-dimensional information particle (IP)* that travels within the confines of a 5-cube (the location of the IP at any moment in time—i.e., in the course of a session—is defined by five values, or addresses). It is these five dimensions that have proven to be the basis for our science of emotional cognition; they have carried us to a deeper level of nature, where lawfulness seems to prevail (Rapp et al., 1991).

The five dimensions, scored for every two lines (8–10 seconds) of transcribed dialogue, are:

1. *Newness of theme (NT)* [the scale ranges from 0 (no new theme) to 1–2 (minor new themes) to 3–4 (major new themes)].
2. *Degree of narration and imagery versus the use of intellectualization and speculation (NI)* [the scale ranges from 0 (brief utterances) to 1–2 (intellectualizations) to 3–5 (increasingly strong narratives or vivid images)].
3. *Positive cast or tone of image (PosT)* [the scale ranges from 0 (no positive quality) to 1–3 (increasingly strong gratifying, helpful, positive images)].
4. *Negative cast or tone of image (NegT)* [The scale ranges from 0 (no negative quality) to 1–3 (increasingly hurtful, frustrating, negative images)].
5. *Continuity of dialogue (CTY)* the scale ranges form 0 (Unscorable brief utterance) to 1–2 (breaks in the flow of the dialogue) to 3 (the present comment follows logically from the prior comment) to 4 (a rigid and exact repetition of the prior comment)].

The first four dimensions carry the weight of most of our findings. This suggests that the psychodynamics of human communication are notably more powerful than system dynamics and, by implication, that the vicissitudes of how and when we convey unconscious meaning are a strong factor in human expression. As other variables are explored, the validity of these propositions can be further tested. For now, there is much to support these contentions (see below).

As we move towards presenting our results, it is well to obtain a clear sense of the central phenomenon that we are investigating. Indeed, it takes some effort to become accustomed to the 5-dimensional vector and the implications of its vicissitudes. We are, for example, *not* studying meaning per se, *nor* responses to therapists' interventions. We *are* on the other hand, tracing *the vicissitudes of non-conscious choices of communicative vehicle or configuration*—combinations of the five scores—as they unfold over the course of a session.

The interactional science that we created, then, was founded on the investigation of the vicissitudes of an IP that, as we later learned, rotates within a 5-cube, moving towards new communicative configurations (new combinations of the five scores—*new states*) even as it seeks to return to configurations already used—*prior states*. Uniqueness and redundancy in *choice of communicative vehicle* is at the heart of this new science. In time, we found that one of the driving psychological forces for this activity involves unending swings from encoded (derivative or symbolic) to unencoded (non-derivative or non-symbolic) expression.

In this context, note should be made that we did garner some support for the *validity* of our contention that these four dimensions (NT, NI, PosT, and NegT) do indeed reflect the vicissitudes of unconscious expression. We ran correlations for the interviews with both patients between our NT and NI measures and an independently derived index of unconscious expression called *Referential Activity* (Bucci, 1984; Langs et al., submitted). There was significant agreement between the two measures for all three consultations.

With all of this in mind, let us turn now to the models and methods we used, and the results that we obtained.

Statistical approaches

We began with *statistical models* to get a 'feel' for the data and the results it could generate. These models summarize with a single score, such as an average, an entire, complex trajectory; they reveal trends and differences between subjects and P/T systems, but no laws or underlying mechanisms. They cannot form the basis for a formal science, but nonetheless they are a valuable first step (Langs & Badalamenti, 1992).

To cite some interesting results, we found that the extent to which a therapist was silent during a session correlates positively with levels of NT and NI (Langs et al., submitted)—that is, the more silent a therapist, the more a patient communicates through encoded messages. This result supports communicative theory, which states that silent listening tends to facilitate encoded or derivative expression. On the other hand, the finding runs counter to classical analytic thinking, which proposes that questions and clarifications enhance unconscious expression (Boesky, 1989).

At issue is the clinical definition of unconscious communication. The communicative approach, as we saw earlier, stresses derivative expressions, while classical thinking emphasizes the implications of manifest contents. Still, as just noted, there is research support for the validity of the communicative formulation. Nonetheless, this dispute may serve as warning that competing paradigms can produce clinical evidence garnered with scientific spirit—though not strict science—that support diametrically opposed positions. Statistical findings related to specific measurements can generate evidence for one proposition compared to the other, but only a formal science with properly designed experiments and mathematical techniques can provide irrefutable evidence for one idea versus another.

A complementary statistical study supported the importance of silence for therapists who wish to enhance a patient's use of unconscious expressions. We found that the levels of NT and NI were consistently *reduced* after a therapist intervened in these consultations. This, too, suggests that therapists' interventions reduce rather than enhance unconscious expression.

One explanation for these findings involves the traumatic aspects of recorded sessions of this kind. There is clinical evidence that the derivative images from these patients are incisively and perceptively critical and attacking of the therapist—for the recording itself, as well as his or her errant interventions. We can therefore speculate that these therapists, quite unconsciously, were strongly motivated to interrupt the flow of such material by becoming active and probing the patient directly—a way of closing off these unconsciously hurtful derivatives. Our study of the specific instabilities of the speaker duration sequence in the psychotherapy with the HIV-positive man lent strong support for this hypothesis.

* * *

Another statistical study revealed unexpected evidence that therapist needs and interests—and not those of these patients—dominated these consultations. We studied the vicissitudes of gender themes—parenting, love relationships, sexuality, family, and the like—from Patient B in her three consultations and found significant differences in the extent to which this kind of material appeared in each session. The consultation with the international interpersonalist was almost devoid of gender material, that with the American interpersonalist was overloaded with family gender material, and, finally, with the unstable analyst, there was a plethora of sexual material and allusions to intimacy and dating. The influence of the therapist on these statistically significant results was quite evident in reviewing the protocols. Later studies supported and amplified this theory contradicting finding—the fact that these were consultation sessions not withstanding (Langs et al., 1992b).

We also had the privilege of carrying out the first measure of informational complexity, carried out with psychotherapy data. We used a Kolmogorov type of measure (Kolmogorov, 1965; Jimenez-Montano, 1984); the program was borrowed from geneticists who were studying DNA sequences. The program determines the minimum number of symbols needed to characterize a given sequence of numbers—here, the sequence of gender theme scores. The results were straightforward and rather simplistic: the session with the American interpersonalist produced the least complex sequence of gender material scores for the patient (they were repeatedly about family issues), while that with the unstable analyst produced the most complex configuration.

Statistics may at times produce unexpected results, but often the outcome merely provides systematic evidence for results whose nature and implications are or become self-evident. These findings may extend our thinking in small ways and may be reassuring for a particular theory, but they seldom disturb or dislodge a theory or lead to notable revisions in prevailing clinical thinking (Strupp & Bergin, 1969).

* * *

In straightforward fashion, these results support the notion that there is indeed a strong interactional influence between therapists and their patients during psychotherapy sessions. The findings also speak for systemic thinking in that each P/T system had its own characteristics, even though one party was the same for each set of three consultations. And, as noted, communicative thinking is far more compatible with these findings than prevailing classical thought and its variants.

An interesting hypothesis suggested itself from these early results. It may well be that some therapists create sessions low in unconscious expression—and perhaps low in complexity as well (there was too little data to investigate that particular correlation). In contrast, other therapists allow for considerable expression of unconscious meaning, perhaps with considerable complexity as well. Each mode could bring relief to a patient suffering from an emotional disturbance: the first by blocking out disturbing encoded images and maintaining a fairly simple interaction; the second by allowing for rich encoded expression and considerable complexity. While the first approach would require little in the way of interactional interpretations, the second, having opened up derivative meaning, would in all likelihood need sound interactional interpretations to be effective.

Another statistical technique we applied involved a *linear regression analysis* that was used to study the intercorrelation between our six scored items within the communications of a given speaker, and between speakers as well. The most notable finding was that my consultation with patient A was the only interview in which interpersonal effects were seen. This foreshadowed a number of later results that revealed the relative interactional power of the communicative approach in a number of spheres.

* * *

Perhaps the most elaborate statistical technique we applied involved a study of lagged relationships through the use of a ten-minute window within which we could measure cross-correlational effects between the scores on our five main dimensions for the patients and their therapists. This study could answer questions such as: was there any regular or consistent change (at a level of statistical significance) in the *therapist's* new theme (or any other item) scores at any time interval up to five minutes *before* a *patient's* narrative imagery (or any other item) increased (or decreased). The complementary question is: *after* the *patient's* narrative imagery (or any other item) scores increased (or decreased), was there any consistent change in the *therapist's* new theme (or any other item) scores in the *following* five minutes?

One can see, then, that the method is sensitive to lagged statistical effects by and on the therapist five minutes before and after a given score change for the patient; the same exploration can be applied to the therapist. Effects in both directions—patient to therapist, and the reverse—can be determined.

The results for the six consultations were quite varied. We used the number of seconds of significant correlational effect as a *measure of deep linear influence*. Given that the maximum total possible effect per case for all possible cross-correlations was 75,000 seconds, the intensity of this deep interaction across cases was rather small. We found that there was no significant deep lagged effect at all in the consultation with the international interpersonalist, while the sessions with the self-psychologist and the unstable analyst each showed a slim 30 seconds of influence. The woman analyst, however, showed 150 seconds of effect, most of it related to the tone of the narratives. The American interpersonalist, on the other hand, showed 250 seconds of influence, while my consultation showed 2,250 seconds of significant lagged cross-correlational results (Langs et al., 1991).

All of these effects were in both directions—patient towards therapist and therapist towards patient. They provide sample evidence that on the level of deep nature, especially as it relates to the vicissitudes of unconscious communication between patient and therapist, therapists vary greatly in the extent to which they affect patients and are themselves responsive in some deep way to their patients' communicative changes as well. The strongest deep influence by far was found in my interview in which I used—more-or-less—communicative principles of listening and intervening. The weakest effects were seen with the international interpersonalist, who conducted a highly intellectualized consultation, and with the self-psychologist, whose use of empathy and related interventions was evidently quite detached from deeper sensitivities.

Though this work is scientific in spirit only and tells us nothing of underlying mechanisms, it does facilitate a sense of how dimensions of the therapeutic interaction can be strictly measured and yield unexpected results that begin to question existing clinical precepts and theory. While this pilot study offers only preliminary impressions, we certainly did not expect an interaction between a psychoanalyst and his patient to be devoid of this kind of deeper communicative effect. Nor did we anticipate the extensive interactional influence between my patient and myself, a finding well beyond anything I—or anyone else—experienced subjectively or observed in my patient.

At the very least, these results point to vast aspects of the therapeutic experience of which we have not only little or no theory, but also little or no sense of their existence. The findings also call into question various approaches to therapists' work with patients; low degrees of influence raise unanticipated questions about how these particular analysts conducted their consultations with their patients. And once sensitive measures of outcome are available, we will be able to move beyond the establishment of a basic science for the field and indications of issues with theory and practice into definitive issues of clinical effects.

We can already see that there is evidence here that many clinical beliefs shared by the practitioners of psychotherapy will not hold up under statistical and mathematical scrutiny. It may well be that this kind of work will soon put us on the threshold of an entirely new view of the therapeutic process and its means of cure. Perhaps, too, new and more effective modes of therapy will materialize through this work.

Stochastic models

We move next to a series of *stochastic studies*, which generate mathematical equations that account for both deterministic and random factors in a series of observations. When successful, stochastic models involve relatively simple equations that predict in retrospect (account for) the trajectory of time-series values. We used the Box–Jenkins models (Box & Jenkins, 1976; Box & Tiao, 1975) as a first approach; these models have been used to characterize mathematically the behaviour of such diverse phenomena as the vicissitudes of volcanic activity, forest yield, sunspot activity, the vicissitudes of chemical viscosities, and economic indicators. Successful application of these models with psychotherapy data would bring the field into the family of sciences—at least in a preliminary way—and into line with other aspects of nature.

There are two major components to the Box–Jenkins equations that we used with our data. The first of these is an *auto-regressive component or parameter*, which reflects the influence of *the prior state of the system on the present state*. For speaker duration data, auto-regression implies that the present speaker was the speaker at the prior second in the dialogue and is likely still to be speaking the next second into the session. Clearly, a high auto-regressive parameter speaks for a relatively stable (inertial) system. Indeed, the model is systemic in nature because it characterizes the *switching of the speaker role*, which is, of course, a systemic attribute stemming from characteristics within each party related to listening, interrupting, and speaking as they are interpersonally affected by the entire communicative interchange.

The second element in the model is a *shock value*, a measure of a random shock that perturbs the system and whose nature must be determined through other studies. High levels of shock destabilize the P/T system, and in some cases the effects may be so extreme that no model can be fitted to the data (in our studies, this occurred in only one of the psychotherapy situations—the outpatient therapy with the HIV-positive man, with whom a second-level model was fitted). If the influence of these shocks moves past a single time increment, then it introduces a lagged relation that is referred to as *moving average* (Badalamenti & Langs, 1991, 1992).

On inspection, the usual speaker duration data series appeared to wander about and to be without evident pattern. But the Box–Jenkins models consistently indicated that in these consultations there was a strong underlying auto-regressive structure in all of the P/T systems we studied. There was in each case a significant fit between a first-order auto-regressive Box–Jenkins model and the speaker duration data; in substance of all of these P/T systems showed considerable inertia with respect to the switching of speaker roles—i.e., strong prior state sensitivity. Systemic stability was in evidence, and in general, this deep stability prevailed on the level of deeper nature, despite considerable back-and-forth dialogue on the surface.

Within the general consistency of these findings, there were individual differences as well. In the main, the greatest degree of inertia was seen in my consultation and the session with the American interpersonalist, the least with the unstable analyst and the woman analyst. In general, then, high levels of speaker duration inertia were associated with high indices of linear influence as measured by the cross-correlations described above.

* * *

It was reassuring and affirming to realize that internal consistencies were surfacing in these studies. The outcome of these various investigations enabled us to begin to develop *deeper nature profiles* of these patients, therapists, and P/T systems. The resultant images began to present an entirely unprecedented picture of these psychotherapists and their techniques. As results accumulate, pressure for reformulation and revised practice should mount. The goal is both to create a new science and to find incontrovertible ways of identifying flawed techniques and their best replacements.

We were able to develop another view of the switching of the speaker role by making histograms that counted the number of utterances of a given length (e.g., one second, two, three, etc.); in all cases, short utterances dominated the graph. Carried forward separately for each patient and therapist in this sample, the method yielded *rate constants* that characterize a speaker's tendency to maintain the speaker role and his or her inclination to interrupt the other speaker when that party is talking (Langs & Badalamenti, 1990).

The histograms were consistently fit by a negative exponential. This specific configuration brought these results into another family of processes and entities found in nature—the *Poisson processes*. Processes like component failures in large systems and the rate of radioactive decay belong to this group. In addition to this basic result, we found that the curves for each patient–therapist pair tended to clone each other. In a way, this is a rather remarkable result, since the histograms summarize the speaker duration data for an entire consultation.

Individual differences were also in evidence. The American interpersonalist and I were the least interrupting therapists (my scores were adjusted for repetitive uh-huhs), while the woman analyst and the unstable analyst were the most frequent interrupters of the patient. Indeed, the rate constants indicated that the woman analyst was so active that she assumed the role of the primary speaker, and the patient found it necessary to interrupt her to get a word in edgewise. Strange indeed are the revelations of measurement; again—they contrast greatly with clinical impressions and mythology.

* * *

One final effort we made with the speaker duration data is of some clinical import (Badalamenti & Langs, 1991). Using these results alone (and blind to identifying markers), one of us (Badalamenti) attempted to identify the four analysts who had each seen two patients in consultation. He was successful in three of the four cases—a statistically significant result. (The erroneous choice was of an analyst whose speaker duration profile resembled the missed analyst in many ways.) But when the attempt was made to identify the three patients who were interviewed more than once (two were actually seen by three different analysts), none of the correct pairings was made. This failure was worse than expected by chance—a significantly negative result.

Here too, then, therapist dominance is in evidence: the therapists' speaker role tendencies are identifiable across interviews, but the comparable attributes of the patient are not; apparently they are subverted to the therapists' propensities. Even though these are consultation sessions, we would not, given psychoanalytic writings, have expected this level of therapist control in these sessions. Results of this kind indicate that there are undoubtedly many clinical myths that we have been perpetuating that fall far short of actual practice. We need to re-examine our clinical work to see if, even at the level of clinical experience, we can detect other principles that have been advocated and seemingly accepted but not truly explicated. Beyond these inconsistencies lie many actual practices that are not recognized as detrimental in existing theory and use, yet are nonetheless actually harmful to sound therapeutic progress as revealed through interactional scientific research. In this way, science can serve to identify clinical delusions and mispractices and to provoke healthy scepticism and a fresh sense of humility and openness in those clinicians ready to heed these warnings.

* * *

As far as these results are concerned, they speak directly to those therapists who are indeed interested in allowing the patient a maximal degree of unconscious expression, in the belief that this engenders the most insightful and effective form of cure. They indicate that relative silence is the best means of accomplishing this goal—silence that is maintained until the patient has conveyed sufficient material for a clear interactional interpretation or framework management response (this, of course, mixes research findings with likely implications—the latter open to scientific validation). The findings also help to explain the pervasive use of active interventions in all forms of therapy—apparently, psychoanalysis included; they are, in part, a means of reducing a patient's unconscious expressions. The deep and universal dread of unconscious meaning seems unwittingly to have been a powerful force in shaping how therapy is conducted.

Mathematical models drawn from physics

We began our use of models from physics with a measurement of *the power spectral density function (PSD)* for each of the five dimensions of communication and the speaker duration data. The model was taken from the study of electrical thermodynamics and the power that is carried by direct currents (*the DC component*) and by each cycle of an alternating current (*the AC component*). Thus, the PSD function is a measure of *cyclical and non-cyclical (DC) power for an entire session*. Technically, the *variance* or degree of variability of the scores for a given item is identical to its total power across frequencies. Measured separately for patient and therapist (though results for each P/T system can be culled from these separate findings), these PSD values gave us a first measure of the power or strength of six aspects of communication and, in sum, of each therapy session we investigated.

The power under consideration is tied to harmonic components or cyclicity—to repetitive sequences of scores. Since the study is centred on the four measures of unconscious expression—NT, NI, PosT, and NegT—we are dealing primarily with a form of power that is in some way related to the vicissitudes of unconscious communication; the greater the power, the stronger the unconscious component in what the patient and/or therapist has communicated.

For insight psychotherapy, we intuitively proposed in advance of the study that high levels of cyclical power would be optimal for these insight-oriented interviews. More broadly, this was a first attempt to answer the question of what types of therapists and therapeutic interactions actually produce measurably strong and weak dialogues and sessions, and which dimensions of communicated material are the strongest and weakest. These are some of the new questions and issues of clinical import that are raised by and through the research itself (Langs & Badalamenti, in press).

* * *

The results were, again, in keeping with communicative theory. Across cases, the most powerful items were degree of narration, newness of theme, and negative tone—all strong aspects of the vicissitudes of unconscious expression. As for the consultations themselves, the most powerful sessions once again belonged to myself and the American interpersonalist, while the weakest involved the woman analyst and the international interpersonalist.

We can see, then, that the results from this study, carried out *in the frequency domain*, bear a relationship to studies mentioned earlier in the *time domain*—the lagged cross-correlation study of linear influence and the investigation of the switching of the speaker role (both are time-dependent)—that is, the analysts whose interviews were most strongly auto-regressive and stable, and who allowed the patient the greatest opportunity for communicative expression, generated the sessions with the greatest degree of cyclical power in our sample. In addition, high levels of cyclical power were associated with a strong degree of cross-correlational linear influence—both with regard to the specific dimensions that showed the interpersonal effects and the sessions in which these effects were the strongest (Badalamenti & Ferguson, 1991).

Once discovered, these results, generated through rather different mathematical models, seem to interdigitate with considerable logic. Therapist silence evidently promotes derivative expressions from patients, which, in turn, fosters deep interpersonal influence and high levels of cyclical power. Driven by an abundance of derivative (encoded) material, these are powerful sessions both in terms of unconscious expression and their delineation by means of strictly defined deep measures and mathematical models.

It appears, then, that it is quite feasible to identify and develop specific techniques designed to enhance a patient's use of encoded material—narratives that embody unconscious expressions that then become available for (interactional) interpretation. Contrariwise, techniques that diminish the extent to which unconscious messages are conveyed can also be identified and correctly understood for their effects.

* * *

Finally, two striking general findings emerged from this study. First, we were surprised to discover that for every item we measured, *peak power was always in the DC component*; in fact, there were no significant indications of high levels of power for any cyclical component from any of these patients or therapists. This indicates again that well beneath the rather chaotic manifest contents or surface of a therapeutic dialogue, where meaningful prediction is virtually impossible, and below the more ordered level of unconscious communication and expression, there is a deep and abiding *stability* to therapeutic—and all emotional—dialogues (DC power speaks for steadiness and stability). Emotional experience and even moments of interpersonal turmoil evidently unfold in the context of a deeply stable foundation.

The second finding is that there were no signs of cyclical coherence between these patients and therapists. That is, in the frequency domain, there were no harmonic or cyclical rhythms that were deeply shared by these dyads. The cycles of the patient and therapist failed to co-ordinate or match in any way—a finding that ran counter to later results in the time domain, where complementary rhythmicity was in evidence.

Work, force, and the geometry of human communication

Using strict mathematical definitions, we have been able to track the motion of the 5-dimensional IP within the 5-cube in which it lives. Again to our surprise, in all cases—and these investigations were carried out separately for the patient and therapist—the data points or scores for the 5-vector fell consistently within an ellipsoid shell that is shaped like a longitudinal slice through a watermelon rind. Within this constraint, individual differences were once again in evidence in the exact location of the ellipsoid, the angle at which it lies, and its foci.

It took extensive exploration and considerable time before some of the clinical implications of these exquisite mathematical results began to come through. To get there, we applied a powerful theorem from the calculus—Stoke's theorem—which relates the motion of a fluid on its surface to its internal motion. The theorem revealed that the activity of the IP is powerfully rotational. Specifically, as noted earlier, it could be shown that in all cases the IP tends to rotate to new states (new communicative configurations) while tending also to return to prior states (to configurations of the 5-vector that have been utilized previously). The motion to new states diminishes as the session moves along, but it never ceases entirely.

This activity has a number of important clinical ramifications and has proven to be critical to most of the results we obtained through the models that we took from physics (see below). The key phenomenon pertains, as we said, *to the selection, automatically and unwittingly, of vehicles with which human beings express themselves emotionally*—i.e., make use of particular combinations of newness of theme, degree of narration, positive and negative tone, and continuity. At bottom, the key driving force clinically appears to be the movement from derivative (symbolic) to non-derivative (non-symbolic) space in an unending circular fashion.

* * *

There is evidence, too, that this rotation is strongly driven by needs within the speaker, and that it is also promoted by the listener, who, in general, does not tolerate extended encoded expressions. These tendencies are therefore a fundamental property of human communication (and of the human mind) and of P/T systems as well. Thus, this trend is seen in monologues where there is no listener to interact with, no one who can affect the speaker's immediate communications (we omit for the moment any consideration of the expected and/or fantasied audience for the monologue). The interpersonal-systemic element to this finding is evidenced in the reduction of encoded expressions following interventions by therapists. It is also supported by the finding that individuals show higher levels of derivative expression in emotional monologues compared to the emotionally charged dialogues in which they participate.

There appears, then, to be a universal tendency to diminish derivative expression in others, to drive them out of derivative space soon after they enter it. This indicates that humans have a limited tolerance for unconscious expression—though, interestingly enough, the listener tends to be more disturbed by encoded material than the primary communicator.

It seems that well beneath the issues of unconscious meaning and defence lies the more fundamental issue of how we express ourselves communicatively. The basic nature of the therapy a patient experiences is determined on this deeper level. The mathematical models compel us to explore this domain extensively—an area whose existence was barely known before this work (communicative theory did, of course, have a sense of these matters, but did not realize their fundamental importance). Research of this kind can actually begin to reshape our thinking about the clinical situation and the process of cure; it adds fresh dimensions to the accustomed ways of thinking about clinical experience that open up new avenues for exploration and insight.

* * *

Moving to our next model, we found a basis on which we assumed a fixed mass for the IP and measured the distance it travels second-by-second in the 5-cube; this gives a value for the *velocity* with which the IP moves from moment to moment. The rate of change of the velocity of the IP is its *acceleration*, and *force* is mass x acceleration; in turn, *work* is the integral of force along its path of action—more simply, force x distance. The capacity to do work, and its outcome, involves changes in *energy* (it is energy that moves the IP, and kinetic energy is the energy of motion). However, not all energy achieves a change of velocity—e.g., energy may change the inner state of the IP—the person—without altering its motion.

With all this in hand, it is possible to explore these issues in our communicative data. We asked basic questions like: how much work is done in a session on a given patient's and therapist's IP? How much energy exists in the communicative force field created by each P/T system? And how much energy does a patient retain in a particular session—energy that may well be available for inner structural change?

We first studied the work—*psychical or communicative work*—done on the IP's of these patients and therapists. This is a measure of *instantaneous power*—an aspect of power that is different from our earlier measure of cyclical power. It was here that we discovered our first deep law: in all of these cases, as measured separately for the patients and therapists (and for everyone else we have studied to date), *work is a linear function of time.* That is, the same amount of work or expenditure of energy occurs in each time segment of a session, regardless of subjective feelings or where you are in an hour.

As we know, there is both a subjective sense of the passage of time, and a measured value. The personal sense is under strong psychological influence and may differ greatly from the measured elapsed time. Similarly, in psychotherapy sessions there is a subjective sense in both patients and therapists as a session unfolds of just how hard they are working and how much energy they feel they are expending. Yet even though this inner sense varies greatly—at one moment there is a feeling that the work is intense, the next that it has slackened—the measured amount of communicative work performed is quite unvarying. It is the slope of the curves—the rate at which work is done—and the total amount of work done by the force field on the individual IP's that show individual differences. Indeed, it appears that each P/T system creates a *communicative force field* with a certain amount of available energy that is then distributed between patient and therapist in distinctive fashion (Badalamenti & Langs, in press).

In the consultations that we have been considering, the force field consistently performed more work on the patient's IP than her therapist's, though in the consultation with the unstable analyst these values were nearly equal. Further, the least amount of work was done on the patient's IP in my consultation and that with the American interpersonalist, while the most work on the patient's IP was done in the interviews with the woman analyst and self-psychologist. It seems, then, that therapists who are relatively silent and likely to create deep interpersonal effects and considerable cyclical power generate with their patients force-fields that do less work on their patient's IP than do therapists who are relatively more active and inclined to disrupt the flow of their patients' material. Low levels of work are seen as reflecting efficient therapeutic effort. In general, then, a therapist's basic style of working with his or her patient has many deep consequences that distinguish P/T systems and their subsystems of patient and therapist. The broader consequences of these distinctions are presently being explored.

Two measures of entropy/complexity

There are two ways of measuring entropy or the degree of informational complexity of the trajectory of the 5-dimensional vector through which we characterized these patients and therapists and their communications. The first method stems from *probability theory*; it was developed for gases and thermodynamics by Boltzmann and then applied to communication and information in general by Shannon (Shannon, 1984; Shannon & Weaver, 1949). The second arose in the study of engines and their work capacity, heat loss, and efficiency; it is called the *caloric method* and involves *the calculus*. In the first technique, the complexity of a numerical sequence is measured, while in the second, the rate of reversible heat absorption is divided by the absolute temperature of a physical system and summed along a path of action. The first strategy, the *Shannon–Boltzmann method*, allows for relatively simple calculations; it is rather easy to measure the complexity of any sequence of numbers. However, the second method requires the development of accurate and meaningful analogues in human communication for the two variables that go into the equation—reversible heat absorption and temperature.

* * *

As for the probabilistic approach, the five variables in our vector allow for 2,400 possible combinations of scores; maximum entropy—where all scores are equally probable and there is a total loss of definable structure—is 7.78, while an optimal degree of entropy would be in the 4.0 range (low entropy values reflect a lack of variety and of richness, while exceedingly high values reflect randomness and uncertainty).

The study of cumulative Shannon entropy produced another law of human communication for which we have as yet seen no exceptions: in all instances, *entropy proved to be a logarithmic function of the time elapsed in the session*. This indicates that the complexity of these sequences of communicative configurations increases continuously in psychotherapy sessions and emotional dialogues, though the rate at which this increase occurs tends to diminish as a session elapses. The finding is in keeping with the discovery that patient and therapist IP's, in their rotation through 5-dimensional space, continually press towards new states or communicative vehicles, while more and more frequently returning to previously used or old states (Badalamenti & Langs, in press).

As for the final or cumulative entropy values themselves, we found that all of the patients and therapists on our study reached final/maximal cumulative entropy levels in the 4.0 range. This suggests that human communication is optimally complex—it has seemingly ideal degrees of freshness and redundancy. As for the expected individual differences, the most striking finding was that in all cases except the consultation with the unstable analyst, final patient entropy exceeded therapist entropy—that is, as we would expect, patients tend to show more complexity in their use of communicative vehicle than do their therapists, though exceptions do occur.

As for the individual cases, the patient whom I interviewed had the highest levels of complexity for the sample in her sessions with me and with the woman analyst. The lowest level of complexity was found in Patient B in her consultation with the unstable analyst.

It seems likely that the sources of the high levels of variety seen with Patient A were different in her session with me as compared to the interview with the woman analyst. In my case, the richness probably stemmed from the freedom I allowed the patient to communicate as diversely as she wished (unconsciously), while with the woman analyst the richness probably arose from the agitating qualities of her work with this patient. On the other hand, the unstable analyst's extreme agitation seems to have had a constricting effect on his patient—a consequence we found in other domains as well (e.g., the low measure of linear influence). In general, these results indicate that a therapist's style of working with his or her patients has a compelling and distinctive effect on how the patient communicates—and in all likelihood, experiences and reacts to the treatment situation.

* * *

The search for the means through which we could measure caloric entropy was considerably more convoluted and also far more interesting. We were able to formulate a distinctive value for reversible heat absorption in that the equations indicated that the work done to move the IP (kinetic energy) used up only half the available energy; the other half, we reasoned, must involve heat/energy dissipation.

As for temperature, we sought an analogue to physical systems where temperature reflects motion and internal agitation. Since we knew that the motion of the IP involved rotation to fresh states while returning to old configurations, we assigned these two activities—our clearest indications of motion and agitation—distinctive temperature increment values. In the end, after much empirical experimentation, we produced an equation that replicated and preserved for all cases the logarithmic dependence of entropy on time and the rank order of final entropy values for all of the patients, therapists, and couples in our sample.

This equation has five internal factors; three involve measurements related to the speaker, while two reflect measures of the non-speaker. That is, the equation showed that entropy values and, perhaps more importantly, the amount of heat or energy kept internally by each party to these dyads (the probable source of inner change), are fundamentally systemic and inductive dimensions. The amount of energy retained by a patient is inherently a factor of the amount of energy that his or her therapist takes from the force field.

We have here reached a level of results in which the entire P/T system must be taken into account mathematically in order to understand the results and effects experienced by either party to a therapy session or emotional dialogue. Clinically, it no longer seems tenable to isolate patient from therapist, or vice versa; they are an intertwined total system in every sense.

Quantification and the scientific approach to countertransference

The translation (decoding) of surface images into unconscious messages, while fraught with risk, proves to be a far easier task than the translation of findings from mathematical models touching on deeper nature into clinical understanding. Before all of the specific results can be integrated, we will need a broader perspective—a general sense of the measures we have used and how, in general, they illuminate clinical experience. What are the clinical ramifications of the vicissitudes of power, force, complexity, energy distribution, and the like? And how do they bear on human emotional experience in general?

We have tried to offer some initial answers to these compelling questions, though with each fresh model we develop, our insight extends and deepens. More will come forth as we expand the dimensions that we model and investigate; classifications of new categories like those of *comments made* and of *themes* in a manner that allows for scaling and quantification should greatly advance this work. These efforts are now under way.

* * *

In concluding this chapter, we will attempt to highlight some clinical consequences of this work by showing in a preliminary fashion how this particular interactional science can help to define freshly and to illuminate the seemingly intractable issue of the nature and manifestations of countertransference in a psychotherapist.

The models described above lend themselves to a scientific and quantitative approach to the issue of *therapist dysfunction* (to use a distinctive term) within a therapeutic interaction. The ability to identify quantifiable measures of therapist disturbance will move us a long way towards an irrefutable definition of countertransference. In time, this will enable us to define sound therapeutic techniques more clearly and assist us in enhancing their use, and in addition, guide towards discarding measures that are, in general, deeply doubtful and hurtful.

The central issue lies in finding definitive criteria with which to define countertransference-based interventions and techniques. This is an all-but-impossible task in today's clinical world, where an error identified by one approach or individual therapist is seen as a sound intervention by another. Even the efforts made by the communicative approach to use encoded validation as a criterion for sound versus unsound (countertransference-based) interventions is marred by the many subjective judgements involved. What, then, can science do to clear the air?

In tracking the six consulting analysts who conducted the assessment interviews that we used for our pilot studies, a number of patterns emerged that promised scientific insight into how to resolve this dilemma. These impressions were developed entirely on the basis of the mathematical results; we then looked at the interview protocols to develop a sense of the possible clinical referents—identifying features—for the quantified indications of therapist dysfunction that we had developed from our models. The sweep was broad and general, yet it revealed notable dysfunctions in two of the consulting therapists and suggested difficulties in two others. We saw the results as a most promising beginning.

* * *

By way of orientation, we will begin with the offer of a brief clinical appraisal from the vantage point of the communicative approach of these six consultations. By these standards, all six interviews—including my own—showed notable signs of therapist countertransference. These were defined through the lack of encoded validation of the therapists' interventions from the patients and through the strikingly negative and uncomplimentary disguised material that followed most of the comments from these therapists. The latter were understood to represent valid encoded perceptions of the errant efforts of the therapists and of the conditions of the consultations—e.g., the recordings, the potential audience, the single meeting with the therapist. (I myself made two interventions that were unconsciously validated, though my other comments were not confirmed and did, indeed, depart from communicative principles to some extent. However, two other consultations that I carried out more closely in terms of communicative principles produced results comparable to those described above.)

Though we made no effort to quantify these impressions, it was our clinical sense, shared with several other therapists who reviewed these protocols, that countertransferences difficulties were most prominent in the interviews with the woman analyst (she was hyperactive, irritatingly repetitive in her comments, and, at times, flagrantly directive and suggestive to the patient), the self-psychologist (he attempted to deprecate the other analysts who had interviewed the patient and had pressed the patient forcefully to discuss topics she was clearly reluctant to explore), and the unstable analyst (he was erratic and often grossly provocative in his comments). Nonetheless, each of these analysts is widely published and respected, and each has a large number of followers who consider their work elegant and sound. It would be impossible to reach a consensus on the issue of who showed the most dramatic degree of therapist difficulty.

* * *

What, then, was the picture of these analysts that developed through the lens of the scientific studies—the mathoscope? Given the strangeness of the realm and its configurations, our first task was to see if we could detect on the level of deeper nature a sensible and promising set of scientific indicators of therapist dysfunction. Were there idiosyncratic violations of these laws that could be taken as indicators of disturbance? Were there other kinds of indicators suggested from our results?

At the time, we did not have quantitative measures of patient responses to specific interventions; our markers of difficulty would have to be inherently self-evident or highly probable. And since we had no measures of therapy outcome, the assessment of the likelihood that we were dealing with therapist dysfunction would have to be based on the appearance of an idiosyncratic result—*a departure from the established norms*. This criterion could be supported by being blind to who was being assessed and the use of logic, intuition, sensibility, and fair assessment until means of validation could be established. At the very least, this search for scientific markers of therapist dysfunction could have considerable heuristic value and might well produce some intriguing and promising initial results.

We had our first inkling that therapist dysfunction could be identified through our results when we discovered the existence of a single departure from the basic auto-regressive Box–Jenkins models used to characterize the speaker duration data. This divergence from the norm did not appear in the consultations series, but did materialize in each of three sessions studied from the psychotherapy of the HIV-positive man. The failure of these sessions to fit the basic model (though the data did satisfy a more complex one) was taken as a sign of considerable instability in the switching of the speaker role in the course of these sessions. And a study of the data showed that almost all of the departures from the norm were initiated by the therapist—here too, therapist dominance was in evidence.

We reviewed these sessions clinically in an effort to comprehend intuitively the basis for the mathematically identified instability. Our clinical impression was that the therapist initiated these erratic interludes by creating a disturbance in the switching of the speaker role when the patient's negative unconscious perceptions of the therapist's interventional errors became excessively intense. It was this first sense of having a quantified marker of therapist dysfunction (Badalamenti & Langs, 1992) that encouraged us to seek other indicators.

* * *

As our work unfolded, we noticed that rather consistent trends appeared with each of the models we developed from physics. All parties studied conformed to the laws we had unearthed, but the ratios between patient and therapist values tended to vary. In general, patient values exceeded therapist values; exceptions to this rule appeared to indicate therapist dysfunction (recall the evidence for therapist dominance in our results).

For example, as a rule, both work done on a patient's IP and patient entropy were greater than the work done on a therapist's IP and therapist entropy. Similarly, patients were virtually always higher than their therapists on total cyclical power and on the cyclical power for the five dimensions treated separately. While other indications of dysfunction also emerged, we had a general principle to guide us; *we would take as a sign of therapist dysfunction any departure from the general norm of our results across mathematical models.*

These data also allowed us to identify systemic (P/T system) disturbances to which the therapist undoubtedly contributed. We spoke above of instabilities in the switching of the speaker role—a systemic indicator for which we had clear evidence of the therapist's contribution as the initiator of almost all of the disequilibria. In addition, the speaker duration data yielded measures of dysfunction through the simple measure of who spoke longer in a session (only the woman analyst spoke more than did her patient), and who assumed the role of the leading speaker and who was the main interrupter (here too, only the woman analyst showed a rate constant that revealed her to be the primary speaker in the consultation). Still another measure of systemic dysfunction was seen with the time lagged cross-correlation functions—absence of deep effects suggested therapist dysfunction (the value was zero for the international interpersonalist, and very low for the self-psychologist and the unstable analyst).

* * *

Our first models, then, provided us with a series of markers of therapist dysfunction. We found that the idiosyncratic results were not distributed randomly among these therapists, but that particular therapists were prone to show repeated departures from the usual results. Not surprisingly, the most dysfunctional therapist in our sample was the unstable analyst. He was erratic on the surface of the interview he conducted and evoked many negative derivatives (encoded perceptions) in his patient. In our models, he showed several reversals in the values he obtained compared to his patient. The work done on his IP was equal to (rather than less than) that done on his patient's IP; his temperature value (a sign of IP activity) was higher than his patient's, as was his level of final entropy (complexity of information). In addition, the measure of linear influence for his consultation was quite low in the lagged cross-correlation study. Finally, in our investigation of irreversible heat (energy) absorption—a likely measure of energy available for structural change and inner adjustment—he drew a relatively large percentage of the energy from the communicative force field; as a consequence, his patient took the least amount of irreversible heat/energy for herself at the end of her consultation (Badalamenti & Langs, in press–a).

This last indicator of dysfunction is a single example of another approach to the measurement of therapist dysfunctions—though it has not as yet been fully developed. The method involves a study of the comparative results among patients and therapists on the various models we applied. In general, extreme values in either limiting direction for the results are a probable sign of therapist difficulty (cf. the comparatively low measure of linear influence noted above). We suspect that these mathematical models will eventually provide us with a variety of ways of identifying therapist—and patient—dysfunction.

* * *

The second analyst to show strong evidence for dysfunction is the woman analyst, who was so active that, as we noted, she emerged as the more frequent and leading speaker in the speaker duration data. And much like the unstable analyst, her P/T system showed a comparatively low auto-regressive parameter, an indication of an unstable sequence of speaker duration data with low levels of inertia. A striking sign of dysfunction was the high level of irreversible heat/energy that she took from the communicative force field, and the complementary low value for the patient.

The international interpersonalist was marked for dysfunction because his P/T system showed a zero index of linear influence. This suggests deep disengagement between himself and his patient, a sense reflected in the very intellectual and grossly distant surface qualities of the session he conducted (a realization that came a posteriori). Similarly, the low index of deeper influence obtained by the self-psychologist suggests therapist difficulty, while the concentration of influence in the session with the woman analyst in the areas of positive and negative tone also suggested some type of aberration (all of the other P/T systems that showed strong effects did so mainly in the areas of degree of narrative and newness of theme).

* * *

Much work needs to be done in further developing these signs of therapist dysfunction and in understanding the clinical implications of the markers that we use. The quantitative net made a distinctive kind of sweep, one that is far different from any net created through clinical criteria. The models used reflected overall signs of dysfunction and did not as yet investigate specific interventions. Nonetheless, the effort convincingly identified two therapists with strong signs of dysfunction and identified lesser signs in two other therapists. Grounded as they are in mathematical techniques and entirely devoid of subjective judgement, the results produced by these models are difficult to dispute; in time, we should have a sound scientific approach to the problem of countertransference.

We have tried in this chapter to introduce an unprecedented approach to these issues. If the reader has gained a sense of the methodology and its potential, then we have conveyed our intended message as well as we hoped we could. We will not pursue the specific findings further for now, except to indicate that a presentation of these markers to the therapists who generated them could and should lead them to question their techniques and their validity. We are of course still far from such practical consequences from this kind of effort; yet hopefully the consequences for clinical practice will soon be appreciated and explicated. These studies raise serious questions about psychotherapy and psychoanalysis as they are now practised.

* * *

We have come now to the end-point of our journey—at least for now. A new psychoscope has been present, one that offers a new view of the data and domain of psychoanalysis and psychotherapy. It has led to a strong interactional viewpoint of the therapy experience and to a powerful systems theory, and from there to a fresh and sharp critique of the existing science of psychoanalysis. Not content with criticism alone, the final step has been the presentation of the beginnings of an interactional science of psychoanalysis replete with initial results—and with an opportunity to quantify therapist dysfunctions. Though much of the territory we explored is new and, as yet, strange and probably a bit discomforting, it is our hope that the ways in which this work has, we trust, expanded your clinical purview and your insight into human nature will, in the end, have made the reading a satisfying and illuminating experience.

THE WORKS OF ROBERT LANGS

Books

1. *LSD Personality and Experience* (with H. Barr, R. Holt, L. Goldberger, and G. Klein). New York: Wiley, 1972 .
2. *The Technique of Psychoanalytic Psychotherapy, Volume 1*. New York: Jason Aronson, 1973.
3. *The Technique of Psychoanalytic Psychotherapy, Volume 2*. New York: Jason Aronson, 1974.
4. *The Bipersonal Field*. New York: Jason Aronson, 1976.
5. *The Therapeutic Interaction: Abstracts of the Psychoanalytic Literature, Volume 1*. New York: Jason Aronson, 1976.
6. *The Therapeutic Interaction: A Critical Overview and Synthesis, Volume 2*. New York: Jason Aronson, 1976.
7. *The Therapeutic Interaction: A Synthesis*. New York: Jason Aronson, 1977.
8. *The Listening Process*. New York: Jason Aronson, 1978.
9. *Technique in Transition*. New York: Jason Aronson, 1978.
10. *The Supervisory Experience*. New York: Jason Aronson, 1979.
11. *The Therapeutic Environment*. New York: Jason Aronson, 1980.

12. *Intrapsychic and Interpersonal Dimensions of Treatment: A Clinical Dialogue* (with H. Searles). New York: Jason Aronson, 1980.
13. *The Therapeutic Experience and its Settings* (with Leo Stone). New York: Jason Aronson, 1980.
14. *Interactions: The Realm of Transference and Countertransference*. New York: Jason Aronson, 1980.
15. *Classics in Psychoanalytic Technique* (Editor). New York: Jason Aronson, 1981.
16. *Resistances and Interventions: The Nature of Therapeutic Work*. New York: Jason Aronson, 1981.
17. *Psychotherapy: A Basic Text*. New York: Jason Aronson, 1982.
18. *The Psychotherapeutic Conspiracy*. New York: Jason Aronson, 1982.
19. *Unconscious Communication in Everyday Life*. New York: Jason Aronson, 1983.
20. *Madness and Cure*. Emerson, NJ: Newconcept, 1985.
21. *Workbooks for Psychotherapists, Volume 1: Understanding Unconscious Communication*. Emerson, NJ: Newconcept, 1985.
22. *Workbooks for Psychotherapists, Volume 2: Listening and Formulating*. Emerson, NJ: Newconcept, 1985.
23. *Workbooks for Psychotherapists, Volume 3: Intervening and Validating*. Emerson, NJ: Newconcept, 1985.
24. *A Primer of Psychotherapy*. New York: Gardner Press, 1988.
25. *Decoding Your Dreams*. New York: Henry Holt & Co., 1988.
26. *Rating Your Psychotherapist: The Search for Effective Cure*. New York: Henry Holt, 1989.
27. *Take Charge of Your Emotional Life*. New York: Henry Holt, 1991.
28. *A Clinical Workbook for Psychotherapists*. London: Karnac Books, 1992.
29. *Science, Systems, and Psychoanalysis*. London: Karnac Books, 1992.

Books in press

The Physics of the Mind (with A. Badalamenti). New York: Ballantine Books.

Books in translation

1. *The Technique of Psychoanalytic Psychotherapy, Volumes 1 and 2* [Italian].
2. *The Psychotherapeutic Conspiracy* [German and Swedish].
3. *Madness and Cure* [Italian].
4. *Interactions: The Realm of Transference and Countertransference* [Italian].
5. *Psychotherapy: A Basic Text* [Italian].
6. *Technique in Transition* [French].
7. *Unconscious Communication in Everyday Life* [Italian].
8 *A Primer of Psychotherapy* [Italian].
9. *Decoding Your Dreams* [German, Italian, French, Dutch].
10. *Rating Your Psychotherapist* [German, Italian].
11. *Take Charge of Your Emotional LIfe* [French, Italian].

REFERENCES

Abbott, E. (1884 [1984]). *Flatland.* New York: New American Library.

Alexander, L., & Luborsky, L. (1986). The Penn helping alliance scales. In: L. Greenberg & W. Pinsof (Eds.), *The Psychotherapeutic Process: Research Handbook* (pp. 326–366). New York: Guilford Press.

Arlow, J., & Brenner, C. (1964). *Psychoanalytic Concepts and the Structural Theory.* New York: International Universities Press.

Badalamenti, A. F., & Ferguson, R. (submitted for publication). Some dimensions of power and cyclicity in psychotherapy consultations.

Badalamenti, A. F., & Langs, R. (1991). An empirical investigation of human dyadic systems in the time and frequency domains. *Behavioral Science, 36*: 100–114.

Badalamenti, A. F., & Langs, R. (1992). Stochastic analysis of the duration of the speaker role in the psychotherapy of an AIDS patient. *American Journal of Psychotherapy, 46*: 207–225.

Badalamenti, A. F., & Langs, R. (in press–a). The thermodynamics of psychotherapeutic communication. *Behavioral Science.*

Badalamenti, A. F., & Langs, R. (in press–b). Work and force in psychotherapy. *Journal of Mathematical and Computer Modeling.*

Basch, M. (1976). Theory formation in chapter VII: A critique.

Journal of the American Psychoanalytic Association, 24: 64–100.

Bateson, G. (1972). *Steps to an Ecology of Mind.* New York: Ballantine.

______. (1979). *Mind and Nature.* New York: Bantam Books.

Bertalanffy, L. von (1968). *General System Theory: Foundations, Development, Applications.* New York: George Braziller.

Bird, B. (1972). Notes on transference: Universal phenomenon and the hardest part of the analysis. *Journal of the American Psychoanalytic Association, 20*: 267–301.

Boesky, D. (1989). The questions and curiosity of the psychoanalyst. *Journal of the American Psychoanalytic Association, 37*: 579–603.

Bochner, S. (1966). *The Role of Mathematics in the Rise of Science.* Princeton, NJ: Princeton University Press.

Bornstein, M. (1989). Prologue. *Psychoanalytic Inquiry, 9*: 165–168.

Box, E., & Jenkins, G. (1976). *Time Series Analysis: Forecasting and Control.* San Francisco, CA: Holden Day.

Box, E., & Tiao, G. (1975). Intervention analysis with applications to economic and environmental problems. *Journal of the American Statistical Association, 70*: 70–79.

Brenner, C. (1974). On the nature and development of affects: A unified theory. *Psychoanalytic Quarterly, 43*: 532–556.

Broadbent, D. (1958). *Perception and Communication.* London: Pergamon Press.

Bryant, R. (1990). Patterns of interaction between patient and therapist in terms of three attributes of communication: Emerging themes, degree of narration and quality of tone. (Doctoral dissertation, Adelphi University, Garden City, New York.)

Bucci, W. (1984). Linking words and things: Basic processes and individual variation. *Cognition, 17*: 137–153.

______. (1987). A reconstruction of the 'tally argument': A program for psychoanalytic research. (Unpublished manuscript.)

Butterfield, H. (1957). *The Origins of Modern Science.* New York: Free Press.

Chertok, L. (1968). The discovery of transference. *International Journal of Psycho-Analysis, 49*: 560–575.

Conti, J. (1989). *Paradigms Lost.* New York: William Morrow.

Davies, P. (1989 [1987]). *The Cosmic Blueprint.* London: Unwin.

Dell, P. F., & Goolishian, H. A. (1981). 'Order through fluctuation': An evolutionary epistemology for human systems. *Australian Journal of Family Therapy, 2* (4): 75–184.

Dixon, N. (1971). *Subliminal Perceptions: The Nature of a Controversy*. New York: McGraw-Hill.

______. (1981). *Preconscious Processing*. New York: Wiley.

Edelson, M. (1984). *Hypothesis and Evidence in Psychoanalysis*. Chicago: University of Chicago Press.

______. (1989). The nature of psychoanalytic theory: Implications for psychoanalytic research. *Psychoanalytic Inquiry, 9*: 169–192.

Ellenberger, Henri F. (1970). *The Discovery of the Unconscious*. New York: Basic Books.

Ford, D., & Urban, H. (1963). *Systems of Psychotherapy*. New York: Wiley.

Freud, S. (1895d) (with J. Breuer). Studies on Hysteria. *Standard Edition, 2*: 3–335. London: Hogarth Press, 1955.

______. (1900a). *The Interpretation of Dreams. Standard Edition, 4–5*: 1–625.

______. (1905d). Three essays on the theory of sexuality. *Standard Edition, 7*: 185–243.

______. (1905e [1901]). Fragment of an analysis of a case of hysteria. *Standard Edition, 7*: 3–122.

______. (1908a). Hysterical phantasies and their relation to bisexuality. *Standard Edition, 9*: 155–166.

______. (1912b). The dynamics of transference. *Standard Edition, 12*: 99–108.

______. (1915e). The unconscious. *Standard Edition, 14*.

______. (1916–17). *Introductory Lectures on Psychoanalysis. Standard Edition, 15 & 16*.

______. (1917a). A difficulty in the path of psycho-analysis. *Standard Edition, 17*: 135–144.

______. (1923a [1922]). Two encyclopedia articles. *Standard Edition, 18*: 234–259.

______. (1923b). *The Ego and the Id. Standard Edition, 19*: 1–66.

______. (1925d). *An Autobiographical Study. Standard Edition, 20*: 1–74.

______. (1926e). The question of lay analysis. *Standard Edition, 20*: 179–258.

______. (1926f [1925]). Psycho-analysis. *Standard Edition, 20*: 261–270.

______. (1933a). *New Introductory Lectures on Psycho-Analysis. Standard Edition, 22*: 3–182.

______. (1937d). Constructions in analysis. *Standard Edition, 23*: 256–269.

______. (1940a [1938]). *An Outline of Psycho-Analysis. Standard Edition, 23*: 141–207.

_____. (1950a [1887–1902]). Project for a scientific psychology. *Standard Edition, 1*: 281–397.

Galatzer-Levy, R. (1978). Qualitative change from quantitative change: Mathematical catastrophe theory in relation to psychoanalysis. *Journal of the American Psychoanalytic Association, 26*: 921–935.

Gardner, H. (1985). *The Mind's New Science.* New York: Basic Books.

Gazzaniga, M. (1985). *The Social Brain.* New York: Basic Books.

Gill, M. (1963). *Topography and Systems in Psychoanalytic Theory. Psychological Issues. Monograph 10.* New York: International Universities Press.

_____. (1982). *Analysis of Transference. Vol. 1: Theory and Technique. Psychological Issues, Monograph 53.* New York: International Universities Press.

Goleman, D. (1985). *Vital Lies, Simple Truths.* New York: Simon & Schuster.

Glover, E. (1940). *The Technique of Psychoanalysis.* New York: International Universities Press.

Greenberg, J., & Mitchell, S. (1983). *Object Relations in Psychoanalytic Theory.* Cambridge, MA: Harvard University Press.

Greenberg, L., & Pinsof, W. (Eds.) (1986). *The Psychotherapeutic Process: A Research Handbook.* New York: Guilford Press.

Greenson, R. (1967). *The Technique and Practice of Psychoanalysis, Vol. 1.* New York: International Universities Press.

Grunbaum, A. (1984). *The Foundations of Psychoanalysis: A Philosophical Critique.* Berkeley, CA: University of California Press.

Holt, R. (1967). The development of the primary process: A structural view. In R. Holt (Ed.), *Motives and Thought. Psychological Issues, Vol. 5.* New York: International Universities Press.

_____. (1972). Freud's mechanistic and humanistic images of man. *Psychoanalysis and Contemporary Science, 1*: 3–24.

_____. (1985). The current status of psychoanalytic theory. *Psychoanalytic Psychology, 2*: 289–315.

Horowitz, M. (1976). *Stress Response Syndromes.* New York: Jason Aronson.

Jimenez-Montano, M.A. (1984). On the syntactic structure of protein sequences and the concept of grammar complexity. *Bulletin of Mathematical Biology, 46*: 641–659.

Kiesler, D. (1966). Some myths of psychotherapy research and the search for a paradigm. *Psychological Bulletin, 65*: 110–136.

Kline, M. (1985). *Mathematics and the Search for Knowledge.* New York: Oxford University Press.

Kohut, H. (1971). *The Analysis of the Self: A Systematic Approach to the Psychoanalytic Treatment of Narcissistic Personality Disorders. Psychoanalytic Study of the Child Monograph 4.* New York: International Universities Press.

_____. (1984). *How Does Analysis Cure?* Chicago: University of Chicago Press.

Kolmogorov, A. (1965). Three approaches to the definition of the concept of quantity of information. *Information Theory, 14*: 662–669.

Kuhn, T. (1962). *The Structure of Scientific Revolution.* Chicago: Chicago University Press.

_____. (1970). Logic of discovery or psychology of research. In: I. Lakatos & A. Musgrave (Eds.), *Criticism and the Growth of Knowledge* (pp. 1–22). Cambridge: Cambridge University Press.

Langs, R. (1976a). *The Bipersonal Field.* New York: Jason Aronson.

_____. (1976b). *The Therapeutic Interaction.* New York: Jason Aronson.

_____. (1978). *The Listening Process.* New York: Jason Aronson.

_____. (1979). *The Therapeutic Environment.* New York: Jason Aronson.

_____. (1980). *Interactions: The Realm of Transference and Countertransference.* New York: Jason Aronson.

_____. (1981a). Mode of 'cure' in psychoanalysis and psychoanalytic psychotherapy. *International Journal of Psycho-Analysis, 62*: 199–214.

_____. (1981b). *Resistances and Interventions.* New York: Jason Aronson.

_____. (1982a). *The Psychotherapeutic Conspiracy.* New York: Jason Aronson.

_____. (1982b). *Psychotherapy: A Basic Text.* New York: Jason Aronson.

_____. (1984–85). Making interpretations and securing the frame: Danger situations for psychotherapists. *International Journal of Psychoanalytic Psychotherapy, 10*: 3–23.

_____. (1985a). *Madness and Cure.* Emerson, NJ: Newconcept.

_____. (1985b). *Workbooks for Psychotherapists, Vols. 1, 2, and 3.* Emerson, NJ: Newconcept Press.

_____. (1986). Clinical issues arising from a new model of the mind. *Contemporary Psychoanalysis, 22*: 418–444.

_____. (1987a). A new model of the mind. *The Yearbook of Psychoanalysis and Psychotherapy, 2*: 3–33.

_____. (1987b). Clarifying a new model of the mind. *Contemporary Psychoanalysis, 23*: 162–180.

_____. (1987c). Psychoanalysis as an Aristotelian science: Pathways to Copernicus and a modern-day approach. *Contemporary Psychoanalysis, 23*: 555–576.

______. (1988a). *A Primer of Psychotherapy*. New York: Gardner Press.

______. (1988b). *Decoding Your Dreams*. New York: Henry Holt.

______. (1988c). Mathematics for psychoanalysis. *British Journal of Psychotherapy, 5*: 204–212.

______. (1988d). Perspectives on psychoanalysis as a late arrival to the family of sciences. *Contemporary Psychoanalysis, 24*: 397–419.

______. (1989a). *Rating Your Psychotherapist*. New York: Henry Holt.

______. (1989b). Models, theory, and research strategies: Toward the evolution of new paradigms. *Psychoanalytic Inquiry, 9*: 305–331.

______. (1989c). A systems theory for psychoanalysis. *Contemporary Psychoanalysis, 25*: 371–392.

______. (1991). *Take Charge of Your Emotional Life*. New York: Henry Holt.

______. (1992). *A Clinical Workbook for Psychotherapists*. London: Karnac Books.

Langs, R., & Badalamenti, A. F. (1990). Stochastic analysis of the duration of the speaker role in psychotherapy. *Perceptual and Motor Skills, 70*: 675–689.

Langs, R., & Badalamenti, A. F. (1991). Statistics and mathematics in psychotherapy research. *Bulletin of the Society for Psychoanalytic Psychotherapy, 6*: 13–21.

Langs, R., & Badalamenti, A. F. (1992). The three modes of the science of psychoanalysis. *American Journal of Psychotherapy, 46*: 163–182.

Langs, R., & Badalamenti, A. F. (in press). *The Physics of the Mind*. New York: Ballantine Books.

Langs, R., Badalamenti, A. F., & Bryant, R. (1991). A measure of linear influence between patient and therapist. *Psychological Reports, 69*: 355–368.

Langs, R., Badalamenti, A. F., & Cramer, G. (1992a). The formal mode of the science of psychoanalysis: Studies of two patient/therapist systems. *American Journal of Psychotherapy, 46*: 226–239.

Langs, R., Rapp, P., Pinto, A., Cramer, G., & Badalamenti, A. F. (1992b). Three quantitative studies of gender and identity in psychotherapy consultations. *American Journal of Psychotherapy, 46*:183–206.

Langs, R., Bucci, W., Udoff, A., Cramer, G., & Thomson, L. (submitted for publication). Two methods of assessing unconscious communication in psychotherapy.

Laszlo, E. (1987). *Evolution: The Grand Synthesis*. Boston: New Science Library (Shambhala).

Lewin, K. (1931). The conflict between Aristotelian and Galilean modes of thought in contemporary psychology. *Journal of General Psychology, 5*: 141–177. Reprinted in: D. Adam & K. Zener (Eds.), *A Dynamic Theory of Personality: Selected Papers of Kurt Lewin*. New York: McGraw-Hill, 1935.

Little, M. (1951). Counter-transference and the patient's response to it. *International Journal of Psycho-Analysis, 32*: 32–40.

Loewald, H. (1960). The therapeutic action of psychoanalysis. *International Journal of Psycho-Analysis, 4*: 16–33.

Marmar, C., Horowitz, M., Weiss, D., & Marziali, E. (1986). The development of the therapeutic alliance rating system. In: L. Greenberg & W. Pinsof (Eds.), *The Psychotherapeutic Process: A Research Handbook* (pp. 367–390). New York: Guilford Press.

Maturana, H. R., & Varela, F. (1987). *The Tree of Knowledge*. Boston: New Science Library (Shambhala).

Meissner, W. W. (1989). A note on psychoanalytic facts. *Psychoanalytic Inquiry, 9*: 193–219.

Meissner, W. W. (1991). *What Is Effective in Psychoanalytic Therapy: The Move from Interpretation to Relation*. Northvale, NJ: Jason Aronson.

Miller, G. A., Galanter, E., & Pribram, K. H. (1960). *Plans and the Structure of Behavior*. New York: Henry Holt.

Mitchell, S. (1988). *Relational Concepts in Psychoanalysis*. Cambridge, MA: Harvard University Press.

Newton, P. (1971). Abstinence as a role requirement in psychotherapy. *Psychiatry, 34*: 391–400.

______. (1973). Social structure and process in psychotherapy: A sociopsychological analysis of transference, resistance and change. *International Journal of Psychiatry, 4*: 480–526.

______. (1989). Free association and the division of labor in psychoanalytic treatment. *Psychoanalytic Psychology, 6*: 31–46.

Noy, P. (1969). A revision of the psychoanalytic theory of the primary process. *International Journal of Psycho-Analysis, 50*: 155–178.

Orlinsky, D., & Howard, K. (1978). The relation of process to outcome in psychotherapy. In: S. Garfield & A. Bergin (Eds.), *Handbook of Psychotherapy and Behavior Change* (pp. 283–329). New York: Wiley.

Penrose, R. (1989). *The Emperor's New Mind.* New York: Oxford University Press.

Peterfreund, E. (1971) (in collaboration with J. Schwartz). *Information, Systems, and Psychoanalysis: An Evolutionary Biological Approach to Psychoanalytic Theory. Psychological Issues, Monograph 25/26.* New York: International Universities Press.

Popper, K. (1959). *The Logic of Scientific Discovery* (rev. ed.). New York: Harper & Row, 1968.

Potzl, O. (1917). Experimentell erregte Irraumbilder in Ihren Beziehungen zum indirekten Sehen. *Zeitung Gesammelte Neurologie Psychiatrika, 37*: 278.

Pribram, K. H. (1991). *Brain and Perception: Holonomy and Structure in Figural Processing.* Hillsdale, NJ: Lawrence Erlbaum Associates.

Pribham, K., & Gill, M. (1976). *Freud's 'Project' Reassessed.* New York: Basic Books.

Prigogine, I. (1980). *From Being to Becoming.* New York: W. H. Freeman.

Prigogine, I., & Stengers, I. (1984). *Order Out of Chaos.* New York: Bantam Books.

Rapp, P. E., Jimenez-Montano, M. A., Langs, R. J., & Thomson, L. (1988). *Quantitative Characterization of Patient-Therapist Communication.* Preprint. New York: Beth Israel Medical Center.

Rieff, P. (1979). *Freud: The Mind of the Moralist.* Chicago: University of Chicago Press.

Rosenblatt, A., & Thickstun, J. (1977). *Modern Psychoanalytic Concepts in a General Psychology. Psychological Issues, Monograph 42/43.* New York: International Universities Press.

______. (1984). The psychoanalytic process: A systems and information processing model. *Psychoanalytic Inquiry, 4*: 59–86.

Sandler, J., Holder, A., Kawenoka, M., Kennedy, H., & Neurath, I. (1969). Notes on some theoretical and clinical aspects of transference. *International Journal of Psycho-Analysis, 50*: 633–645.

Searles, H. (1975). The patient as therapist to his analyst. In: P. Giovacchini (Ed.), *Tactics and Techniques of Psychoanalytic Psychotherapy: Vol. 2. Countertransference* (pp. 95–151). New York: Jason Aronson.

Shannon, C. (1948). A mathematical theory of communication. *Bell System Technical Journal, 27*: 379–423, 623–656.

Shannon, C., & Weaver, W. (1949). *The Mathematical Theory of Communication.* Urbana, IL: University of Illinois Press.

Shengold, L. (1989). *Soul Murder.* New Haven, CT: Yale University Press.

Shevrin, H. (1988). Unconscious conflict: A convergent psychodynamic and electrophysiological approach. In: M. Horowitz (Ed.), *Psychodynamics and Cognition* (pp. 117–167). Chicago: University of Chicago Press.

Shevrin, H., Williams, W., Marshall, R., Hertel, R., Bond, J., & Brakel, L. (1988). Event-related potential indicators of the dynamic unconscious. (Paper presented at the Fourth International Conference on Psychophysiology, Prague, Czechoslavakia.)

Shulman, D. (1990). The investigation of psychoanalytic theory by means of the experimental method. *International Journal of Psycho-Analysis, 71*: 487–497.

Silverman, L., Lachman, F., & Milich, F. (1982). *In Search of Oneness.* New York: International Universities Press.

Smith, D. (1991). *Hidden Conversations: An Introduction to Communicative Psychoanalysis.* London: Routledge.

Spence, D. (1982). *Narrative Truth and Historical Truth.* New York: Norton.

Sperry, R. (1961). Cerebral organization and behavior. *Science, 133*: 1749–57.

Stone, L. (1973). On resistance to the psychoanalytic process: Some thoughts on its nature and motivation. *Psychoanalysis and Contemporary Science, 2*: 42–74.

______. (1975). Some problems and potentialities of present-day psychoanalysis. *Psychoanalytic Quarterly, 44*: 331–370.

Strupp, H., & Bergin, A. (1969). Some empirical and conceptual bases for coordinated research in psychotherapy: A critical review of issues, trends and evidence. *International Journal of Psychiatry, 7*: 18–19.

Sullivan, H. S. (1953). *The Interpersonal Theory of Psychiatry.* New York: W. W. Norton.

Szasz, T. (1963). The concept of transference. *International Journal of Psycho-Analysis, 44*: 432–443.

Wallace, E. (1989). Pitfalls of a one-sided image of science: Adolf Grunbaum's *Foundations of Psychoanalysis. Journal of the American Psychoanalytic Association, 37*: 493–529.

Wallerstein, R. (1986). Psychoanalysis as a science: A response to the new challenges. *Psychoanalytic Quarterly, 55*: 414–451.

Weiss, J., & Sampson, H. (1986). *The Psychoanalytic Process.* New York: Guilford Press.

Winnicott, D. (1953). Transitional objects and transitional phenomena: A study of the first not-me possession. *International Journal of Psycho-Analysis, 34*: 89–97.

Young, R. (1986). Freud: Scientist and/or humanist. *Free Associations, 6*: 7–35.

INDEX